SOVIET PSYCHIA

The Shadow over W

SOVIET PSYCHIATRIC ABUSE:

The Shadow over World Psychiatry

by

SIDNEY BLOCH

and

PETER REDDAWAY

LONDON
VICTOR GOLLANCZ LTD
1984

For

Felicity and Kathy

British Library Cataloguing in Publication Data
Bloch, Sidney, *1941–*
Soviet psychiatric abuse.
1. Psychiatry—Soviet Union—Political aspects
I. Title   II. Reddaway, Peter
362.2'0947   RC455.2.P/

ISBN 0-575-03253-7

Printed and bound in Great Britain at
The Camelot Press Ltd, Southampton

CONTENTS

LIST OF ILLUSTRATIONS

Following p. 96

PREFACE

WHEN IN 1977 we completed *Russia's Political Hospitals (Psychiatric Terror* in the American edition), our first book on the subject of the political abuse of psychiatry in the USSR, the issue was coming to a head in international psychiatric circles. It seemed then that concerted action by the profession might well pave the way for the abolition of political psychiatry. Alas, this was not to be—the Soviet practices continued more or less unabated, and have done so until the present. During this period of six years, psychiatry throughout the world has undergone a traumatic experience, as the campaign to try to combat psychiatric abuse, and official Soviet opposition to that campaign, have both intensified. The battle finally culminated in the resignation of the Soviet Psychiatric Society from the World Psychiatric Association in January 1983, and in momentous repercussions at the Association's World Congress six months later. The outcome was a profession subject to division and schism. It is with these dramatic developments that the present volume is chiefly concerned.

In the first chapter, we briefly recapitulate the contents of *Russia's Political Hospitals* by covering the main aspects of the misuse of psychiatry to suppress dissent. In doing so, we have brought the original account up to date. The body of the book, which follows, consists of a detailed description and evaluation of international developments in this field from the time of the Sixth Congress of the World Psychiatric Association, held in 1977 in Honolulu, up to and including the Seventh Congress in 1983 in Vienna. We start in chapter two with an account of the Honolulu congress, at which the Russians' unethical conduct was formally condemned and a Review Committee was created to investigate the abuse of psychiatry wherever it might occur. In chapter three we turn to the opposition movement that evolved in the Soviet Union around the time of Honolulu and gave an extra impetus to the international campaign against psychiatric abuse. We focus particularly on a remarkable human rights group, the Working Commission to Investigate the Use of Psychiatry for Political Purposes, charting its growth, mode of operation and effectiveness, and its final destruction by the KGB.

In chapter four we examine the Review Committee of the World Psychiatric Association—the hurdles confronted by the Association in setting it up, its *modus operandi*, and its ultimate impotence in the face of Soviet psychiatry's failure to co-operate with its investigations. Chapter five deals with the efforts of various psychiatric and other bodies to bring political psychiatry to an end, including the clinical examination of ex-dissenter-patients, the support given to victims and their families, the application of pressure on the Soviet psychiatric leadership, and attempts to establish contact with ordinary Soviet psychiatrists.

Whether to pursue dialogue or confrontation with the Soviet Union is the theme of chapter six, which traces the evolution of a movement to expel the Soviet Psychiatric Society from the World Psychiatric Association, and the official reaction of the Society to this radical intent. The dénouement of this contest is covered in the next chapter, which provides our account of the dramatic resignation of the Soviet Union from the world body—the reasons for the decision, the reactions of other member societies, and the broader repercussions for world psychiatry. In chapter eight we focus on the Vienna congress, examining the decisions taken there in the light of the withdrawal of the Soviet Society and some of its allies. We consider the immediate effects of these resignations on the organization, and speculate briefly about the likely implications for the psychiatric profession both within the Soviet Union and throughout the world.

A short appendix follows containing some key documents which illuminate various facets of the subject. All translations are by us.

We would like to record our sincere thanks to many people who helped us, directly or indirectly, in the preparation of this book. First and foremost, we thank the members of the

Moscow-based commission on psychiatric abuse, many ex-dissenter-patients, émigré Soviet psychiatrists, and human rights dissenters both in and outside the USSR, all of whom have been indispensable in our research. The contributions of our colleagues in the Special Committee on Political Abuse of the Royal College of Psychiatrists, the London Working Group on the Internment of Dissenters in Mental Hospitals (of which we are members), and the International Association on the Political Use of Psychiatry have been exceedingly helpful and are much appreciated. Jane Manley of the Royal College of Psychiatrists and Ellen Mercer of the American Psychiatric Association were always willing to help with our enquiries. Our special thanks go to Robert van Voren for his constant encouragement.

Pauline Madden did a superb typing job, and Marie Vickers was helpful in all sorts of ways. We are grateful to Kathy Reddaway for her compilation of the Index. One of the authors (SB) would like to express his gratitude to his mother, Rachel Bloch, to Frieda and Mark Verstandig, and to Gery Low-Beer for making life considerably easier during his period of study-leave. Finally, we thank our wives, Felicity and Kathy, for their endurance and constant support.

S. B. and P. R.
JULY 1983

CHAPTER ONE

POLITICAL ABUSE: WHAT IS IT?

The Vulnerability of Psychiatry

BECAUSE OF ITS particular nature, the profession of psychiatry has to wrestle constantly with a wide range of ethical questions. Although many of these are shared with medicine in general, the practice of psychiatry involves some exceptional quandaries. Consider, for example, the question of compulsory hospitalization.[1] The psychiatrist, uniquely, has the awesome authority, invested in him by society, to place a person in a psychiatric hospital without his consent. Although granted legal sanctions to fulfil this role, the relevant statutes are frequently ambiguous and ill-defined. Even when the law is more explicit, its translation into practical guidelines is exceedingly complex. A person posing a danger to himself or to others is the usual reason for commitment—on the face of it, reasonable enough—but the psychiatrist's predicament lies in the lack of objective criteria to predict dangerous behaviour. His best efforts to arrive at a clinically-scientific judgement are inevitably influenced by pressures from several sources including his own tendency to play safe in the face of doubt.

The slender scientific basis for a judgement about dangerousness also applies elsewhere in psychiatry. In contrast to other spheres of medical work, objective criteria to establish whether a psychiatric condition is present or not are unavailable in many cases. Even more problematic is the whole question of what *is* mental illness. An influential body of opinion—Thomas Szasz[2] is its most vocal representative—holds that psychiatry does not deal with ill people at all but rather with their problems in living. Thus, to label a young married mother's unhappiness as "morbid depression" constitutes a camouflage of the real issue: namely, that she feels harried and overwhelmed by her responsibilities and consequently has difficulty in coping. The picture is all the more complex since the diagnostic process is closely intertwined with social factors; this is evidenced by the sometimes considerable differences among various cultures and in the same culture from one epoch to another in the clinical approach to such patterns of behaviour as homosexuality and the use of alcohol and other drugs. The relationship is patently illustrated by the decision of the American Psychiatric Association some years ago to alter radically its view of homosexuality by declaring that the term did not in itself signify a clinical condition.[3]

In this new view American psychiatry echoed society's profound shift in attitude towards homosexuality during the 1960s. This example reveals another feature of psychiatry universally—the tendency to align itself with the *status quo*. Not unexpected, therefore, is the concept of "adjustment to society" as a commonly used criterion of mental health. A person is adjudged well if he adapts to the customs and conventions of the culture wherein he functions. The argument is advanced, most cogently by the American psychiatrist Seymour Halleck,[4] that the psychiatrist, whether he realizes it or not, assumes a political role when he attempts to modify a person's "maladaptive behaviour" in order that he may resume his membership of society.

All three above issues—compulsory hospitalization, the question of what is mental illness, and the widely-supported link between mental health and social adjustment—are made the more involved by psychiatry's vague boundaries. The optimal extent of its role and responsibility is subject to heated debate. The position is trenchantly held at one extreme that psychiatrists would do well to limit sharply their sphere of activity to the treatment of patients who can be confidently diagnosed as suffering from a recognized clinical illness. The opposite camp avers that as most illnesses are attributable to social factors—unemployment, racism, lack of opportunity, and divorce, for example—a rational approach entails an active political role for the psychiatrist so that he may contribute to an amelioration of undesirable conditions in his society.

The special character of psychiatry—to which the

aforementioned ethical issues point—constitutes an Achilles heel of considerable danger for its practitioners, because they may harness their professional skills, intentionally or unwittingly, to purposes in such a way that their patients lose paramountcy. The vulnerability of psychiatry to misuse, for non-medical reasons, is always present. Periodically, though happily this is rare, an individual psychiatrist perpetrates an abuse. This is inevitable in a profession made up of ordinary men and women who share the same foibles and weaknesses as any other group of people. While statutory regulations, review by peers, and codes of ethical practice contribute to the safeguarding of proper ethical standards, occasional infringements are bound to occur. More sinister is a pattern of abuse which involves an entire professional system and relies on the active connivance of its representatives with non-medical forces of influence.

It is to this form of unethical conduct that we now turn as we provide an outline of the misuse of psychiatry for political purposes in the Soviet Union. In so doing, we will follow a similar format to that used in our earlier book;[5] anyone wishing to obtain a comprehensive picture is advised to read this basic volume. We feel a summary of what we covered there is appropriate now, serving as it does as a *mise-en-scène* for the material we shall deal with in the chapters that follow.

We highlighted earlier the unavoidable relationship between the psychiatrist and his society, and the problems this generates. The association could not be better exemplified than in the Soviet Union where an exceptionally authoritarian State is coupled with the espousal of a doctrinal ideology. Both the particular structure of government and the central place given to ideology facilitate an intimate bond between Soviet society and its psychiatric profession.

The supremacy of ideology in all fields was a feature of the early revolution period and has remained solidly intact throughout the Soviet era. Stalin's call for political awareness in the professional work of scientists specifically—psychiatrists are included here together with all fellow scientists—is obvious from the following quotation:

... there is one branch of science which Bolsheviks in all branches of science are duty-bound to know, and that is the

Marxist-Leninist science of society . . . a Leninist cannot be just a specialist in his favourite science; he must also be a political and social worker, keenly interested in the destinies of his country, acquainted with the laws of social development, capable of applying these laws and striving to be an active participant in the political guidance of the country.[6]

For Stalin political qualifications were of greater relevance than professional ability and experience, and entailed the professional's commitment to Communist principles, reflected chiefly in his loyalty to the Communist Party. The Party then played a dominant role in all professional matters, as indeed it still does.

History of the Abuse

The first recorded case in Russia of the suppression of dissent by means of psychiatry occurred in 1836 when the philosopher, Pyotr Chaadayev (1793–1856), was labelled by Tsar Nicholas the First as suffering from "derangement and insanity". Ostensibly benevolent—". . . the Government in its solicitude and fatherly concern for its subject . . ."—Nicholas had in one neat stroke punished Chaadayev for publishing an article critical of his regime, and at the same time discredited the ideas expressed therein by declaring that they were those of a sick mind. This episode was, however, localized and in no way constituted a State policy.

The advent of the Bolshevik Government saw no basic change, in that the psychiatric repression of dissent continued to be sporadic and *ad hoc*. The most noteworthy case, in the very early days of the new regime, was the prominent political figure Maria Spiridonova. 1918 saw the collapse of the alliance of the Bolsheviks and the Socialist Revolutionary Party. Spiridonova and her Socialist Revolutionary colleagues posed a marked threat to the fledgling Government, and were energetically suppressed. Undeterred by a prison sentence, Spiridonova mustered her party's forces and launched a vehement attack on the Bolsheviks. Her growing power and influence had to be curbed, but rearrest and a second prison sentence would have proved embarrassing and risky to the Government; Spiridonova was by then too popular and celebrated a figure. The dilemma was soon resolved in a judgement by the Moscow Revolutionary Tribunal: in the interests of her health Spiridonova was to be "banished for one year from political and social life and isolated in a 'sanatorium'—there she would have the opportunity of healthy physical and mental work".[7] While in detention Spiridonova had predicted such an outcome, presumably in the knowledge that a declaration of insanity would discredit her political ideas as well as deprive her of the opportunity to continue her campaign. In the event, she escaped and the tribunal's scheme never materialized.

The Bolsheviks resorted to a similar device a year later in an effort to check another persistent critic, Angelica Balabanoff. In 1920 she attacked the leadership, including Lenin, pointing out the errors she believed they had committed. Again, the quandary faced the Government of what to do with a prominent political figure. The plan devised for Spiridonova was revived, albeit in modified form: Balabanoff was ordered to enter a sanatorium for the sake of her health although her "mental condition" was only hinted at. As in the case of the tough-minded Spiridonova, the plan was foiled by an uncooperative and unswerving critic. An alternative scheme was then concocted to dispose of Balabanoff, and before long she was bound for distant Turkestan at the command of a propaganda train.

During the Stalin period, the picture of psychiatric abuse is rather obscure but it does seem as if an embryonic policy to detain political dissenters in mental hospitals evolved in the late 1930s. Evidence comes from a psychiatrist who worked on the staff of a psychiatric hospital in Kazan during the second world war (he remained silent following his move to the United States, but in 1970, when allegations of current Soviet abuses were first made in the West, he reported vividly on his experiences in Kazan).[8] The institution, under the direction of the NKVD (the secret police), catered for the treatment of politicals from throughout the USSR. Most patients were in fact ill, the content of their disturbed minds being political in nature. A small proportion, however, were mentally healthy and detained there only on the grounds of their political convictions. The case of a Moscow factory worker exemplifies this second group. Following his persistent refusal to contribute to the war effort, then a "voluntary" State requirement for all workers, he was arrested, diagnosed as schizophrenic, and transferred to Kazan. His psychiatrist could not detect any mental illness but obviously felt under considerable pressure to collude with the police authorities; not to do so would have spelt personal danger for the psychiatrist himself. A humanitarian motive also operated—the hospital ward was undoubtedly less punitive than a prison or labour camp; at the least, he would remain alive!

This humanitarian motive on the part of psychiatrists is understandable in the face of the inhumanity of Stalin's penal policy. We obtained reliable corroboration of its existence from the poet Naum Korzhavin, when he provided us with an account of his experiences of 1948 in the Serbsky Institute for Forensic Psychiatry. (We discuss the Serbsky later in this chapter.) Following his arrest for writing "anti-Soviet" poems, he was examined by the Serbsky staff. Although finally declared sane and thus responsible before the law—he was sent into Siberian exile for several years as a result—he gained the distinct impression that the motive for psychiatric detention of healthy "politicals" was benevolent, not punitive. The staff, he suspected, were hoping to pin a diagnostic label on him in order to prevent his dispatch to a labour camp, with all its attendant horrors.

Korzhavin's testimony is buttressed by that of Ilya Yarkov, another victim of the thoroughly arbitrary legal procedures that typified the Stalin period. In his vivid autobiography he paints a similar picture of the practice of psychiatric abuse as he witnessed it in three different mental hospitals—in Gorky, Kazan and Chistopol. As in Korzhavin's experience, Yarkov never received any treatment, most doctors were kind and cordial, and conditions in the hospital were reasonably pleasant. No matter how humanitarian the motive of psychiatrists was, despite their benevolent management of the healthy dissenter their profession was obviously being manipulated during the 1940s and early 1950s to serve non-medical interests—as a tool to repress dissent.

It was Sergei Pisarev, a long-standing Party member, who first campaigned for the abolition of this political misuse of psychiatry. He himself had suffered from it between 1953 and 1955 following his open criticism of the secret police for fabricating the notorious "Doctors' Plot". His arrest, a spell in the Serbsky Institute, and then some eighteen months' detention in the Leningrad Prison Psychiatric Hospital enabled him to witness numerous cases—among them writers, artists and Party workers—in which misdiagnoses had been intentionally made. On his release he pressed the Party's Central Committee to rid psychiatry of this evil. The resultant commission of enquiry inspected the Serbsky, Leningrad and Kazan Hospitals, but its findings were completely ignored by the Party.

Were the revelations too embarrassing to allow their dissemination? Were there influential figures in the committee or in the secret police who wished to retain a useful option in the battle against political deviation? Stalin had by this time been succeeded by Khrushchev who was keen to cleanse the tarnished image of the USSR and to convey to the West that the ruthless methods of Stalin had ceased and the country no longer held political prisoners. The advantages inherent in psychiatrically-based repression, especially the discreet silencing of dissenters without recourse to a major trial or blatantly trumped-up charges probably appealed to Khrushchev as he tried to project a new image of the Soviet regime.

The actual reasons for sweeping the report under the carpet were, in the event, of little consequence—political psychiatry evidently continued unabated; in 1970, with the development of a human rights movement, Pisarev felt compelled to resume his protest. On this occasion he wrote to the Academy of Medical Sciences (the Government's most senior and prestigious advisory body in medicine) expressing his bitter disappointment that no substantial changes had taken place since the Central Committee's investigation. Indeed, if anything, matters had worsened, with an "increase in the illegal political repressions facilitated by the Serbsky Institute . . ."[9] (the foremost Soviet centre for forensic psychiatry which also doubles as the apex of psychiatric abuse). Although there is no way of corroborating Pisarev's statement about an escalation in political psychiatry, sufficient cases were learned about—Yarkov and Pisarev have already been mentioned but others that came to light were the mathematician Alexander Volpin, the artist Mikhail Naritsa, the geophysicist Nikolai Samsonov and the pensioner Fyodor Shults—to suggest that

during the 1950s and early 1960s a proportion of dissenters
were charged with a political offence, diagnosed as mentally
ill, and detained in a psychiatric hospital for indefinite
treatment.

Hitherto, only flimsy details that something was amiss in
Soviet psychiatry had percolated to the West. Then, in 1965,
two events brought the matter into much sharper focus. The
first was the British publication of *Ward 7* by Valery Tarsis.[10]
Although in novel form, it was obviously an account of the
author's own personal experience in a Moscow psychiatric
hospital. Party officials had engineered his forcible admission
there when they learned that Tarsis planned to publish in the
West *The Blue-Bottle*, an account of the constraints imposed on
intellectuals under Khrushchev. This "anti-Soviet" behaviour
required nipping in the bud, and what better deterrent than
an indefinite stay in a mental hospital? The second event, in
1965, which attracted Western attention concerned Evgeny
Belov, a student interpreter. The discovery of his politically-
based psychiatric internment was entirely fortuitous. A year
earlier a group of British students had met him whilst on a
tour of the Soviet Union and during a follow-up visit they
learned of his psychiatric confinement. On their return to
Britain they immediately launched a campaign on his behalf
which attracted widespread support from the media, public
and Amnesty International.

It soon emerged that Belov had, in the period between the
British students' two visits, become dissatisfied with certain
features of the Communist Party of which he was a member
and had voiced his criticism openly, his discontent culminating in his dispatch of proposals for change to the Soviet
leadership. Although beyond verification, and despite an
article in *Izvestia* which dubbed the British campaign on
behalf of Belov as a "filthy soap bubble" and "yet another
anti-Soviet forgery", all the evidence pointed to his detention
as another example of political psychiatry.

Finally, in this brief sketch of the history of psychiatric
misuse, we focus on Alexander Volpin. Forcibly hospitalized
on no less than five occasions between 1949 and 1968, his case
illuminates clearly the practice of political psychiatry during
this period. His poetry, regarded by the authorities as anti-
Soviet, led to his arrest, a diagnosis of schizophrenia and a

year in a prison psychiatric hospital. All subsequent admissions were clearly associated with political factors. The fifth episode, for example, followed his application for a visa to visit the United States where he had been invited to attend a scientific conference. On this occasion and for the very first time in the USSR in the context of psychiatric abuse, a large-scale protest ensued—99 of Volpin's colleagues petitioned the authorities for his immediate release. Several paid a high price for this action—demotion or dismissal from their posts. One signatory, Yuri Shikhanovich, would himself later share Volpin's fate. One of the authors (SB) interviewed both Volpin and Shikhanovich and failed to detect any evidence to warrant a diagnosis of mental illness.

Nineteen sixty-eight also saw the first generalized protest in the Soviet Union when a dozen human rights activists appealed to a conference of Communist Parties to react to the suppression of human rights including "the most shocking form of reprisal—forcible confinement in a mental hospital".[11] This act heralded two notable and interrelated developments: the emergence of a regular *samizdat* (underground, non-official publication) journal, the *Chronicle of Current Events*, which recorded accurately and dispassionately violations of human rights in the Soviet Union; and the establishment of the first formally-constituted group of dissenters—the Action Group for the Defence of Human Rights. Amid the Group's initial appeals were references to "a particularly inhuman form of persecution: the placing of normal people in psychiatric hospitals for their political convictions".[12] Ironically, four of the fifteen foundation members were destined to suffer from the very persecution about which they were protesting (we have interviewed three of them in depth—Natalya Gorbanevskaya, Vladimir Borisov and Leonid Plyushch—and confidently concluded that none was in need of any sort of psychiatric treatment).

Perhaps the most courageous and indefatigable of activists who battled to publicize political psychiatry was another of its victims—Vladimir Bukovsky. His remarkable effort to attract the attention of Western psychiatrists undoubtedly paved the way for their ultimate recognition of, and resistance to, the blatant misuse of their profession. We focus briefly on these developments at the end of this chapter.

The Pattern of the Abuse

At this point we need to examine the pattern of the abuse as it has occurred over the last fifteen years. First, we look at the routes along which dissenters have reached the psychiatric hospital. Then we provide brief accounts of the hospitals in which the dissenters have been placed and the treatment they have received there, the psychiatrists involved in this treatment and the diagnoses they have used, and the victims themselves—who are the dissenters confined to mental hospitals?

The dissenter is hospitalized by way of either a criminal or a civil commitment. A typical criminal commitment begins with an arrest. The ensuing investigation of the alleged offence includes a clinical examination by a psychiatric commission charged with the task of determining the presence or otherwise of any mental illness, whether the defendant is responsible or not, and the need or not for treatment. Charges are then drawn up and a lawyer brought in to serve the defendant. Articles 70 and 190-1 of the Criminal Code are the two most commonly used charges levelled against dissenters. Article 70 is the more serious, dealing as it does with subversive activities against the State, and it provides for a maximum punishment of seven years of imprisonment and five years of exile. Article 190-1 covers the discrediting of the Soviet political and social system and has a maximum sentence of three years of imprisonment.

Dissenters who undergo a psychiatric evaluation are usually declared mentally ill and not responsible for the alleged offence. The court almost always adopts the psychiatrists' recommendations. Their involvement ushers in a number of procedural changes: the dissenter is usually excluded from the trial on the grounds of his ill-health; his family and friends are normally kept out of court by extra-legal means; and the number of witnesses is substantially reduced. The trial, as a result, is often transformed into a mere formality.

What about the role of the defence counsel? He usually challenges the psychiatric findings and may request a second opinion, or a third if two previous reports are discordant. The court virtually always refuses such a request and does so invariably if a report from the Serbsky Institute is available.

The court has several "psychiatric" options at this point,

ranging from an order for outpatient medical supervision to compulsory placement in a special psychiatric hospital (SPH). The latter is the customary destination for a dissenter (on the grounds that he poses a special danger to society), less often used is an ordinary psychiatric hospital (OPH). Defence counsel may then lodge an appeal to a higher court but almost always to no effect—the most that this court does, very occasionally, is to substitute an OPH for an SPH as the institution for internment. Once the defendant has been transferred to hospital, his relatives can petition, but no more than this, for the cessation of compulsory treatment, and he must be examined every six months by a psychiatric panel whose report is submitted to the regional court. However, the dissenter himself has no right of appeal because he is deemed mentally incompetent; and the court is not obliged to accept a panel's recommendation for release or transfer to an OPH.

Release from hospital—usually from an OPH since most cases are transferred there from a prison hospital en route to liberty—does not necessarily mark the end of a dissenter's ordeal. Thereafter, the court usually orders his registration with his local clinic, in which event he is subject to regular supervision. This, coupled with a system of rating the level of social danger posed by the dissenter, is tantamount to an omnipresent sword of Damocles hovering over him. The rating—made first by the psychiatrist, and then by the security authorities in the light of all available information—guides the latter in the application of any necessary "preventive" actions (the degree of tenacity with which the dissenter holds to his convictions seems to be the key criterion in this rating). For example, the dissenter with a high rating of social danger may be detained briefly during major public holidays and important events like Party congresses. Also associated with systematic internment have been one-off occasions like the visit to the Soviet Union of President Nixon in 1972 and the holding of the Olympic games in Moscow in 1980.

Civil commitment is the dissenter's other potential route into the psychiatric hospital. By contrast with criminal commitment, it is a relatively straightforward procedure, especially because no criminal charges are laid and therefore no trial is held. Soviet psychiatrists, as is the case universally,

have the legal authority to place a person in hospital without
his consent if he is regarded as mentally ill and as a result
dangerous to himself or to others. They follow directives,
formulated in 1961 and marginally revised ten years later, in
which the crucial provision states: "If there is a clear danger
from a mentally ill person to those around him or to himself,
the health organs have the right ... to place him in a
psychiatric hospital without the consent of the person who is
ill or his relatives or guardians".[13] Only a single psychiatrist is
necessary to effect the commitment but once in hospital the
dissenter must be examined by a panel of psychiatrists within
24 hours to determine the need or otherwise for further
compulsory treatment. Thereafter, examinations are manda-
tory at least once monthly. The same conditions that affect the
release of a criminally committed person may, under certain
circumstances, also apply to the discharge of his counterpart
under civil commitment.

Mental health law throughout the psychiatric world constantly grapples with the question of indications for civil
commitment and particularly the tricky issue of dangerousness. The Soviet directives, if compared to those of other
countries, fare reasonably—their explicit specification of the
person's dangerousness to himself or others is a distinct
attribute. On the other hand their stated catalogue of mental
conditions which warrant urgent hospitalization is severely
limited by vagueness and poor definition. What is one to make
of "psychomotor excitement with a tendency towards aggressive actions"? This is merely dressed-up jargon which refers to
nothing more than it states, and no particular psychiatric
connotation can be extracted from it. This vagueness appears
to pave the way for the security organs to "persuade"
psychiatrists that a dissenter's behaviour is a risk to society.
Yet the evidence is overwhelming that civil commitment has
been used in the case of dissenters who constituted no danger
whatever to others and certainly not to themselves and who
did not fulfil any of the directives' indications.

Only if the concept of danger is extended radically to cover
"political" as well as the customary physical form—an interpretation which is wholly unjustified by a reading of the
published text—can we locate any possible basis for the
detention of dissenters. In the Soviet context, the argument

can be made that they pose a "danger to society" (more accurately a "danger to the regime") in that their views on human rights, their practice of religion, their wish to emigrate, and the like, are viewed by the regime with hostility and as a threat to the prevailing order. But the incorporation of such types of danger into a procedure of civil commitment is, in our view, completely indefensible as well as lacking foundation in the authoritative Soviet text. Even the most objective expert in mental health law could not possibly accept such an extension of the dangerousness concept. This is not to negate the possibility of a mentally-ill person harbouring delusions that he, for instance, possesses extraordinary powers or is a latter-day prophet and will "lead his followers to triumph over the wicked State". In such a case it is obvious that mental illness has robbed the person of contact with reality and placed him in a precarious social position from which he could act dangerously to others; but surely he is not dangerous because of the ideas he is attempting to propagate.

One other serious flaw of the Soviet civil commitment procedure, which is of striking relevance to the plight of the healthy dissenter confined to hospital, is the complete absence of judicial review. The detainee has no right of appeal at any point during his commitment and no access to legal counsel. The Soviet position on this absence of judicial review is as follows: psychiatrists are fair and impartial in their clinical judgements; the Ministry of Health constantly ensures the proper application of procedures; and third parties can protest against improper commitment. But this argumentation is extremely weak. As Judge David Bazelon, an American expert in mental health law, has observed, all these points fail to substitute adequately for the safeguard of legal review to check that no mistake has been made.[14]

The Dissenter's Treatment in Hospital

The nature of the commitment procedure has a crucial bearing on the sort of experience the dissenter is likely to have once he passes through the portals of the psychiatric institution. The reason is simple: generally (though we should note that there are exceptions to this pattern) civil commitment means a relatively brief and bearable internment in an OPH, whereas criminal commitment usually leads to a lengthy and harsh stay in an SPH.

Putting aside momentarily the sheer horror of a mentally-well person being forced into a psychiatric hospital, the dissenter can still be thankful when he is detained in an OPH rather than an SPH. The OPH is under the aegis of the Ministry of Health and serves as a facility for the community living around it; it is a relatively accessible institution and liable to scrutiny by patients and their families. The SPH is another matter altogether. There the dissenter is immersed in a highly disturbed environment, surrounded on all sides by genuine patients with severe mental illnesses, many of whom have committed violent crimes such as rape, assault and murder. The SPH is in fact little more than a prison and perhaps worse, as the inmate lacks the basic rights still retained by prisoners. He is left vulnerable and without hope. As an instrument to oppress him the SPH succeeds all too well.[15]

Fully to understand the SPH's horror, we need to describe its organization and staffing. It is controlled by the Ministry of Internal Affairs—not the Ministry of Health—and with this Ministry also responsible for the police and prisons, its foremost priority is without question the maintenance of security. Staffing in the SPH demonstrates this clearly. Medical personnel work alongside non-medical security officers in whose hands lies ultimate responsibility. For example, the chief psychiatrist is subordinate to the hospital's director, himself not usually a psychiatrist. So too are the junior personnel—the warders and orderlies—involved in the day-to-day management of the wards. The warder operates essentially as a guard and is not subordinate to the psychiatrist. Although the orderly is under the direction of both medical and non-medical seniors, his activities are mainly supervised by the warder. In practice, the orderly seems to be a law unto himself, for much of his work is unsupervised. He is, amazingly enough, a common criminal serving out his sentence and because of his own particular situation—imprisonment, poor living conditions, doing an unattractive job—is easily corrupted. We have as yet said nothing of the role of nurses, and little of that of psychiatrists; this reflects their comparatively insignificant place in the SPH. Any efforts by them to act humanely are apt to be thwarted by the security demands of the institution.

All these features contribute to a system in which any therapeutic impulse is squelched at birth. The testimony of several dissenters—Vladimir Bukovsky, Leonid Plyushch, Vladimir Gershuni and Viktor Fainberg have written especially vivid accounts—reveals a harrowing picture: the words punitive, inhumane, cruel and oppressive emerge as common epithets. Corroboration by outside forces is unavailable since, to our knowledge, no Westerner has ever been allowed in an SPH. But the dissenters' accounts of various SPHs are highly consistent. Brutality by the staff, especially the orderlies, is commonplace. Punishments are regularly meted out. Beatings seem to be the commonest form but have been supplemented by other more "exotic" methods such as the "wet pack". Wet canvas is tightly bound around the patient from head to foot and as it dries out the canvas gets progressively more taut causing great difficulty in breathing.

The administration of drugs is also applied as a punitive measure. Several dissenters have cited the role of Sulphazin. A preparation of purified sulphur, this drug was used in the 1930s but soon found to have no therapeutic effect and discarded. As a mode of punishment Sulphazin appears to be most effective: the victim suffers high fever and pain at the site of injection and throughout the body. By all accounts it is a gruesome experience. More commonly, drugs conventionally prescribed by psychiatrists are administered for non-therapeutic reasons. Virtually all drugs used in psychiatric practice share the unwelcome feature of producing side-effects. Such is the case especially with the major tranquillizers, a group of chemicals customarily given in the treatment of serious mental illness such as schizophrenia. Perhaps their most unpleasant and certainly most hazardous side-effect involves the system of the brain responsible for normal bodily movement and co-ordination. Tremor, purposeless movement of lips, tongue, face and other parts, restlessness, rigidity and slowness are possible consequences. Scrupulous attention to the setting of dosage, the careful monitoring of side-effects, and the prescribing of a specific drug to counteract the side-effects, reflect the conscientious psychiatrist's caution when prescribing the major tranquillizers. Several dissenters have described the indiscriminate use of these drugs—as punishment or as intimidation. The account by Plyushch of his own experience and that of fellow patients in the Dnepropetrovsk SPH in the Ukraine shows how devastating the "chemical weapon approach" can be: ". . . I was horrified to see how I deteriorated intellectually, morally and emotionally from day to day . . . my speech became jerky and abrupt. My memory also deteriorated."[16] He was soon unable to read or write.

In the case of Plyushch the intimidatory function of drug misuse was probably more relevant than its punitive function. A Marxist intellectual and leading figure in the then growing human rights movement, the authorities were determined to break him and to neutralize his "dangerous thinking", and by so doing deal a grievous blow to his colleagues. Specifically they sought to extract a recantation. The pattern of Soviet psychiatric abuse suggests strongly that the dissenter's renunciation of his convictions, coupled with his admission that they are the result of mental illness and his commitment not to readopt them in the future, is a primary objective of the political and security authorities. "Release requires recantation" might well be their slogan. As Vladimir Bukovsky describes it: ". . . admit openly and officially to the doctors that you were sick—yes, I was ill, yes; I didn't know what I was doing when I did it. The second condition is to admit you were wrong, to disavow what you did."[17] Elsewhere, in a *Manual on Psychiatry for Dissidents*[18] which Bukovsky authored with the dissenting psychiatrist Semyon Gluzman, he advises dissenters to pretend to their psychiatrists that they have reappraised their previous pathological thinking, in order to show their newly gained insight. "Tactical devices" such as this will enable survival. Bukovsky mentions examples of dissenters who refused to recant and were consequently detained for many long years. Certainly Plyushch's lengthy commitment was due to his steadfast determination not to renounce his views. At first sight we might regard Plyushch and his ilk as unduly stubborn, too highly principled, unrealistic. But we need to pause and consider some basic qualities of much of the dissenting community. Imbued with idealism and dedicated to their convictions, be they social, political or religious, they see recantation as tantamount to self-abnegation, to spiritual death: "moral suicide" is Fainberg's apt label.

Recantation or not, one distinct advantage of psychiatric repression as compared to prison, labour camp or exile is its indefiniteness. A dissenter subjected to one of the latter punishments lives with the anticipation of release at a defined point in time. Not so the psychiatrically confined dissenter. If a case of civil commitment, he has no right of appeal—his destiny is completely in the hands of doctors, and these hands, as we have seen, are tied by non-medical authority. No right of appeal is granted in the case of criminal commitment either. The court is the ultimate arbiter of his fate, through the mechanism of the recommendations of the six-monthly psychiatric commissions. The result may be a period of detention lasting several years, sometimes more than a decade. General Grigorenko, one of the most prominent dissenter-patients, refers to the "lack of any real hope of release" as particularly "harrowing".[19] And so it must be when the detainee has no idea at all about his chances of release. The epithet "Kafkaesque" could not be more appropriate to depict such an ordeal.

Added to this frightening insecurity is the sense of complete impotence experienced by the dissenter. Not only is he deprived of the right to judicial review but he also has no legal redress whatever concerning any aspect of his conditions. For example, he cannot mount a malpractice suit against a cruel staff member; unlike prison or camp authorities, the SPH director is not obliged to submit a dissenter's protest to the local prosecutor; and although the family does have the right to petition the prosecutor to initiate criminal proceedings against hospital personnel, such a procedure is bound to be futile (we know of no SPH staff member who has ever been prosecuted, let alone convicted, by these means).

The prospect of being placed compulsorily in a psychiatric hospital as a healthy person is so ghastly as to be almost unimaginable. But this has been the fate of many hundreds of Soviet citizens over the past two decades. We now focus on these victims of political psychiatry and consider the sort of activities which have led to their suppression.

The Victims of Psychiatric Abuse

Who, then, are the dissenters labelled as mentally ill and forced to be treated? We have produced a classification consisting of five categories, derived from an analysis of over 200 well-authenticated cases, covering the period 1962–1976. A further 300-odd cases that have come to light during the period from 1977 to the time of writing (see chapter three) roughly confirm the original pattern.

All these dissenters share one basic feature: they have deviated in some way from social conventions and norms firmly laid down by the State, and by virtue of their activities have been identified and labelled as suspect. They can be classified as: (1) advocates of human rights or democratization; (2) nationalists; (3) would-be emigrants; (4) religious believers; and (5) citizens inconvenient to the authorities. We now describe the categories briefly and provide representative case-illustrations.

The advocates of human rights and democratization comprise about half the dissenters repressed psychiatrically. They have through various legal means appealed to the Soviet Government to respect the civil rights of citizens as accorded in the Constitution, and to permit democratic processes to operate. Viktor Davydov is a typical example.[20] A law student born in 1956, Davydov comes from the Volga city of Kuibyshev. For his part in a human rights group of young people, and in demonstrations, and for writing *samizdat* works on Stalin and the failings of the Soviet system, he was subjected to psychiatric examination from 1976 onwards. In October 1979 he sought an independent examination by Dr Alexander Voloshanovich, then consultant to the Moscow Working Commission to Investigate the Use of Psychiatry for Political Purposes (see chapter three). Voloshanovich concluded that he was in no way schizophrenic, and "fully responsible for his actions". A month later Davydov was arrested and charged with "slandering the Soviet system". Examination by a psychiatric commission, which found him responsible, was immediately succeeded by his transfer to the Serbsky Institute. Here, in mid-1980 he was diagnosed as a mild schizophrenic and judged not responsible. At his trial the court accepted the Serbsky report alone, declaring that: "In view of the great social danger he represents he needs to undergo compulsory treatment in a psychiatric hospital of special type."[21]

After a brief period in the Kazan SPH Davydov was

dispatched to the Blagoveshchensk SPH near the Pacific coast—4,500 kilometres from his wife and friends. He has been confined there ever since.

Nationalists comprise about one-tenth of the dissenter population victimized by means of psychiatry. They have protested about the lack of rights—usually in the sphere of language, culture and education—of ethnic groups such as the Crimean Tatars, the Ukrainians, the Georgians, the Estonians and the Latvians, or appealed for the granting of political autonomy to the Soviet Union's fifteen national republics in accordance with the Constitution.

A good example is the Georgian Nikolai Samkharadze, who was born in 1915 and graduated in both history and medicine. First he taught history and became the headmaster of a secondary school in the Georgian capital of Tbilisi. In 1958 he attended a meeting of history teachers at the Ministry of Education, and made a critical speech about the inadequate teaching of Georgian history in Georgian schools. For this, he was soon arrested, ruled not responsible and interned by a court in an OPH. Eight months later he was discharged. However, for ten years he found himself constantly barred from jobs in teaching or medicine. In desperation, he cabled Mr Brezhnev in 1969, renouncing his citizenship and seeking emigration for himself and his family. Almost at once he was given a job as a doctor. In 1974 he joined the Group to Defend Human Rights in Georgia, and was soon subjected to police harassment.

In an appeal of 1982 his son brought the story up to date: "On 23 September 1980 my father was arrested by the KGB and charged with anti-Soviet agitation. In reality he was involved in no agitation: he demanded the realization of the Georgian people's constitutional rights, criticized certain officials and their actions, and fought for Georgian history to be taught in Georgian schools. . . . Now my father, aged sixty-seven, . . . has again been put in a mental hospital for telling the truth, for his integrity. He, a completely healthy person, is languishing in the psychiatric prison in Oryol. . . . I appeal to all people of good will to raise their voices against this terrible act of KGB oppression, to defend our family from persecution, and to save my father from the 'treatment' of the psychiatric butchers."[22]

The third category, of would-be emigrants, makes up about one-fifth of dissenters subject to psychiatric abuse. They have campaigned or physically tried to emigrate from the USSR. In some cases this has been influenced by a national motivation—Volga Germans wishing to return to West Germany, Jews seeking emigration to Israel; for others, it has been simply the desire for a better life. The Jews and Germans have been relatively spared political psychiatry, probably because their movements are large and well-known in the West. Individual would-be emigrants have, however, been tackled head-on. Consider two typical cases, those of Alar Kume and Zita Šalaševičiute. Kume, an Estonian worker, was arrested in December 1981 when he was twenty-four.[23] He was attempting to cross the Norwegian border in the north of the Kola Peninsular. Examined at the Serbsky Institute, he was judged not responsible for his crime—probably Article 83, "illegal crossing of the frontier"—and at the trial that ensued was sent for compulsory treatment to the Leningrad SPH. He continues to be detained to the present.

Zita Šalaševičiute, a Lithuanian teacher of English born in 1947, exemplifies the psychiatric saga of a person applying legally to leave the USSR.[24] The first penalty she paid after seeking permission to migrate was the loss of her job. Soon thereafter, in May-June 1976, she was interned in a small local psychiatric clinic. Presumably frustrated by the futility of her quest, she demonstrated in January 1981 on Red Square in Moscow with a placard "I demand the right to emigrate". She was quickly interned in a Moscow OPH and held there until March, being given intensive insulin shock treatment. She then returned to Lithuania and renounced her citizenship. Since then her fate is unknown.

People belonging to a variety of church groups, who have been detained solely because of their religious activity, constitute our fourth category and account for about fifteen per cent of dissenter-patients. They wish to practise their religion freely and to see a complete separation of Church and State. Although all four Soviet Constitutions to date contain the principle of freedom of conscience, Marxist ideology has in fact led to the imposition of severe restrictions on religious practice, even to the point of making certain facets—notably the teaching and dissemination of religious belief—criminal offences liable to imprisonment. Psychiatric repression has proved a useful addendum to the State's programme of deterrence.

From the many cases we can choose as illustrative, covering several religious denominations including Catholic, Baptist, Christian Orthodox, Pentecostalist and Buddhist, that of Anatoly Runov is typical.[25] A preacher in the unofficial Baptist Church, he was forcibly hospitalized in the Gorky Regional OPH on three occasions in the mid-1970s, with a diagnosis of paranoid schizophrenia. Undeterred, he continued his work as a preacher. In an effort to thwart the authorities from adopting the psychiatric option yet again, he had himself examined in February 1979 by Dr Voloshanovich who did not find him mentally ill. Notwithstanding, a few months later the local procurator asked a court to rule him mentally incompetent apparently so that he could be deprived of a driving licence, and his preaching thus made more difficult to carry out, and his psychiatric internment easier to expedite. In October 1979 he was arrested for throwing from his motor-bike a few slips of paper containing the times of foreign religious broadcasts, charged with hooliganism and ruled mentally ill at the Gorky City Mental Hospital. He was sent to the Leningrad SPH and later transferred to the one in Volgograd. In late 1981 he was moved yet again to an OPH and was still there at the time of writing.

The fifth and smallest category—about five per cent of dissenters dealt with psychiatrically—is a more amorphous group. It consists of those who are inconvenient to Party or State officials because of their "obdurate" complaints about bureaucratic excesses and abuses. It is clear, for example, that in Moscow the highest official bodies such as the Party's Central Committee, the Presidium of the Supreme Soviet and the Council of Ministers have ready access to a psychiatric first-aid service in order to dispose of complainants regarded as unduly troublesome. An illuminating example is the case of Mrs Gusyakova, a sixty-one-year-old housewife. She went to complain to Government officials about what she saw as malpractices of the district authorities but was soon forcibly shoved into a car and driven to a local OPH. It took her a week to get out. Later, she commented bitterly: "Simple people cannot obtain elementary justice: the most persistent protesters, those who doggedly press for fairness, are dispatched to lunatic asylums from the reception rooms of the Supreme Soviet Presidium and the Central Committee. No, not dissenters, just the persistent—to stop them complaining."[26]

With such a large range of options open to quash dissent—prison, labour camp, internal exile, forced emigration—why do the authorities resort to psychiatric internment of certain dissenters such as those described above? Though we have just cited Mrs Gusyakova's comments about the detention of ordinary citizens, they comprise a very small proportion of the known psychiatric victims. Our impression is that the mental hospital has, at least until recently, been used for the more persistent, determined dissenter. And even more so if there is the slightest psychiatric taint in his background. Were he to be brought to trial in the usual manner, there would be an opportunity for a fiery "political" speech by the defendant and the possibility of its subsequent dissemination. As we commented earlier in our discussion of criminal commitment, the prosecution's psychiatric device paves the way for a trial that is a simple formality—the defendant is absent, only minimal evidence of a crime needs to be produced, and the risk of a demonstration by supporters outside the court is virtually eliminated.

The dissenter's experience in the SPH highlights the artfulness of the KGB's design: he is isolated from his family, friends and fellow dissenters; implanted in a highly disturbed milieu; deprived of all legal rights; detained indefinitely; often given drugs as punishment or intimidation; and pressed to make a recantation as a condition of release. In a phrase, the KGB's goal is: break the dissenter, even the toughest, and so help to crush his movement. And throughout, the dissenter's views, regarded as so "socially dangerous" by the State, can be ascribed to his sick mind. This ploy is especially valuable against those dissenters who, because of their Party membership or their status as Marxists, or their prominent public position, should be seen to be loyal and devoted Soviet citizens under all circumstances.

The above catalogue of factors seems coherent enough but the overall pattern of the regime's battle against dissent is in practice much more inconsistent. Often it is well-nigh impossible to ascertain why the KGB has opted for the psychiatric gambit rather than the labour camp; why criminal commitment was used in preference to civil commitment; why an OPH and not an SPH was chosen as the place of internment. The KGB obviously keeps its motives and rationales mostly to itself, and we can do little more than speculate about the factors that influence its decisions. One factor about which we can have some confidence is international publicity. As we shall discuss at length in later chapters, psychiatric repression has over the past decade and a half fluctuated in prevalence and varied in form according to the level and intensity of reaction both in the Soviet Union and in the West.

The Role of the Psychiatrist and His Diagnosis

Thus far we have barely mentioned the psychiatrist's role in the misuse of his profession. It goes without saying that he is indispensable—without his co-operation the practice would evaporate. Does this indicate that all psychiatrists are equally involved? We believe not. Interviews with ex-dissenter-patients and émigré Soviet psychiatrists have led us to the following classification: (1) core psychiatrists—pivotal participants in the abuse; (2) average, ordinary psychiatrists—the large mass of the Soviet profession—who reluctantly collude with the politicization of their discipline out of a blend of indoctrination, passive conformism and sheer fear; and (3) dissenting psychiatrists—a minuscule group—who are openly or covertly critical of the unethical practice. We now focus on each group, particularly on what motivates their actions. In this account we also note the uneasy relationship between psychiatrists and authoritarian State, an extension of the points we made in our discussion of the vulnerability of psychiatry to non-medical influences.

The core group, probably no more than several dozen in number, contains psychiatrists who have participated in the examination of dissenters or who have been consulted in some way about them. They tend to occupy senior administrative, academic or hospital positions, from which they exert considerable power and influence. Some are known to Western observers, for example: Professor Andrei Snezhnevsky, director of the prestigious Institute of Psychiatry of the Academy of Medical Science, doyen of Soviet psychiatry and probably the most influential figure in his profession (later we will consider his crucial contribution to diagnostic theory); Professor Georgy Morozov, director of the Serbsky Institute for Forensic Psychiatry and in recent years the President of the All-Union Society of Neuropathologists and Psychiatrists; Professor Ruben Nadzharov, Snezhnevsky's deputy director; Drs Margarita Taltse and Yakov Landau, senior psychiatrists at the Serbsky; and Professor Marat Vartanian, director since its foundation in 1982 of the All-Union Scientific Centre for Mental Health, who has had a distinctive role for over a decade as chief apologist for Soviet psychiatry to the world medical community.

Several lines of evidence converge to indicate that these figures, and fellow core psychiatrists, are active participants in the abuse. What drives them to co-operate so readily with their political masters? A blend of the following motives, complex and manifold, probably pertains. The first is ideological—a conviction (whether held sincerely or opportunistically, it is difficult to say) that the Party's interests are paramount and call for unswerving respect and loyalty. The critic of the Party or of Marxism–Leninism, the State's institutions, and Soviet political doctrine, may therefore well be mentally disordered and poorly adjusted to his society. We suspect the sincerity underlying this ideological factor. Even if genuinely believed in, the core psychiatrists' usual recommendation for a dissenter's compulsory treatment in a SPH, when they know full well what he will encounter there, is extremely dubious. We need to recall here that the SPH is primarily designed for mentally-ill offenders with a propensity for violence. In the case of many dissenters their diagnosis has been a relatively mild form of schizophrenia which by no stretch of the imagination could call for such a radical measure.

We believe that another more cogent motive also operates—the desire to rise to a high professional position, with its attendant exercise of power and influence, the satisfaction of ambitious striving, and the more tangible benefits of the "good life". Of course, this desire is not limited to Soviet psychiatry, but the means whereby it is fulfilled *is* most distinctive. As we mentioned earlier, the political qualifications of professionals have always been regarded as vitally important. In essence, this amounts to a strong loyalty to the Communist Party, a strict adherence to its ideology, and unquestioning fulfilment of its directives. The psychiatrist, as a professional person, will have been obliged, as a medical student, to devote about a quarter of his studies to political subjects. Later, as part of his oath on graduating he will have sworn: ". . . in all my actions to be guided by the principles of Communist morality . . ."[27]

In practical terms the political factor is seen in the concentration of Party members in the top echelons of psychiatry. Their presence there facilitates the regime's control and manipulation of all policy. Implementing Party programmes through its "loyal" representatives is thus assured. The vulnerability of psychiatry now becomes apparent: the psychiatrist in a senior post has a dual allegiance—to Party and to patient, but in order to preserve his privileged status he must submit to the Party's will. If that entails collaboration with the State in its programme to curb dissent, so be it; particularly if he can rationalize that his actions are based on the ideological motive we mentioned earlier. Moreover, the core psychiatrist is comforted by the knowledge that his patron, the Party, will ensure his "safety" in the face of any victim calling him to account, legally or otherwise. Meanwhile, in addition to the power he enjoys, he can obtain material benefits—foreign travel, high salary, a country cottage, special holidays, access to stores selling luxury goods—all the rewards for dutiful service.

We will come across some core psychiatrists in later chapters, when we look at their role as apologists for Soviet psychiatry in the international arena. But now we turn our attention to the smallest category in our classification, that of the dissenting psychiatrist. Since we focus in detail on two of its foremost representatives in chapter three, our discussion here is relatively brief. This minute group consists of those psychiatrists openly criticial of colleagues who have perpetrated political psychiatry. Some of them, like Semyon Gluzman and Anatoly Koryagin, have been punished severely for voicing their criticism whilst others—Yuri Novikov, Marina Voikhanskaya, Boris Zoubok, Avtandil Papiashvili and Alexander Voloshanovich—have emigrated to the West and there condemned Soviet psychiatric perversion. Koryagin and

Voloshanovich are particularly interesting in that they served as consultants to the previously mentioned commission investigating the abuse of psychiatry. In this capacity they undertook a task unprecedented in psychiatric practice—the examination of dissenters who had been hospitalized in the past or who had good reason to anticipate psychiatric victimization in the future. This vulnerable group hoped that a clean bill of health by an independent psychiatrist, publicized both in the USSR and abroad, might deter the authorities from deploying political psychiatry on them in the future. In chapter three we will look at this remarkable assignment in more detail.

There is probably a sizeable group of psychiatrists—the number is impossible to estimate—who condemn the misuse of their discipline as much as those we have listed but who are too petrified, with justification perhaps, to voice their sentiments openly. When the price of such action is so costly—Gluzman received a ten-year sentence and Koryagin is presently serving twelve years, both on trumped-up charges—even the morally outraged psychiatrist is likely to think long and hard before "declaring" himself. He knows only too well that in his country there are no half measures, that the expression of criticism against a State-directed system entails a transmogrification from conformist, law-abiding Soviet citizen to labelled dissenter and with that change a precipitous slide into a whirlpool of personal risks and hazards, ranging from professional ostracism to punishment like that meted out to Gluzman and Koryagin.

The only pragmatic way out of this moral dilemma is the exercise of passive, veiled dissent, namely, acting with implicit benevolence towards the dissenter-patient. The case of Ilya Rips illustrates this well. During his eighteen months of detention in a hospital in Riga, Rips told us, his doctors were mostly kind and helpful. Their benign attitude was probably reinforced by the resentment they themselves felt as Latvians towards the Russian *force majeure*.

The phenomenon of veiled dissent more properly fits into our final category of the average psychiatrist, which is composed of the many thousands of ordinary Soviet practitioners, the bulk of the profession. These psychiatrists, motivated by fear and a strong need to conform, have probably colluded with the misuse of psychiatry, using denial and rationalization to avoid facing painful ethical dilemmas. Their fear and conformism stem from a basic awareness of Soviet reality. The ordinary psychiatrist observes the norms and conventions of his society, knowing only too well that taking a single deviant step embodies great risk and danger. One strategy for self-protection is complete avoidance, if at all possible, of any activity that contains even a hint of personal threat. If compelled to enter hazardous territory, a second tactic is applied, namely retreat to safer ground as promptly as circumstances permit.

The testimony of one émigré psychiatrist (who wishes to remain anonymous) reveals the typical thinking of an average psychiatrist faced with the examination of a "political" case. He told us that like every Soviet citizen the psychiatrist has learned over many years how to "understand"—to ascertain in the absence of explicit instructions what the "authorities" expect of him in particular situations. Thus a request by the KGB, a local Party Committee, or other authority, for ·the psychiatric examination of a person who has manifested dissent, even a whiff of it, is recognized as a covert message that psychiatry has been selected as a potential option to deal with that dissent. Now the first of the two defensive strategies comes into play: "Is there any way that I can evade this task? Yes, let the Serbsky staff fret over this." And so the case is referred for specialist opinion. This tactic is not always available, and in the absence of an alternative evasive ploy, reluctant participation ensues.

From the information given us by several émigré psychiatrists, it appears that the average psychiatrist unavoidably involved with a case of dissent plays out a charade. This is what he might tell his dissenter-patient if he felt free to do so: "I know you're not mentally ill, or at least you don't need to be hospitalized, but do appreciate my own position—I have no choice but to play along with the KGB (by whom he feels intimidated). If I don't, I'll be in the same boat as you. Let us co-operate with one another—you play the patient role properly and I shall do what I can to get you out of here as soon as possible. Bear in mind, however, that if my efforts do not succeed, it is because my clinical freedom is severely hamstrung by the authorities. One thing you can be assured of is that I hate this sordid business as much as you do".

This picture would be overly simplistic were one to ignore the other motive we mentioned earlier—conformism. This aspect of the average Soviet psychiatrist is well described by Bukovsky and Gluzman in their *Manual on Psychiatry for Dissidents*.[18] He is of average intellect, with highly conventional opinions and interests; for example, he is sceptical of modern forms of art and of poetry. He finds it difficult to comprehend the dissenter's poor adjustment to Soviet society—why he should risk his all for some futile cause: "But you had a flat, a family, a job. Why did you do it?"[28] There is nothing surprising about this view of dissent—a general intolerance of non-conformist behaviour has always permeated Soviet culture; conformity has dominated Soviet consciousness; and the threshold for deviance from convention has been correspondingly low. The average psychiatrist is as much an example of Soviet conformism as any other citizen.

This brings us to contemporary Soviet diagnostic theory and its relevance to dissent. Over the past quarter century the view of what constitutes mental illness has been markedly influenced by the culturally-held view of deviant behaviour. The ascendancy of Professor Snezhnevsky's theories during this period has led, in particular, to a stretching of the boundaries of illness such that even the mildest behavioural change is construed as evidence of mental disturbance.

Part of this development is the broadening in the USSR of the diagnosis of schizophrenia and the prominence given to it. Snezhnevsky's classification of this illness, one of the most serious encountered in psychiatry, postulates the existence of three distinguishable forms, with several subtypes in each. The mildest of the progressive form, labelled sluggish schizophrenia because of its very slow rate of development, is the sinister "new" illness of Soviet psychiatry–sinister in that it allows the most subtle behavioural change to be readily interpreted as a severe psychiatric condition. So subtle may the change be that the concept of "seeming normality" has been invoked. Thus, in the case of Olga Iofe—diagnosed as a sluggish schizophrenic—a psychiatrist responded in this way to the defence counsel's observations that his client had performed well in her scholastic pursuits over several years despite allegedly harbouring a severe illness: "The presence of this form of schizophrenia does not presuppose changes in the personality noticeable to others." Professor Lunts, in defending his diagnosis of sluggish schizophrenia in Natalya Gorbanevskaya, contended that the condition was "theoretically", but not clinically, present at the time of her offence!

Before delving further into the peculiarities of diagnostic practice *vis-à-vis* dissent, we need to consider one final characteristic of the ordinary psychiatrist, the possibility that his ostensible adherence to the Snezhnevsky diagnostic schema results from the absence of any competing theoretical approach. The Snezhnevsky school triumphed during the 1950s over its rivals during what was then an intensely ideological era. Subsequently, the new concept of schizophrenia was launched and refined. With Snezhnevsky virtually dominating the psychiatric profession over the past 30 years (through its hierarchical structure which ensures control of all teaching, research and clinical activities throughout the country as well as firm control of the sole professional journal), most psychiatrists who have been trained during his "reign" know of no other approach and are therefore not in a position to question it.

We would be on shaky ground in arguing that the average psychiatrist errs in using the Snezhnevsky scheme. His approach cannot be objectively judged as more or less valid than other theories, because there is simply not sufficient scientific evidence for that judgement to be made as yet. But we are on much firmer ground, and in the company of many national psychiatric associations who have studied the Soviet labelling of dissent as illness, when we aver that the application of a diagnosis such as sluggish schizophrenia to dissenters is without justification, at least as regards the cases with which we are personally acquainted.

Consider some of the key phrases commonly used in their clinical reports to buttress a diagnosis of schizophrenia (or one of associated paranoid personality): "reformist delusional ideas"; "uncritical attitude to his abnormal condition"; "overestimation of his own personality"; and "poor adaptation to the social environment". These clinical features simply do not apply to dissenters. "Reformism" and its companion, "uncritical attitude to . . .", are a distortion of a dissenter's clear and insightful views that a specific act or policy of the regime warrants criticism—a violation of the Constitution, the 1968 invasion of Czechoslovakia, the lack of rights of the national republics, and the like. By contrast, in Western countries the expression of social criticism, such as is made by Soviet dissenters, is regarded as an intrinsic attribute of democratic society. "Over-estimation of his own personality" implies a delusion of grandeur. This is not the case with the dissenter who appreciates, often painfully, that his campaign will necessarily be frustrating and laborious, and prone to all the forces of suppression mustered by the State. He is also aware of the risks inherent in his activity, but his strong convictions compel him to take these risks. Finally there is no evidence that dissenters are poorly adjusted to their social environment (unless one accepts—as we certainly do not— the notion that anyone who attempts to tackle the "great Russian bear", the Soviet totalitarian regime, must necessarily be "out of his mind"). On the contrary, dissenters wage their campaigns within the boundaries of Soviet law and without recourse to violence, while concurrently continuing their work as academics, writers, artists, manual workers, priests, technicians (unless dismissed arbitrarily because of their dissent). Attitudes of family and friends to the dissenter reflect in an additional way his satisfactory social adjustment. Almost invariably, he has their support in his activity and in the fight against his psychiatric victimization.

Conclusion

With this brief sketch of the misuse of psychiatry as background, we are now in a position to embark on what is the chief focus of this book—the battle in the Soviet Union and in the West to bring these politically motivated abuses to an end.

The opening shots in the battle—those prior to 1971—have been sketched earlier in the chapter. The subsequent engagement of the two sides, and the clashes of the next few years, occupy chapters four and ten of our first book, and we outline them here only in brief.

In January 1971 Vladimir Bukovsky took the crucial initiative of compiling 150 pages of documentation and sending them to Western psychiatrists. They included the texts of ten official psychiatric reports on dissenters. Aware of the problems involved in commenting from afar, he asked them in his accompanying letter only one question: "Do the above-mentioned reports contain enough scientifically-based evidence to indicate the necessity of completely isolating these people from society through internment?"

Over the subsequent couple of years many psychiatric groups studied Bukovsky's materials, and some replied, directly or indirectly, to his question. All the replies were couched in the spirit that he had clearly hoped for, although they also stopped short of unequivocal condemnation of Soviet abuse. They came, notably, from the World Federation for Mental Health and medical bodies in Britain, the USA, France, Switzerland, and Holland.

Other organizations, however, most conspicuously the World Psychiatric Association (WPA), remained silent. Strong pressures were exerted on the WPA to debate the issue at its congress in Mexico in December 1971, and the congress president declared in his opening speech: "To keep silent about such an ignominious situation would weigh heavily on our conscience." However, the USSR's threat that its delegation would walk out if silence was *not* kept, was—thanks to strong-arm support from WPA Secretary-General Denis Leigh—effective. Bukovsky was thus betrayed and, soon, heavily sentenced.

Following the congress the Soviet authorities developed a fairly clear policy with which to confront their critics. While ceasing to intern dissenters of any renown, they continued to intern others, camouflaged their limited retreat with a smokescreen of self-righteous counter-attacks, and tried hard to manipulate foreign psychiatrists so as to neutralize, as far as possible, current and future pressures.

The year 1973 was climactic. Western campaigns of pressure mounted, as it became widely known that Dr Gluzman had received a ten-year sentence for writing an analysis of Grigorenko's case which demonstrated the fraudulence of the psychiatric report on him. Andrei Sakharov emerged fully into public view with cogent appeals for Western action against political psychiatry. And the Soviet hosting of a WPA conference on schizophrenia in October led to an unprecedented Western debate in advance, and then to a tense conference and a visit to the Serbsky Institute by thirteen foreign psychiatrists. The last was designed to convince them that Western criticism was groundless. But it failed to do so.

This, however, did not prevent Dr Vartanian from claiming that the WPA Executive, to which he belonged, had "agreed that all five of the so-called dissenters who had been discussed at the meeting had been suffering from mental illnesses at the times when they had been examined by psychiatric commissions". Although caught at once in this deception, and corrected, Vartanian, with characteristic brazenness, printed it unchanged some months later in the leading Soviet psychiatric journal. Even more breathtaking was Morozov's publishing of the same lie in the *British Medical Journal* in July 1974. Finally, and most remarkable of all perhaps, it was not until August 1975 that Dr Leigh saw fit to deny the false statements by the president of his second-largest member-society.

The Soviet mendacity and the near-complaisance of the WPA helped to fuel mounting Western protests in the mid-1970s. Another key stimulant was the multi-pronged campaign to free Leonid Plyushch, whose internment we discussed above. The success of this extraordinary campaign in January 1976 and Plyushch's horrifying and persuasive testimony finally clinched, for many observers, three vital points: the abuses were authentic, they were genuinely sinister, and the outside world could play an effective role in, at the very least, mitigating them.

It was against this background that in August 1977 at the Sixth World Congress of the WPA in Honolulu, resolutions were passed to condemn the Soviet practices and to establish a review committee to monitor political psychiatric misuse wherever it might occur. These developments were a prelude to a stormy six-year period in international psychiatry which culminated in the resignation of the Soviet psychiatric society in January 1983 and momentous events at the Seventh World Congress in July 1983 in Vienna. We describe and analyse this dramatic era in the history of contemporary psychiatry in the chapters that follow.

CHAPTER TWO

THE HONOLULU CONGRESS:
THE FIRST GREAT CLASH

USUALLY AN OCCASION for many hundreds of psychiatrists from all over the world to meet, exchange ideas, and learn about new developments in their field, the World Congress arranged every six years by the WPA has, since the latter's foundation in 1961, always been a major event in the psychiatric profession's calendar. The Sixth Congress, held in August 1977 in Honolulu, was notable for more than these professional concerns; the Soviet misuse of psychiatry emerged as the most critical issue on the conference agenda. Because of this, the occasion assumed quite exceptional and extraordinary proportions.[1]

Three weeks before the 4,000 participants gathered in Honolulu, Vladimir Bukovsky had submitted an appeal to them to react vigorously to the Soviet abuse.[2] Bukovsky was internationally-renowned by this stage: he had been one of the most active members of the Soviet human rights movement for more than a decade; he had been severely dealt with by the authorities during this time by means of sentences to prison and labour camp, and through prolonged internment in psychiatric hospitals (he was thus exceptionally well qualified to make his appeal); and he had been freed from a prison and deported to the West in December 1976 in a dramatic exchange with the Chilean Communist Luis Corvalan. His appeal was therefore heeded by many psychiatrists who were at that point aware of the gravity of the unethical practices in the USSR.

As noted earlier, a similar appeal made by Bukovsky six years before on the eve of the previous World Congress in Mexico City, had met with a different response.[3] Then, he had submitted substantial documentation on the forcible psychiatric internment of named dissenters, including the official psychiatric reports on them. Although this material constituted the first solid evidence of political psychiatry, for many psychiatrists such practice was beyond the limits of credulity. The possibility that colleagues had assumed the role of jailer strained their imagination. In any event, in order to forestall complications for the WPA, its Executive Committee ruled that Bukovsky's appeal could not be considered because the organization's statutes did not provide for submissions from lay individuals. This was a relatively painless way out of a tricky situation but also tantamount to sweeping the very serious allegations of psychiatric abuse under the carpet.

The same strategy was quite beyond application at the time of the Honolulu World Congress. The extensive new evidence that had emerged in the intervening six years convinced a number of national psychiatric bodies, notably in the United States, Britain, Australasia and Canada, that the original allegations were well grounded and warranted collective action. Bukovsky argued in his appeal of 1977 that indifference at Mexico City had permitted the perversion of psychiatry to continue, indeed to escalate: the number of victims had increased, other dissenters had been threatened with psychiatric detention, and protesters including psychiatrists had been punished. (The indifference had undoubtedly led also to the severity of the prison sentence handed down to Bukovsky himself immediately after the congress.) He was putting the ball squarely in the court of the WPA by declaring that the position psychiatrists took in Honolulu would: "determine the fate of hundreds of people and, in the shorter term, the fate of Soviet psychiatry itself". Specifically, the abuse could be halted through "unambiguous international condemnation".[4]

Condemnation was precisely what was sought by two member societies of the WPA—the British and the Australasians. Each had submitted resolutions to that effect for debate by the General Assembly, the WPA's governing body composed of a delegate from each of the 76 member societies. The key portion of the British resolution read: "The World Psychiatric Association, taking note of extensive evidence of the systematic abuse of psychiatry for political purposes in the USSR, joins in the condemnation of these practices which has already been made by the British Royal College of Psychiatrists as well as other bodies."[5] The Australasian version whilst similar in intent was broader in form inasmuch as the Soviet abuses were also forthrightly condemned, but, in addition, reference was made to abuses "in all countries in which they occur". The full text reads: "That the WPA take note of the abuse of psychiatry for political purposes and that it condemn those practices in all countries in which they occur and call upon the professional organizations of psychiatrists in those countries to renounce and expunge those practices from their countries, and that the WPA implement this Resolution in the first instance in reference to the extensive evidence of the systematic abuse of psychiatry for political purposes in the USSR."

The eve of the congress, Sunday 28 August, was a festive occasion. At a large welcome reception for the participants, there was evidence aplenty of reunions and the birth of new professional ties and friendships. But the atmosphere was not entirely one of conviviality. The local press, obviously well acquainted with the potentially divisive issue which the Soviet issue represented, had devoted prominent space to the impending debate on the resolutions of condemnation. This attention was soon to be matched by that given by the international media. Throughout the conference, in fact, the Soviet issue was destined to grab the headlines, whereas reports on the scientific programme would be reduced to a trickle.

For the moment, at this early phase of the congress, opinion appeared divided into three camps. In the first, psychiatrists were unwaveringly committed to the idea of explicit condemnation. They wished to make it abundantly clear that world psychiatry dissociated itself from its Soviet colleagues and that inaction at Mexico City had amounted to a betrayal of Bukovsky. Equally entrenched in its view was a group of psychiatrists who saw the criticism of the USSR as nothing more than cold-war tactics; the allegations of abuse were without foundation.

In the middle, perched on a fence, sat the third group. Its members were motivated by one of two considerations: they either remained sceptical about the validity of the evidence marshalled by critics of the Russians, or, accepting the critics' case, believed it would be detrimental to the welfare of the

WPA to allow political matters to intrude into what was essentially a scientific gathering. Confrontation would inevitably lead to schism, with the distinct possibility of a walkout by the Soviet Society accompanied by its "satellites" and perhaps by other sympathetic member societies. Furthermore, an "anti-holier-than-thou" factor seemed to operate. Abuses of psychiatry of all forms probably occurred elsewhere: was it therefore not unfair to pick out the Russians alone?

At this point the exact size of the three camps was quite uncertain and hence the way in which the societies would vote later in the week unpredictable. Unknown to the voting delegates, much was to happen over the next few days which would draw the pertinent issues into sharp relief. The first of these happenings took place at the opening plenary session, held on Monday evening, 29 August. Devoted to a discussion of ethical aspects of psychiatry, it was especially noteworthy for the unveiling of the Declaration of Hawaii (see Appendix I). For the first time in the annals of psychiatry, its international representative body had devised a code of ethics to serve as guidelines for psychiatrists universally. The idea for such a set of principles had germinated at Mexico City and an Ethical Sub-Committee had been created especially to do the ground work. Its members, Drs Wretmark, Eitinger and Blomquist (interestingly, at that time, the last was probably the only psychiatric occupant of a special chair in Medical Ethics—his tragic, early death occurred in 1979) laboured at the assignment for three years preparing no less than nine drafts. One was submitted to member societies of the WPA in early 1977 for comment. The code was then being presented for consideration and discussion by the congress. Couched in the most general terms, it would have occasioned considerable surprise if the declaration had not been accepted by all those present.

The Executive had quite possibly entertained the hope when it set up the Ethical Sub-Committee in late 1973 that the code of ethics, although unenforceable, might deal with the Soviet "problem" and help to defuse it. Clauses relevant to potential misuse were contained in the document; for example: "The psychiatrist must never use the possibilities of the profession for the maltreatment of individuals or groups, and should be concerned never to let inappropriate personal desires, feelings or prejudices interfere with the treatment"; even more pointedly: "The psychiatrist must not participate in compulsory psychiatric treatment in the absence of psychiatric illness." Moreover, implicit recognition that abuses had already taken place was conveyed by the content of one passage in the preamble of the declaration, to wit: "Conflicting loyalties for physicians in contemporary society, the delicate nature of the therapist-patient relationship, and *the possibility of abuses of psychiatric concepts, knowledge and technology in actions contrary to the laws of humanity* [our italics], all make high ethical standards more necessary than ever for those practising the art and science of psychiatry."

The plenary session was intended to launch the Declaration of Hawaii, although it would still require formal endorsement by the General Assembly, scheduled to meet three days later. In fact, no difficulties were encountered in the Assembly. It was however recognized that while certain ethical principles might be sacrosanct, professional practice was prone to change, and this might have ethical implications. Delegates therefore decided to formalize the original Ethical Sub-Committee by creating a new Committee on Ethics. Its function would be to study areas of ethical concern to psychiatrists and more particularly to recommend any necessary revision of the declaration. Under the chairmanship of Professor C. Stefanis of Greece and comprising representatives from the United States, Iran, West Germany, Japan, Brazil and the USSR (ironically Marat Vartanian, who, as we shall see in later chapters, came to play a central role as apologist for Soviet psychiatry), the committee worked unobtrusively at its task.

If we now return to the task before the participants in the plenary session, it was presumably to examine the content and form of the declaration in an academic fashion. This plan was soon shattered by Eduard Babayan, the chief Soviet delegate to the congress. At this meeting, and thereafter on numerous other occasions during the week, it was this forceful, tough-minded physician, a high level administrator in the echelons of the Ministry of Health of the USSR, who would act as aggressive defender of his country's profession. On this first day of the congress, he appeared to be preparing the ground for the Soviet Society's opposition to the resolutions scheduled for debate at the Assembly two days later. Although he made no mention of these resolutions, he undoubtedly had them uppermost in mind when he proclaimed that he and his colleagues were ethically sensitive and responsible. Attacks on Soviet psychiatry in recent years were nothing more than slander—herein was a replay of the counter-offensive by Professor Snezhnevsky six years earlier at Mexico City. Snezhnevsky, the chief Soviet delegate to that congress had dubbed Western criticism as "cold-war manoeuvres".[6] Dr Babayan was more concerned to convince his audience that they need feel no anxiety about the conduct of Russian psychiatrists: first, enlightened legal procedures in the USSR completely precluded any arbitrary practices; second, no one group of psychiatrists enjoyed greater power and influence than any other in the Soviet court, and this included those working at the Serbsky Institute in Moscow (which by then had become a special target of condemnation by critics both within the Soviet Union and abroad); and third, antisocial activity *per se* could not possibly be used as a sole criterion for the compulsory admission of a person to a psychiatric hospital.

To the informed observer Babayan's performance constituted the first round in the contest over the fate of the resolutions of condemnation. His opponents sprang into action the next evening—Tuesday 30 August—at the second of the two plenary sessions devoted to ethical concerns. At the request of the American Psychiatric Association, the congress organizers had scheduled this event and designated it as an open discussion of the abuses of psychiatry. The ostensible motive of those who originated the session was to provide an open forum in which the misuse of psychiatry, whatever its form and wherever its occurrence, could be directly looked at and studied. In reality the dice were loaded against the Soviet Union as its particular misuse of psychiatry to suppress dissent was much to the fore at the time of the congress. That this topic would attract the virtually exclusive interest of participants was a foregone conclusion.

The Russians had clearly expected "trouble" at this session. This is evident from the reaction of Professor Snezhnevsky when he first learned about the proposal for the discussion in January 1977. In a letter to the WPA he stated his society's firm opposition: "It would only give cause to unnecessary excitement around this problem [of ethics]." Snezhnevsky requested that this view be disseminated to all member societies, presumably with the hope of removing the slot from the programme. Of the small number which responded, two-thirds wanted the event to proceed, the rest supported the Soviet position.

Yet there was in theory a semblance of even-handedness. Four speakers representing each of the official languages of the WPA had been invited to lead the discussion. In addition, because the Soviet Union had the right to present its views, a Russian speaker had been solicited several months in advance. In the event, that slot was left unfilled—as we shall see, the Russian voice overall was conspicuously still that evening.

Among the speakers, Professors Pichot and Ehrhardt read papers of a general nature and received polite applause for their contributions. The English-language paper, by contrast, brought the audience to the edge of their chairs. Suddenly the packed hall began to buzz, the atmosphere a blend of tension and excitement. Paul Chodoff, a distinguished figure in the American Psychiatric Association, had obviously decided to dispense with discreetly-toned generalities and come directly to the point: although allegations pointed to psychiatrists in a number of countries collaborating in the suppression of dissent, the most flagrant abuse of psychiatry then operative anywhere in the world was that taking place in the USSR. There was no doubt, Chodoff stressed, that the case was proven—the evidence was voluminous and compelling. The WPA was consequently obliged to react in the strongest terms. The challenge to do so at the forthcoming Assembly debate should not be flinched at. Chodoff unambiguously emphasized the WPA's moral responsibility: "If the world community of psychiatrists is confronted with a major ethical problem then the proper forum where it should be discussed, judged and possibly remedied is the WPA. This is the organization which purports to speak for all psychiatrists and which is superordinate to national psychiatric societies. If the WPA avoids or sidesteps such an ethical issue, it may survive but it will have forfeited its moral vigor."[7] Chodoff concluded with an appeal to delegates to the Assembly to support the resolution of the Royal College of Psychiatrists condemning

the Soviet abuse, and a resolution from the American
Psychiatric Association proposing the creating of a special
committee to review the abuse of psychiatry wherever it might
occur.

The discussion was now open to the floor and it came thick
and fast. Apart from a spirited repudiation by a South African
psychiatrist of allegations of the political misuse of psychiatry
in support of the country's policy of *apartheid*, and an open
invitation to any psychiatrist present to visit and see for
himself,* the focus was exclusively on the Soviet practices.
Speaker after speaker condemned them. Marina
Voikhanskaya, who as a psychiatrist in Leningrad had herself
witnessed the internment of four healthy dissenters in her
hospital, stood out particularly. Here was a Russian psychiatrist with first-hand experience. She offered her testimony
incisively and explicitly but also with dignity. Dr
Voikhanskaya had reason to be more emotive. Over two years
had elapsed since her hasty emigration to the West. On her
discovery of political psychiatry she had begun to share her
concerns with colleagues but been uniformly shunned. Her
subsequent links with the human rights movement had
speedily brought her into hazardous territory; it looked omi-
nously as if the KGB was on the brink of silencing her protest.
Emigration suited the authorities well. The customary levell-
ing of a charge of anti-Soviet activity against her and a trial at
which she would have offered a defiant defence would have
been a source of much embarrassment.

But she did not depart unscathed. At the time of Honolulu
her eleven-year-old son, Misha, was still in Leningrad, ostensibly as a result of legal wrangling over custody (the
Voikhanskys had divorced some years earlier), but obviously
filling the role of political pawn. The KGB had calculated that
Misha as hostage would both punish his dissenting mother
and prevent any criticism of Soviet psychiatry by her in the
West. Voikhanskaya's presence in Honolulu and her personal
report were a clear demonstration that the KGB plan, at least
in its latter component, had failed.

* The American Psychiatric Association took up this invitation the
following year and reported that the use of psychiatry to suppress black
dissent had not in fact taken place; but they were critical of discriminatory
practices in the provision of clinical services, on racial grounds.[7]

As the condemnation of the Soviet abuses mounted, John Spiegel, a past president of the American Psychiatric Association, enjoined the participants to act more fairly towards their Soviet colleagues. After all, they were not present that evening to state their views. Perhaps caught unaware, the audience paused to reflect upon the abrupt realization that the Russians were indeed absent from the proceedings. Probably anticipating a barrage of criticism they had felt it prudent to keep away from the firing line. The moment's reflection was broken by the then president of the American Psychiatric Association, Jack Weinberg. While he appreciated Spiegel's point, he reminded him and the audience that the plenary session was completely open and Soviet psychiatrists had been invited to participate. Regrettable and sad as it was to admonish colleagues, world psychiatry had no choice but to voice clearly its opposition to unethical conduct. Weinberg's position obviously had the overwhelming support of those present, as revealed by their respective responses to Spiegel and himself. Indeed, by the end of the evening, the sentiments of the participants were not in doubt—a shared abhorrence of the perversion of their discipline.

Less clear at this juncture were the views held by most of the official delegates of the Association's member societies represented at Honolulu: their voting intentions at the General Assembly due 24 hours later were quite unknown (55 societies participated in the vote, thirteen societies did not have a vote because they were not paid-up members, and eight appeared not to be represented in Honolulu). A group of about a dozen psychiatrists, mainly from Britain, the United States, Canada, France and Germany, and including two Soviet émigré psychiatrists, were scurrying about the conference halls trying to find out. One of the authors (SB) had written some weeks before, inviting them to participate in a joint action designed to win support for the resolutions of condemnation. At our first gathering we agreed to meet regularly during the course of the congress in order to co-ordinate our activities.

Two goals were identified—to publicize the Soviet abuses among all psychiatrists in Honolulu, chiefly through the use of the public media; and to lobby individual delegates to the Assembly. The first presented no problem. Journalists hovered everywhere eager to catch the newest development in what was turning out to be a dramatic saga. For example, a press conference we convened at short notice with the keen assistance of Neil Abercrombie, a member of the Hawaiian Legislature, yielded newspaper reports both in Honolulu and, as we later learned, throughout the Western world. Leonid Plyushch was particularly persuasive—and not surprisingly. As we noted in the first chapter, his experience in the Dnepropetrovsk SPH had been harrowing in the extreme. Here he was now, a mere eighteen months after his release, providing vivid testimony of his internment. Complementing his account was the evidence given by the two émigré psychiatrists in the lobby group—Marina Voikhanskaya and Boris Zoubok. The latter had once worked under Professor Snezhnevsky.

Although we were satisfied that the conference had been organized responsibly and had proceeded in a dignified and sober fashion, Hans Vladimirsky, the Soviet journalist present, later depicted the event quite differently. He referred to the lobby group as: "a group of traitors to our country, including mentally sick persons, former Soviet citizens, jointly with some Zionists and Ukrainian Nationalists", and labelled the press conference as "anti-Soviet". According to him we had been refused permission to hold the session in any hotel by the local Hotel Association (an utter fabrication!) and had therefore been obliged to go to the building of the Hawaiian Legislature.[8] Vladimirsky's report was a polemic from start to end, obviously designed for domestic propaganda purposes.

The holding of this press conference was soon followed by one convened by the Russian delegation. On Wednesday afternoon, 31 August, leading Soviet psychiatrists—with Babayan at the helm and including Dmitri Venediktov, the Deputy-Minister of Health (his presence in Honolulu was an indication of how crucial were the issues for the Soviet authorities)—made their position abundantly clear: they would have no truck with the politicizing of the WPA; the resolutions scheduled for debate by the General Assembly that evening violated the true purposes and character of the organization. The resolutions were, in any event, totally uncalled for. The allegation of Soviet abuse was strenuously denied. Objective observers would realize, they argued, that

the criticism was mounted by politically motivated individuals. Our own book on the subject, *Russia's Political
Hospitals*, was branded as "well-composed slander" and inade-
quately researched, written as it was by a "so-called psychiatrist" and by a political scientist who was still smarting from
his deportation from the USSR because of antisocial activities whilst on a study visit (PR had indeed been instructed to
leave in 1964 after the authorities had objected to two visits he
had paid for humanitarian reasons to the wife of an engineer
who had defected).

Our lobby group's second objective—to inform delegates to
the Assembly about the nature and gravity of Soviet unethical
practices—was much more complicated than the goal of
publicity. The identity of many delegates was unknown (even
the total number was a mystery), some refused to be drawn,
and others had already been mandated to vote in a specific
way by their national body.

Thus, when they met on Wednesday evening, the outcome
of the pending debate was a complete question mark. The
resolution of condemnation which was, in the event, voted on
was that of the Australasians. Dr Babayan, with impressive
rhetorical and political skill, immediately criticized the time
limit imposed on the debate. But the Executive was determined to avoid any tactics which might prevent a vote being
taken. John Grigor, the Australasian delegate, then pressed
the Assembly to support the resolution. Although it was a
tough critical statement, world psychiatrists had to take a firm
stance against such a blatant misuse of their profession.

Babayan questioned the evidence upon which the charges
had been levelled. He demanded scientific proof—official case
reports signed by forensic psychiatrists on the dissenters
alleged to be improperly interned. He no doubt knew that
such reports were not available but also that Western
psychiatrists had interviewed émigré dissenters and found in
them no evidence of mental ill-health to warrant forcible
hospitalization. Then, quite unexpectedly, Babayan distributed his own "evidence"—a series of case reports on ten
dissenters known in the West (including Viktor Fainberg,
Nataly Gorbanevskaya and Vladimir Borisov—well-known to
us personally and, in our view, clear-cut examples of psychiatric abuse). Ironically, the package also contained reports on

Vladimir Bukovsky, who as we saw earlier had submitted an eloquent appeal to the congress, and on Leonid Plyushch who had provided personal testimony at the press conference we had convened. This material was identical to that sent to the WPA by Professor Morozov four months earlier with the request that it be circulated to member societies; he obviously had hoped that the reports would convince wavering colleagues of the dissenters' mental condition. However, the WPA had declined to circulate them on the grounds that this would jeopardize their confidentiality. With the case histories now thrust into their hands, the delegates were subjected to a further onslaught by Babayan. Conveniently overlooking the fruitless WPA-sponsored visit to the Serbsky Institute in 1973, he asked why Western psychiatrists had never bothered to come to the USSR to examine dissenters?[9] They were welcome to visit any hospital of their choice, not as critics, "but as friends and colleagues".[10] Did they know of the émigré dissenters who had committed suicide?* Dr Grigor, supported by the British and American delegates, retorted that compelling evidence had accumulated over several years, including reports on examinations of dissenters in the West (the British delegate cited his own lengthy interview with Plyushch), and testimony by psychiatrists who had recently left the Soviet Union.

Ironically, a few hours before the Assembly convened, Dr Avtandil Papiashvili had given a press conference in London. A young Georgian psychiatrist who had defected to the West a few months earlier, he described his personal knowledge of three cases of people who had been diagnosed as schizophrenic solely because they had criticized the Soviet political system. He appealed to the WPA to condemn the abuse in the strongest terms.[11]

A contest was clearly under way about the validity of the allegations. The East German delegate could not accept the evidence and regretted the use of the WPA as a "tribunal". The Cuban representative, who divulged that he himself had been accused of practising political psychiatry in the past,

---

* In fact, only one such person, Elena Stroyeva, has committed suicide—while under Soviet pressure to renounce her dissenting views (she had requested permission to return to the USSR because of homesickness).

dubbed the resolution "monstrous and disgusting". The delegate from Bulgaria regarded the resolution as a political manoeuvre, the allegations as "malicious", and Soviet psychiatrists as "deeply humanistic". Professor Ottosson from Sweden believed that the Assembly was not an appropriate forum for discussion of the matter; instead, a Committee should be established to investigate the allegations in a more objective fashion.

By then, the time allotted for the debate had been well exceeded. The WPA president insisted, despite protestations from Babayan, that a vote be taken. The ballot, conducted in secret, soon yielded a result—more of a cliff-hanger it could hardly have been. Of the 186 votes cast, 90 supported the resolution, 88 were opposed, and eight votes were invalid. Because of repeated complaints subsequently by the Soviet delegation about the voting procedure, we should clarify that the WPA statutes stipulated explicitly that only paid-up member-societies were entitled to vote, and then in relation to their size, with one vote for each 100 subscribing members up to a maximum of 30 votes. Had members prepared themselves more thoroughly for the congress, the result might have been quite different. The Royal College, for example, had a mere five votes instead of the 30 to which it would have been entitled had it paid its full subscription. The Soviet Society had, for the same reason, seven votes less than its full allotment of 30. In any event, because of the weighted allocation of the votes, the outcome of the ballot (90–88) did not reflect the balance of opinion between the societies on a one vote for one society basis: 33 were opposed, nineteen were in support, and the ballots of three were invalid.

It was an interesting exercise to try to determine how various societies cast their votes. Definitely in support of the resolution were the national associations of Britain, Australasia, the United States, Canada, the Netherlands and Switzerland—together accounting for 69 of the 90 votes; the remainder probably included societies from Israel, Belgium, France, Luxembourg and Mexico. Backing the Soviet Society almost certainly were associations from Eastern Europe, Cuba, Scandinavia, and most African and Asian States. The geo-political pattern of the ballot is striking. One can only wonder if delegates approached the resolution objectively or were biased by their own country's political affiliations and leanings. Notwithstanding the secrecy of the ballot, political factors were bound to impinge. That the Soviet-bloc States would support their neighbour was totally expected; equally predictable was the grouping together in favour of condemnation of the "liberally minded" English speaking countries, which have for decades at least shared a more or less similar approach to the theory and practice of psychiatry. Third-world support for the Soviet position seemed to parallel the typical pattern found in the lining up of forces in international political forums. The Scandinavians, considering the Swedish delegate's efforts to shift the issue from what he saw as the heated atmosphere of the General Assembly to a more level-headed impartial committee, probably felt that condemnation would shatter the bridges of contact with Soviet psychiatry; in other words, that diplomacy was preferable to confrontation and possible schism. As the Swedish psychiatrist, Clarence Blomquist, whom we cited earlier as one of the authors of the Declaration of Hawaii, put it: "I hate misuse as much as you do, but I think information and negotiations are better than expulsion and closed doors."[12]

But it was confrontation that had won the day. The repercussions for the WPA were anybody's guess but a Russian walk-out was certainly on the cards. As they left the debating chamber, Babayan would not comment on such a dénouement. No doubt he and his colleagues would have to buckle down that very night in an effort to salvage what they could from their defeat. The following morning saw the product of their deliberations.

The delegation, with remarkable efficiency, distributed a document addressed to all member societies and to WPA office-bearers, past and present.[13] The preamble referred to the "clamorous hysterical campaign" that had been waged over several years by certain Western political groups, directed against the USSR and specifically alleging the detention of healthy dissenters in mental hospitals. Some of those dissenters had, following their emigration to the West, been paraded by certain psychiatrists and used by them to bolster their political campaign. This was correct in one sense. As we have noted, Plyushch was indeed in Honolulu. But we should hasten to add, he was there out of his own strong conviction

that the WPA had to act, and to act vigorously, in order to
eradicate abuses from its midst and so re-establish itself as a
responsible professional body of moral integrity.

The Soviet document continued with criticism of the procedure the evening before. In the debate the Soviet delegate had
been granted only a limited opportunity to question his
British, American and Australasian counterparts, and so to
demonstrate the "unfounded nature and tendentiousness" of
their position. A series of objections of a more technical nature
were also cited. For example, the American resolution calling
for the setting up of a committee to review the abuse of
psychiatry for political purposes (which we discuss later in
this chapter) was inadmissible since it had been submitted
less than one month before the congress, the term required by
WPA rules. This was nit-picking in the extreme since the
resolution had in fact been cabled on 3 August, that is 28 days
prior to the Assembly. On the other hand, Babayan pointed
out, a Soviet resolution whose object was to condemn the
exploitation of the psychiatrically ill for purposes of political
propaganda, and which had been submitted "on the last day"
(sic), had received no mention whatever at the debate. The
existence of this resolution remains a mystery to us and we can
find no reference to it in official WPA documents. We can only
presume that it was submitted too late for inclusion in the
agenda.

The voting system was, in the Soviet delegation's view,
decidedly undemocratic, based as it was on the "archaic"
principle of number of votes according to amount of dues
paid. Moreover, the tally procedure had been bewildering—
three ballots corresponding to eight votes had been declared
invalid in the vote on the Australasian resolution. Its passage
by a mere two votes led the Russians to conclude that the
result could, morally, be nothing but null and void.

While the fairest possible voting system for the WPA, as for
any body, is clearly a matter open to debate, the delegation's
view that the result was unacceptable because the USSR had
lost by two votes and some ballots had been declared invalid,
is curious. The objection is comparable to a sporting team
entering a tournament conversant with the rules of play and
participating on the basis of recognition and acceptance of
those rules, then voicing its rejection of the results of the game

played because of the nature of those same rules. The Assembly ballots were conducted with care (several delegates have testified to this including the Royal College representative). Also, the whole voting system was clearly laid out in the Association's statutes. Any society could have tabled for Honolulu a resolution calling for a revamping of the voting procedure (and can do so at any time in the future). The point is that at the Sixth Congress in 1977 a specific procedure was laid down by the statutes which had not been queried *prior* to the votes being taken. Moreover, these statutes had been re-examined at the first session of the Assembly two days earlier, and also the allocation of votes had been approved unanimously.

Soviet Reaction in the Aftermath of Honolulu
The Soviet delegation's criticisms were levelled repeatedly by some of its members over the next few months, both for Soviet and international consumption. Dr Babayan was notably in the forefront of this campaign. He maintained incessantly that the events at the World Congress constituted a politically-inspired attack on Soviet psychiatry. In one interview with a Soviet journalist he highlighted the alleged flaws of the voting system, rehearsing the same points expressed in the delegation's Honolulu document. Again, the three ballots declared invalid were earmarked for special attention—"Why were they declared null and void? Nobody can answer the question!"[14] Babayan's complaints about the absence of a ballot commission and supervisors, and the destruction of the ballot papers immediately after the vote had been taken, conveyed the unsavoury but quite unjustified impression of some underhand conspiracy on the part of WPA officials. His argument that the vote was undemocratic because many societies, each with one vote only, were hopelessly outweighed by the 30 votes of the American Psychiatric Association sounded more like "sour grapes" in a sulking schoolboy than the sober viewpoint of a delegate to an international body with established rules of procedure. Babayan had, after all, never protested about the 30 votes available to the USSR. Two new dimensions were added to Babayan's counter-offensive, both of which revealed the measure of desperation reached by him and his colleagues in the Soviet psychiatric establishment.

First, he referred to the avoidance by critics of the "fact" that "many cases of mentally deranged persons" had been hospitalized in Britain, France, the United States, Israel and Austria, following their emigration from the USSR. To our knowledge this claim is almost entirely spurious. Throughout the twelve years of our research into Soviet abuse, which has included detailed interviews with many émigré victims, the evidence we have accumulated indicates that only three out of 43 have (definitely or apparently) required hospital treatment after reaching the West. In general, we have observed how the great majority have managed, despite their ghastly experience in Soviet mental hospitals, to adapt to Western life. Babayan cites hospitalization in Britain. At the time of his claim, three ex-dissenter-patients were domiciled there: Zhores Medvedev was employed as a scientist for the Medical Research Council, Viktor Fainberg was working full-time in the human rights field, and Vladimir Bukovsky was about to embark on a degree course in biology at Cambridge University (which he later completed; at the time of writing he is pursuing a postgraduate degree at Stanford University in the United States).

The second dimension in Babayan's attack also concerned the "patients". He commented: "Looking through a long list of 'dissenters of sound mind' confined in Soviet mental hospitals, we saw the names of patients who [had] never expressed any political dissent and who [had] had to be subjected to medical treatment after committing criminal offences, sometimes as grave as murder." We surmise that he was referring to the list of 210 dissenter-patients which makes up one of the appendices of our *Russia's Political Hospitals*, and which the Soviet delegation had obviously come across and studied. (As we mentioned earlier they cited the book in their press conference at Honolulu. Later Babayan referred to the book as "a collection of slanderous materials of an anti-Soviet nature, and false information and distorted facts".)[14] We are confident at the time of this writing, as we were when we compiled our list of victims of abuse, that we had applied strict criteria for inclusion—substantial evidence that the individual was a genuine dissenter of some kind, for example, a human rights activist, a religious believer, a would-be emigrant or a campaigner for nationalist and cultural rights; and that he was not suffering from any form of mental illness

requiring forcible admission to hospital.[15] We can only conclude that here was another attempt to mislead—somehow to
convey an impression that we were ill-informed or, perhaps
worse, prepared to convince others by concealing or distorting
our data.

We have referred to Babayan's "counter-offensive" because
it became clear in the aftermath of Honolulu that the Soviet
psychiatric establishment was on the warpath, intent on
destroying the credibility of its critics in order to gain
ascendancy. It must be remembered that further battles were
forthcoming and virtually impossible to evade. The inevitabil-
ity of the formation of a review committee on political abuse in
accordance with the American resolution had to be faced, and
with it the likelihood that the USSR would be tackled head-on
concerning specific cases. In the interim, it seemed, attack was
the tactic selected rather than a passive wait-and-see attitude.
A likely factor too at this point—during the months succeeding the congress—revolved around the establishment's own
fight for survival. Quite probably, the Soviet delegation at
Honolulu had anticipated plain sailing—a ripple here and
there perhaps but nothing more disturbing. After all, the 1971
congress had deftly pushed the issue aside. In any event, a
scientific organization such as the WPA would be little
tempted to entangle itself with political matters. Also, ample
support would be forthcoming for Russia's position from
member societies from Eastern Europe and the third world.
The expected unanimous adoption of the Declaration of
Hawaii would satisfy those societies sitting on the fence that
action had been taken to deal with the problem of ethics.

Having suffered a reverse at Honolulu, the delegation had
to pull out all stops to counter the political pressures, mostly
covert, that impinged on them. They had lost one contest—all
the more urgent was it then to wage the continuing war more
vehemently and steadfastly.

An opportunity soon presented itself. Earlier in the decade,
as part of President Nixon's programme of détente, the United
States and the USSR had entered into an agreement to co-
operate in health research. One project was on the subject of
schizophrenia. The programme had been renewed annually
without fuss—until the review held in October 1977, that is,
two months after Honolulu. On this occasion the Soviet

Deputy-Minister of Health, Dmitri Venediktov who, as we saw earlier, had been a member of the delegation at Honolulu and featured prominently in the defence of Soviet psychiatry, unexpectedly insisted that the final protocol should contain an explicit reference to the allegations of psychiatric abuse. The memorandum, he demanded, should note that the USSR considered these allegations as "groundless and slanderous fabrications". Furthermore, the Americans should dissociate themselves from the allegations by agreeing to this clause: "The American side expressed understanding for the Soviet side".[16]

Evidently, Venediktov was quite vehement. For this reason and because of the considerable political overtones, senior officials of the American Departments of State and Health were apprised of the Soviet demands. Notwithstanding the veiled Russian threat to pull out of the research programme, the Americans responded firmly, indicating that they were totally opposed to the inclusion of any statements not directly connected with scientific issues. An agreement was finally reached, however, and the memorandum was duly signed by the two sides. The section on schizophrenia research referred in rather neutral tone to the attainment of progress in the field and to the need for further research. There was also an allusion, in even more general terms, to the discord that had characterized the review sessions: "Both sides expressed views . . . concerning negative, non-scientific factors affecting the co-operation in this area and agreed to continue as in the past on the basis of mutual respect and trust between the participating scientists of both countries."[17]

It remains unclear whether Venediktov was satisfied or not on his departure. What the incident does portray is how far the Russians were prepared to go in order to recover lost ground. Possibly they sought to extract some compromise statement by starting out with an extreme position. As it was, the result was too bland and too vague to be exploited further, at any rate abroad.

Having failed to obtain the hoped-for American "whitewash", the Soviet offensive continued in high gear. Six weeks after the signing of the research protocol, the Soviet psychiatric Society passed an aggressively-toned resolution whose penultimate paragraph read: "The slanderous anti-Soviet campaign unleashed by the leadership of the psychiatric associations of the US, the United Kingdom, Australia and New Zealand, at the present time, makes it impossible for Soviet scholars to continue their scientific contacts and scientific co-operation with them until they give up their slanderous fabrications and attacks, and until they present their apologies to their Soviet counterparts."[18]

Most blame was directed towards the Americans, who had received the "backing" of certain figures in the WPA leadership. They had intentionally abused their role of organizing the Honolulu congress (the American Psychiatric Association had hosted the meeting on behalf of the WPA) by allowing it to become politicized. For example, the distribution at the congress of "anti-Soviet literature" had been permitted (since the congress was held in a number of public hotels the Americans had no power in this regard); the scientific programme had included "provocative, politically slanted reports" (having participated in the programme and rechecked it at the time of writing, I (SB) am at a loss to understand what reports are being referred to), as well as an open session on concrete abuses of psychiatry (the Russians, as noted, had been invited to participate from the podium and could have done so from the floor as well). Curiously, the Americans were also criticized for placing the British resolution of condemnation on the agenda of the Assembly (the Russians would have known that the agenda was the responsibility of the WPA Executive, as laid down by the organization's statutes).

The Russian statement continued with sharp criticisms of the procedure of the Assembly, similar to those of its delegation in Honolulu. Once again the "undemocratic" voting system and the "amateurishness" of the ballot were highlighted. On this occasion there were also some new complaints: the ballots had been handwritten, there were no ballot boxes, and the ballots were "simply passed on from hand to hand". The society also emphasized how the proposers of the Honolulu resolutions which were critical of Soviet psychiatry had failed to submit written medical reports on the alleged victims signed by psychiatrists. Both the proposers and Western "reactionary circles" had tried to "hush up that many of these individuals [émigré dissenters previously treated in the

Soviet Union] are in mental hospitals in the West (both in the past, as well as at the present time)." We have commented earlier on the spuriousness of this claim.

The inclusion of such a fabrication and the overall vitriolic tone of the document appear to have been designed chiefly for internal purposes. The Soviet psychiatric establishment clearly felt under considerable pressure to curb any suspicion amid the ranks of ordinary Soviet psychiatrists that Western criticism had some foundation, that an abuse most of them had heard vaguely about was a reality. At that time, in December 1977, only a minute number of the many thousands of Soviet psychiatrists had openly condemned the misuse of their profession and they had been promptly punished by the authorities. The threat to these authorities, and to their trusted associates among the top echelons of Soviet psychiatry, of rebellious stirring amongst Soviet psychiatrists must have been keenly felt.

One other tactic deployed to try to recover from the defeats suffered at Honolulu had been regularly brought into play since 1973, namely the misreporting in the Soviet media of comments made by foreign psychiatrists visiting the USSR. It was therefore no surprise to the experienced observer of Soviet affairs to come across quotes of fulsome praise for Soviet psychiatry attributed to a delegation of Austrian psychiatrists in the months succeeding the World Congress.

The story behind these distorted quotes is instructive. It starts in early 1976, when Leonid Plyushch (see chapter one) was released from a mental hospital, following a massive Western campaign, and deported abroad the same day. On arrival in Austria he was examined by a well-known forensic psychiatrist, Willibald Sluga, who found him to be mentally normal. From that time on, a journalist and member of the Central Committee of the Austrian Communist Party, Hans Wolker, started trying to arrange a visit to the USSR by Austrian psychiatrists. In spring 1977 Professor Georgy Morozov came to Vienna and extended a formal invitation for such a visit, which was then organized by Wolker.

On 22 August 1977 a seven-man delegation arrived in the USSR for a week. It consisted of six psychiatrists (including Sluga) and also Wolker himself. They were wined and dined, shown round four mental institutions in Moscow and Leningrad, and impressed by the system of district psychiatric clinics. They had asked to visit the special psychiatric hospitals in Leningrad and Dnepropetrovsk, but this was not arranged for them. There was no outright refusal, but no apparent intention to act either. They had also asked to visit six specific dissenters in particular mental hospitals, but were told—falsely in at least one case—that these people had been released. No arrangements were made to visit the released dissenters in their homes. Case histories of four dissenters (Plyushch, V. Borisov, P. Starchik and A. Argentov) were read out to them and briefly discussed, but, again, no meetings with the last three, who were still in the USSR, were laid on.

By contrast, they were carefully presented to a patient who claimed to be a political dissenter wrongfully interned, and allowed to talk to him at length. They all concluded that he was mentally ill, but were doubtful about whether he would have been involuntarily hospitalized in Austria. Relatively little was known about this man in the West. He had not been adopted by Amnesty International, and no campaigns had been mounted on his behalf. So this encounter did not prove very much.*

Regarding the four cases, the Austrian psychiatrists stated unanimously at a press conference after their return, that as they had not had enough time or facilities to study them properly, they could neither confirm nor reject the Soviet diagnoses and treatment. One of the psychiatrists, however, Dr Heinrich Gross, said that in his view the evidence presented did suggest that the four *might* be mentally ill.[19]

Unfortunately for the Soviet authorities the worth of Dr Gross's conditional approval of their ethics was devalued not only by its hesitancy. In 1978 the press reported that he had joined the Nazi Party in 1933, and, for his involvement in the Nazi euthanasia programme, had subsequently received a prison sentence.[20]

Before this came to light, however, Wolker had rushed into print with no less than ten articles in the Communist Party

---

* We subsequently learned more about this individual, whose name we were told in confidence. He was first arrested in 1968 and charged with "anti-Soviet propaganda".

newspaper *Die Volksstime*,[21] purporting to show at great length that the psychiatrists had admired all they had seen and had emphatically rejected the Western charges about abuse of their discipline. At the subsequent press conference Wolker was sharply criticized for his distortions by some of his travelling companions. Support for him came from only one quarter—Dr Gross.

Professor Gerhard Harrer, by contrast, the delegation's leader, expressed gratitude to Amnesty International for its careful documentation and assistance to the group, voiced concern that psychiatry might indeed be being abused in Russia, and said that a proper investigation could only be carried out by an international commission of the sort which the WPA had just voted in Honolulu to set up.

Dr Sluga was more outspoken. Before the trip, he said, he had been convinced that abuse was taking place, and nothing he had seen in the USSR had changed his mind.

The whole affair became a *cause célèbre* in Austria, with extensive debate and comment in the press. Not surprisingly the psychiatrists were widely criticized for their naïveté in travelling with Wolker and not realizing how thoroughly the Soviet media would exploit his distortions. As we shall see in chapter seven, this exploitation was still in full swing in 1983.

The Committee to Review the Abuse of Psychiatry

To avoid confusion we have deferred until now another critical development that took place at Honolulu and to which we have only alluded. In addition to the two resolutions of condemnation, a third resolution was tabled for debate by the Assembly, one that in the longer term would prove to be of dramatic consequence to Soviet psychiatry as well as to the WPA. The American Psychiatric Association proposed the formation of a special committee to review the political abuse of psychiatry wherever it might occur. Interestingly, this was a repeat of a previous initiative. Five years earlier the Americans had made a similar suggestion in the form of a position statement circulated to all WPA members. That call for an investigative agency, however, fell on deaf ears with not a single society responding to the idea, which promptly withered away. Because of the significance of the 1977 proposal we quote its key paragraph in full:

The World Psychiatric Association opposes the misuse of psychiatric skills, knowledge and facilities for the suppression of dissent wherever it occurs, and will establish a Committee to Investigate Abuse of Psychiatry to review all notices or complaints which are officially addressed to the President of the WPA regarding the political abuse of psychiatry, and if sufficient evidence warrants, may (1) investigate allegations of violation of the WPA policy regarding abuse of psychiatry by seeking additional written information, and/or personal testimony from whatever sources deemed necessary, and/or by site visits; and (2) recommend such corrective actions which seem appropriate to the Executive Committee of the WPA.[22]

The resolution also contained further recommendations for the committee's membership (". . . shall be appointed by the President and approved by the Executive Committee"); for proper procedure to be followed ("to ensure . . . fair and equitable representation of the WPA member societies in the country where the alleged violation(s) occurred"); and for the committee's adequate funding (". . . a special fund . . . for the express purpose of financing the activities . . .").

In framing the resolution the Americans obviously had their sights on the long term. It was well and good to resolve to condemn the misuse of psychiatry, but a form of machinery was required to combat it. The establishment of a Review Committee would enable alleged cases of abuse to be investigated impartially and objectively. If a *bona fide* case was then verified, measures could be taken to try to obtain the release of the person concerned. Although the new committee would lack any legal sanctions to enforce its recommendations it was presumably envisaged that the society involved would co-operate to the extent of investigating the case concurrently and act in conjunction with the Review Committee to ensure that justice was done. It is clear that the Americans had a second purpose in mind—the mere existence of a universal "moral watchdog" or "ombudsman" would help to bring the Soviet practice to an end and prevent its spread elsewhere. The adverse publicity stemming from a series of investigations of dissenter-patients would, in the American calculation, deter the USSR from continuing to resort to political psychiatry.

Conversely, it was realized that the formation of an investigative body might lead to the Soviet Society defiantly boycotting its operations.

As we shall see, the result was indeed a boycott. To understand why, we must remind ourselves of the context in which the American resolution was debated.

Still sensing the setback experienced earlier in the Assembly, Babayan naturally noted the thrust of the proposal from the Russian point of view. The preamble cited the misuse of psychiatry to suppress dissent "wherever it occurs", but not much imagination was needed to realize that the Soviet Union was, at least in the first instance, the intended target of the committee; after all, only moments earlier Soviet psychiatry—*alone*—had been specifically labelled as the offender. Not unexpectedly, Babayan catalogued his opposition to the establishment of an investigative committee: it was clearly directed at the USSR; funding would be a great problem; and it would violate national sovereignty. The last would prove to be the greatest impediment to the functioning of the committee. Another indication of future Soviet non-recognition of the legal status of the committee was the pronouncement the following day by another delegation member, Dr Venediktov: "From a legal standpoint and from a point of view of international law there is only one answer to [the resolution] and that is negative, because no country, including the United States, would permit investigation of its internal affairs."[23] This dubious, legalistic line of argument did not, however, impress the delegates.

Nor were they impressed by other objections voiced by the Hungarian and Greek delegates. Dr G. Pollner, the Hungarian, felt a Review Committee would only complicate the problem. Professor Stefanis could not see the purpose of such a committee; moreover, since the Soviet Society had been condemned earlier without adequate evidence, the Review Committee might act in similar fashion.

Eventually a vote was taken, without the rancour that had typified the earlier proceedings. The resolution was passed by a comfortable margin of 121 to 66 votes. In terms of societies (although this count had no relevance to the official result) 28 voted for, and 26 against. The ballot most likely followed—by and large—the lines of the motion of condemnation; in other words, many Soviet supporters remained loyal, but some had defected. Whatever the case, the Assembly had given the newly-elected Executive a strong mandate for a momentous task, a task that would demand much of its time and energy, especially from the new president, Pierre Pichot from France, and the new secretary-general, Peter Berner from Austria, throughout their period of office and until the next congress in Vienna in 1983.

With the results of the Assembly debates a *fait accompli*—including its official endorsement of the Declaration of Hawaii—the contest had officially terminated, at least for the moment. We noted earlier the grievances expressed by members of the Soviet delegation during the last two days of the congress—the barrage of criticism levelled against their critics and the WPA leadership continued to their very point of departure. Dr Venediktov's last words, for example, referred to the "unprofessional" behaviour of the British, the Americans and the Australasians: "They will be ashamed of themselves, and, I think, will realize soon that their actions were nothing to be proud of."[24]

Jack Weinberg's remarks at the closing session of the congress perhaps best reflected the feelings of those psychiatrists whom Venediktov described. His support of the resolution of condemnation had been accompanied by "a heavy heart". He added: "I know that the vast majority of Soviet psychiatrists are worthy colleagues, and practise ethically. We must all, nonetheless, be willing to search out and condemn the improper actions of even a few. I also believe that in the long run the actions taken here in Hawaii will have greatly strengthened the WPA, and we may now look forward to the future with knowledge that an international body exists that will work to further improve the practice of psychiatry everywhere in the world . . ."[25]

Shame at one's unprofessional behaviour versus heartache and optimism—this huge discrepancy in perspective paralleled the apparently unbridgeable gulf that had developed between the two camps. Could the Review Committee, reinforced by the fine sentiments pervading the Declaration of Hawaii, restore peace to a troubled organization and permit the pursuit of its basic purpose of scientific advancement in psychiatry? And could the WPA succeed in recovering the second of its five stated means to achieve that purpose: "The strengthening of relations between psychiatrists working in various fields and between psychiatric societies existing in different countries"? In the next chapter we examine the mounting opposition to political psychiatry inside the Soviet Union—an opposition which strongly influenced the eventual answers to these questions.

CHAPTER THREE

RESISTANCE AT HOME:
GROWTH AND SUPPRESSION

THE YEARS 1976 to 1979 saw a dramatic diversification of the already far from homogeneous dissenting scene in the USSR. Organized groups emerged in Moscow, the Ukraine, Lithuania, Armenia and Georgia to press for Soviet observance of the recently signed Helsinki Agreements on European Security and Co-operation. Other groups sprang up to promote feminism, free trade unionism, the rights of the disabled, religious freedom, uncensored historical research, and the claims of particular religious denominations or national minorities.

As part of this trend came the formation in January 1977 of the Working Commission to Investigate the Use of Psychiatry for Political Purposes. The growth, intensive activity, and—after four years—destruction of this remarkable pressure group are the main subjects of this chapter. Domestic resistance to political psychiatry did, however, continue after the Commission's demise, if in less co-ordinated, more clandestine ways, and we give a brief account of this at the end of the chapter.

The Scale of the Abuse and the Need for a Pressure Group
To understand why a pressure group to combat political psychiatry became desirable in the late 1970s, we need to note the extent to which dissent was being suppressed by psychiatric means at that time. This is not of course to imply that the exact scale of this or any other type of violation of human rights is, in itself, of fundamental importance. In principle, a violation can be just as sinister and deplorable when committed against one person as when imposed on a thousand. Leaving aside abstract ethical arguments, this is true if only

because a single violation can easily escalate into thousands or millions, especially if it remains unchallenged.

In any case, we have studied carefully the documentation which has reached the West from a variety of reliable sources, and compiled statistics which show that to the 210 dissenter-patients whom we listed in our first book, 276 further names must now be added, making just under 500 over the past two decades. In addition, there are now about 80 others in this whole period for whom the evidence suggests that their internment may well have been politically motivated.[1]

It may seem at first sight as though these statistics point to a sharp increase in the volume of abuse in the last six years. But this conclusion would be wrong—indeed, as we shall see, strikingly wrong. The main reason for this is that many cases on which information appeared in the new period relate, wholly or in part, to the earlier one. In any case, let us now try to get an idea of what the changing rates of internment have been since 1962. To do this, one must count, of course, each internment, not the number of individuals involved, as individuals can easily undergo more than one internment.

On this score, our calculations show that using the data on our 486 individuals for the whole 21-year period, we can—with certainty or near-certainty—assign some 500 internments to particular years.[2] Nothing can be read into the figures for 1962-67, these being highly incomplete because at that time there was no human rights movement to collect data. This movement started operating in 1968. Thus it is not surprising that an average recorded rate of eight new internments per year for 1962-67 should suddenly be followed by 29 internments in 1968. Some of this increase should, however, be attributed to the sharp rise in dissenting activity in that year, and the consequent increase in official counter-measures (whether through psychiatric internment or straightforward imprisonment). The figures for 1968-70 then remain steady, but a jump to 54 in 1971 is notable, and would seem to reflect an increased use of psychiatry to suppress dissent. However, that year also saw the start of serious Western criticism of the practice, and it is instructive to see the annual rate drop steadily back again—as the authorities digest this phenomenon—to reach a mere 24 in 1975. It then remains at around this level until rising suddenly to 42 in 1980. When we

note, though, that nearly half the internments of 1980 were
short-term ones designed to keep certain dissenters locked up
over the wholly exceptional period of the Moscow Olympic
Games, the rise can be discounted.

Most striking of all, however, are the figures for 1981–83.
These were the years when, as we shall see in later chapters,
the international pressure on the USSR became, for the first
time, strong and persistent. Here the figures are: fourteen new
internments for 1981, twenty for 1982, and five for the first
half of 1983. Even if we allow for further cases coming to light
with some delay in the future, the average figure for the years
1981–83 seems sure to remain below the average of 26 which
obtained for 1968–70 and 1975–79, and of course far below the
average of 50 for 1971–72.

But the recent figures take on even more significance in the
light of the fact that since 1979 the overall rate of locking up
dissenters has been running at 200 or more per year, i.e. at
least double the average rate for the preceding years since
1968.[3] So the declining trend for psychiatric internment has
actually taken place during a period when the overall rate of
arrest has sharply increased. To put it another way, the ratio
of psychiatric internments to straightforward imprisonments
has gone sharply down. Although no reliable figures are yet
available for the latter category throughout the whole of our
period 1962–83, the ratio may well prove to have been about
one to four in 1971, and, at the other extreme, one to fifteen or
twenty in 1983.

In 1981 the problem of the statistics of Soviet psychiatric
abuse had fresh light shed on it from a quite new and
unexpected source. The former chief psychiatrist in the Soviet
Ministry of Health, Zoya Serebryakova, who had naturally
been involved in her previous job with the forcible internment
of dissenters[4] and clearly developed an interest in the whole
subject of involuntary hospitalization, co-authored a statistical study on the patients admitted to one Moscow OPH from
its catchment area over one year. Out of the 1,163 patients
admitted, those suffering from alcoholism and those admitted
for special examination (to determine legal responsibility or
fitness for work or military service), or for "compulsory
treatment by order of judicial authorities", were excluded.
This left 817 patients for study. Of these, 1.2 per cent, i.e. ten

patients, were admitted "in connection with visits to state institutions, the lodging of unfounded complaints, or making slanderous statements".[5] Although it is difficult to interpret this information with any confidence, it is nonetheless of considerable interest. The ten patients would seem probably to have displayed no aggressive or threatening behaviour, or else they would presumably have been assigned to another category covering patients acting aggressively (which accounted for 2.9 per cent of the sample studied). Most plausibly they were dissenters like Mrs Gusyakova, whose case we discussed in chapter one, and perhaps also dissenters on the psychiatric register who were interned for two or three weeks over public holidays or state visits—on KGB orders. We should note, though, that the KGB may state or imply to mental hospitals that people in the latter category are displaying "aggressive behaviour", in which case they would be assigned to the "aggressive" category.

We have no idea how many of the 346 patients excluded from the study might be dissenters. Furthermore, although the hospital is clearly an OPH we cannot be sure how typical it is of such institutions in the USSR. After all, there are more government offices in Moscow than in other Soviet cities, and state visits by foreign dignitaries are far more common there. At the very least, however, the paper suggests that throughout the country there must be hundreds of forcible admissions of dissenters to OPHs per year.

To conclude our statistical discussion, we see no reason to change the tentative estimates we published earlier, namely that at any one time the dozen SPHs probably contain a few hundred inmates interned for non-medical reasons, and the OPHs a larger number.

The Working Commission

Given this situation of the regular misuse of psychiatry, it is not surprising that the dissenting community in Moscow should have spawned a group dedicated to investigating and combating it. The most powerful catalyst in this process was a young auxiliary doctor (*feldsher*) called Alexander Podrabinek, who had been prevented from becoming a fully-fledged doctor thanks to officially imposed discrimination against dissenters in the education system. In the mid-1970s, when still in his early twenties, he conducted careful research into political psychiatry which led to his book *Punitive Medicine*.[6] This reached the West just in time for Amnesty International to make a 25-page summary of it for distribution at the WPA's Congress in Honolulu (see chapter 2), where it made a strong impression on participants. The book covers very similar ground to our own *Russia's Political Hospitals*, and reaches the same general conclusions.

Co-founders of the Commission with Podrabinek were his friends Vyacheslav Bakhmin, a computer specialist working in a government research institute, then aged thirty; Felix Serebrov, a self-educated worker of forty-seven; and Irina Kaplun, a young activist who soon left the Commission for personal reasons. Later, as we shall see, three more members joined.

From the start, the Commission was formally affiliated to the Moscow "Helsinki Group" (to monitor Soviet observance of the above-mentioned Helsinki Agreement), its main liaison being with group member General Grigorenko, who was a personal friend and also an ex-victim of political psychiatry.

Throughout the four years of its existence the Commission issued over 1,500 pages of documentation—pages which accurately reflect its intensive activity. To present a clear picture of all aspects of its work would require a book-length study. So the core of this chapter is no more than a sketch. First we consider its aims and methods of work.

The Commission's Aims

The Commission defined its main tasks as follows: "1. To bring to light, and publicize, cases of people being forcibly interned in mental hospitals by illegal means, and to assist in obtaining their release as soon as possible; 2. To give assistance to people who have been unjustifiably interned in mental hospitals, and also their families; 3. To promote the general humanization of the conditions in which people are held in mental hospitals."[7]

To make point (1) more specific, the Commission defined its interpretation of the law regarding both permissible and impermissible internment. As for the former, it "regards forcible hospitalization and compulsory treatment as justified only in relation to ill persons who have committed aggressive acts, or whose mental condition gives a doctor grounds to foresee their possibly committing dangerous acts of this sort against themselves or those around them". This, we would agree, seems to be the only straightforward interpretation which is possible of the "Directives" on administrative commitment discussed in chapter one.

Impermissible internment was defined in these passages: "Considering persecution of people for their beliefs and views to be against the law, the Commission works for the liberation from mental hospitals of people whose forcible internment has been a consequence of their expression of their political or religious views, or of their exercising their civil rights. Here it is essential to stress emphatically that the Commission does not claim (and never has claimed) that all the people for whose release it works have no mental abnormalities and are in perfect mental health. What is important is that they have been interned for political reasons and not on the basis of medical evidence." Internment and treatment are unjustified for "all those who there is reason to believe are mentally healthy"; likewise "for those who have been put in psychiatric hospitals for political reasons and are also (1) people with mental abnormalities who, though responsible for the actions they were charged with, were ruled not responsible by a court without sufficient cause, or (2) people interned in ways which violate the 'Directives of the USSR Ministry of Health on the Immediate Hospitalization of Mentally-Ill Persons who Represent a Social Danger'".

The Commission's second main task—to help such people—required little commentary. But one paragraph explained that while the Commission did not regard it as its duty to carry out psychiatric diagnoses, "nonetheless a psychiatrist who renders the Commission invaluable assistance does, in a number of cases, examine people who turn to the Commission for help, and compiles reports on their mental condition. The Commission uses these reports in its work, and publicly refers to them when this is essential".

The third main task was spelled out as follows: "The Commission is concerned to work for a general humanization and a well thought-out liberalization of the conditions in which all inmates of psychiatric hospitals are held, especially in the special prison hospitals, which ought to be transferred to the Ministry of Health [from the MVD]. The Commission seeks the taking of effective measures to end the illegal practices of orderlies beating patients, of painful methods of treatment being used as 'punishment', and of other abuses. The Commission regards reform of the laws and directives concerning the mentally ill as important and necessary, and is ready to give all the assistance it can in this work. Naturally, all such laws and directives ought to be published in generally available publications."

The document ended with a basic statement of principle: "All the activity of the Commission is conducted openly, within the framework of the law, and is accessible to public scrutiny."

The Commission's Mode of Operation

A more concrete idea of how the Commission set about its tasks is conveyed in its report on the first two years of its work:

> In two years, members of the Commission have sent over 70 letters to various psychiatric hospitals, official health bodies and Prosecutors' Offices. These letters have documented cases in which current legislation has been violated for political reasons in relation to particular individuals. Apart from this, the Commission has issued appeals to the public and the psychiatric associations of various countries; has tried, where necessary, to interview the chief doctors and assistant doctors of mental hospitals, and officials of the USSR Ministry of Health; and has, in a number of cases, given material aid to inmates of mental hospitals and their relatives.
>
> The Commission's work has been consistently reflected in its *Information Bulletin*,[8] of which fourteen issues have so far appeared. The bulletin has published information on 66 people held now or in the past in mental hospitals for political reasons. The section "More Information Wanted" has listed the names of 157 additional people on whom our data are insufficient or not precise enough.
>
> The Commission has no clear idea how many hundreds of prisoners of conscience there are in the ten special psychiatric hospitals of the MVD which are known to us. It is equally difficult to estimate the number of people hospi-

talized without foundation in the ordinary psychiatric hospitals (of which there are several hundred around the country when one includes local psychiatric clinics and the psychiatric sections of general hospitals).

The Commission has received great assistance from its consultant psychiatrist A. Voloshanovich. He has examined 33 individuals who have been interned in mental hospitals or threatened with internment.

Official bodies not only have not facilitated the Commission's work, but have hampered its activity in many ways. In the overwhelming majority of cases the Commission has not received replies from them to its letters and enquiries. Doctors in mental hospitals have tried to evade meetings and conversations. Several inmates have been threatened with intensive drug treatment if they continued their contacts with members of the Commission, and have also been pressured not to accept parcels and financial assistance.

The Commission's members have repeatedly had their homes searched and documents and other Commission materials confiscated. Two members have been subject to criminal prosecution and sentenced. But even in conditions of such pressure from the authorities—not only on the Commission, but also on those who turn to it for help— people who have been confronted by "punitive medicine" are still coming to us, phoning and writing. And as long as such "medicine" continues to produce victims, the Working Commission cannot cease to function.[9]

This report conveys well the spirit of the Commission and its work—sober accuracy, deep humanitarian commitment, no heroics or bravado. Let us now narrow our focus and look more closely at its mirror, the *Bulletin*, which conveys a detailed and accurate picture of its activities.

The Commission's Bulletin
The *Bulletin* appeared in typescript every six or seven weeks, with the Commission members' names and addresses on the title page. It was then circulated in the standard ways—by passage from hand to hand; in broadcasts by Western radio stations to the USSR in Russian, using copies sent abroad to foreign supporters via travellers; and in Western publications

in Russian and other languages. In addition, it was regularly summarized in the main *samizdat* journal of the Soviet human rights movement, the *Chronicle of Current Events*,[10] and individual items were publicized by foreign journalists writing in Moscow or elsewhere.

The methods used to collect information were remarkably effective. Although the Commission never had more than five members at any one time, a large quantity of detailed, reliable and well-edited information was collected in conditions where the authorities were hostile and also exercised considerable control or even "veto power" over the basic means of communication—especially telephone, mail and the printed word. A flexible and resourceful infrastructure was built up, involving the victims themselves and fellow-inmates (before or, more often, after release), friends, relatives, *Bulletin* readers, and medical and other personnel in the mental institutions. In some cases this infrastructure could take advantage of an already existing network of the human rights movement; in others, all the links in the chain had to be forged from scratch. The chains were held together (usually) by bonds of friendship and/or mutual trust, and by a belief that person-to-person mutual aid was the only effective means of resisting official oppression of all sorts.

The Commission stimulated the development of these networks by appealing in most *Bulletins* for more information on listed individuals. It also prepared standard questionnaires so that associates who used them would ask the most important questions of current or ex-victims. The risks involved in such work are illustrated by an incident in 1978, when an ex-victim who had become an associate of the Commission, Sergei Potylitsyn, was detained for a few days by police during a visit to Kiev. Questionnaires and *Bulletins* were confiscated from him, and on his return to his home in the Caucasus area he was forcibly hospitalized for a week—as a warning to stop such activity.[11]

The Commission was always concerned about the *Bulletin*'s accuracy. For this reason it carefully indicated the degree of reliability and up-to-dateness of many items of information, and repeatedly solicited corrections and additions from readers. In this way it was able in many cases to publish more complete and accurate information in subsequent issues.

The Commission collected information not only about victims and their treatment, but also about the nature and extent of the interlocking psychiatric, legal and police systems, as applied to victims of "punitive medicine". It therefore published details of the regulations at particular institutions, and also an informed account of the opening of a new SPH near Volgograd (formerly Stalingrad) in 1978. Listing the institution's address and leading personnel, it added these comments:

> Section 1 contains some solitary cells, and a fifth section is being built which will mostly consist of solitary cells. Criminal prisoners from an ordinary-regime labour camp are used as orderlies. The orderlies sometimes beat the patients. The patients are forced—under threat of "treatment" with neuroleptic drugs—to do unpaid work in a sewing workshop.
>
> The supply of essential goods in the SPH shop is very limited.
>
> Not more than one parcel a month is allowed.[12]

The Commission also took pains to collect information about relevant international developments. It published detailed reports on the WPA Honolulu congress, including the texts of the key resolutions,[13] and then printed translations of long letters by Professor Berner about the process of setting up the Review Committee on abuse (see the next chapter).[14] It also translated a seven-page report about psychiatric abuse by Amnesty International to a sub-commission of the UN Human Rights Commission, most of which concerned a hundred or so cases of abuse in the USSR.[15]

Not surprisingly, the Commission was happy to print a full account of the formal psychiatric assessment of its friend General Grigorenko in the US, which found no trace of mental illness in him (see chapter five).[16] It also demonstrated its concern about evidence of politically-motivated abuses of medical ethics abroad, by enquiring into cases in China and the US.[17]

The importance to the Commission of keeping abreast of world developments was underscored in a private letter it sent to foreign friends who had supplied it with most of the above-mentioned items: "We received your cuttings and materials, and hasten to thank you. They are very important to us, as we know almost nothing about how the matters of concern to us are publicized in the West. Your help is incalculable."[18]

Independent Psychiatric Assessments
A careful study of the Commission's *Bulletin* reveals the usefulness of an aspect of its work which was conducted discreetly for a year and only spelled out to the world when Dr Alexander Voloshanovich gave a press conference in Moscow on 16 August 1978. As the *Bulletin* reported, "he said that he had examined 27 people who had turned to the Commission for help. These people had either been previously interned in psychiatric hospitals, or the threat of such a hospitalization hung over them. In his opinion, the assessments revealed symptoms of mental illness in none of them. Voloshanovich explained that he made no claim that his conclusions were beyond discussion: such conclusions depended on the approach of the psychiatrist to problems of diagnosis, and might be a matter for academic argument. However, he could state for certain that not one of his examinees needed to be forcibly isolated from society." The Commission then reported, correctly, that "the Royal College of Psychiatrists has carefully studied Voloshanovich's reports and has praised highly their professional quality"[19] (see chapter five).

The precise purpose of carrying out such examinations becomes clearer from the rubric printed on each report: "Not for publication or general use. Can be made available to members of commissions investigating the abuse of psychiatry for political purposes, to specialist doctors (psychiatrists), to lawyers." Voloshanovich expanded on this in a private letter to foreign friends, saying that while of course the reports as a whole were confidential, if the passages he had underlined might help a particular examinee who had been interned, or was threatened with internment, then these passages could be publicized. The passages are, in general, his conclusions as to why the examinee is not suffering from mental illness.

These guidelines were followed scrupulously, both by the Commission itself and by bodies abroad like the Royal College of Psychiatrists and Amnesty International. Extensive use was made of Voloshanovich's conclusions because of the thorough, detailed and far from uncritical nature of his examinations and reports. The examinees, too, made use of them when "punitive medicine" threatened to strike, and anyway derived comfort from the knowledge that sympathetic people in Moscow and abroad had this weapon ready for use on their behalf, if need arose. As we shall see, it proved effective in a number of cases.

In all, Dr Voloshanovich compiled 41 reports, totalling some 300 pages, and his successor Dr Koryagin compiled sixteen. Appendix VI indicates most of the individuals they assessed.

In addition, the Commission was able to arrange examinations of nine Moscow dissenters by Dr G. Low-Beer of London (see chapter five) and of one by Dr H. Blomberg of Sweden.

Education, Lobbying and Intervention
Armed with accurate information about the psychiatric, legal and police systems, relevant world developments, particular cases of abuse and, sometimes, independent psychiatric reports, the Commission was well placed to educate the *Bulletin*'s readers and also to lobby on behalf of victims.

In its educational role the Commission was clearly anxious to help readers to understand the subtle, variable, often elusive relationship between, especially, the psychiatrists and the police agencies. This would help them to resist the system and possibly even to exploit loopholes in it. The *Bulletin* often quoted the frank hints of psychiatrists that they had little or no responsibility for internments, and that both internment and release depended on the KGB.

When, for example, the wife of a religious activist, Georgy Fedotov, asked psychiatrists at Moscow OPH No. 14 when her husband would be discharged, "they told her they could not discharge him until they got a signal. 'The people who had him put in here are the same people who decide when to let him out,' they said."[20] The same thing was said even more frankly to would-be emigrant Alexander Shatravka—see appendix IV.

The *Bulletin* often conveyed the feeling that most Soviet psychiatrists do not in fact believe Snezhnevsky's theories about dissent being a symptom of mental illness, and simultaneously indicated that sympathetic and agile doctors do in fact sometimes have the power to manipulate the system and protect dissenters from its worst effects. We give some clear-cut examples of this later in the chapter. But more often the psychiatrists concerned seem to "do good by stealth" and cannot afford to be too explicit.

When, for example, a memoir about the SPH system by ex-victim Oleg Solovyov was published in the West in 1979, he was suddenly summoned to the local psychiatric clinic, even though since his release seven years earlier he had not been on the psychiatric register. Dr D. Feksa first discussed the matter which had served as the false pretext for the summons. Then, at the end of the conversation, the *Bulletin* reported him as saying that "at the present time it was wiser to keep quiet, as 'you won't tell people things they don't know already.' 'Many people think like you, but keep quiet,' the psychiatrist said. 'Follow the example of the majority.'"[21]

This sort of approach, which is typical of sympathetic Soviet doctors trying to be helpful in a difficult situation, seems to be saying beneath the slight camouflage: "Lots of people hold highly critical views like yours, and there's nothing abnormal about them. But if you persist in publicizing them, I won't be able to stop the secret police from having you interned. If, on the other hand, you respond with understanding to what I say, I should be able to convince them in my report that there's no need for that, and you'll stay free." As each proposition in this pragmatic argument strikes us as basically true, it is not surprising in the circumstances that psychiatrists resort to it, even though, by using it, they are in fact—in the gentlest possible way—doing the police's job of intimidation for them. Whatever the truth of this speculation, Solovyov did indeed stay free.

Other psychiatrists are more brutally direct than Dr Feksa, but also find themselves making remarkably confused statements when they add some Snezhnevskian theory to justify an internment. This was what happened to Prof. Valentin Matveyev, a former chief psychiatrist of Moscow, who had ruled that free trade unionist Valeria Novodvorskaya was schizophrenic and must therefore remain in an OPH after an internment. "What condition she was really in (before her internment) we don't know," he told a friend of hers. "That's a matter for the conscience of the doctor who had her committed to our hospital. If she really made the sort of statements she's continuing to make in the hospital, then he had reason to commit her. But if she now . . . [recants?], if her condition changes, if she stops holding meetings, if she draws sensible conclusions from her situation, then it will be possible to discharge her." Matveyev's rather feeble attempt to justify the internment medically broke down almost completely when he then admitted to the friend that "in such cases the hospitalization takes place on the initiative of the KGB, and the local psychiatric clinic has no say in the matter."[22]

Sometimes psychiatrists indicate their inner rejection of Snezhnevsky's theories in a sudden quip. When the young Ukrainian dissenter Viktor Borovsky was adjudged healthy after two weeks of internment in a Kharkov OPH, but then told he would be held for a further week, his mother not unreasonably demanded his immediate release. To this the psychiatrist in charge of him replied sharply: "You'd better not *demand* anything, or he'll turn out to have been healthy this morning, but ill in the evening."[23]

True, the Commission occasionally came across psychiatrists who expressed the Snezhnevsky line with apparent conviction, but these occasions were rare, and also the circumstances sometimes suggested that the sincerity was in reality play-acting designed to justify a politically motivated internment. A psychiatrist at the Kazan SPH, for example, Dr Stanislav Korolëv, claimed to believe that: 'Anti-Soviet convictions simply cannot exist: all anti-Soviet statements or opinions are the result either of mental disturbance, or of cynicism, or of ignorance." At about the same time, however, in 1977, Korolëv and his colleagues conceded that their patient Boris Evdokimov, a dissenting journalist, had only simulated mental illness at his second pre-trial examination (the first had found him normal) and also that he currently had no symptoms of mental illness. Yet Evdokimov told them explicitly that he refused to renounce his political beliefs, and would go no further than promising to desist from dissident activity after his release. Clearly this throws doubt on whether Korolëv genuinely believed the views quoted above.

Whatever the case on this point, however, the psychiatrists insisted that despite their admission of his mental good health, it was "inconvenient" for them to change the official diagnosis of schizophrenia. This was a lightly disguised way of telling him that the KGB demanded a genuine recantation before it would give the signal for his release. In fact, the psychiatrists may have had some sympathy for him, as they had just recommended his transfer to an OPH, but been overruled by a commission from the Serbsky Institute. This commission, the *Bulletin* reports, exerted "psychological pressure and blackmail by telling Evdokimov that his wife had deserted him, by insulting him, and threatening that he would *never* be released." During the Commission's interview she declared: "Say thank you that you're even alive. What else d'you need?"[24]

The blackmail was maintained in even worse circumstances over the next two years, when Evdokimov contracted cancer and the doctors refused to treat him for it. Eventually, in 1979, when he was dying at the age of fifty-six, he was released. During the five months before his death he was denied permission to go abroad for treatment, despite numerous interventions on his behalf. With his last strength he wrote some remarkably dignified accounts of his experience. The Commission devoted much attention—and also space in fourteen issues of the *Bulletin*—to this tragic case, because of the double betrayal of medical ethics involved, and the fatal outcome.[25]

Lobbying Soviet Doctors
Any lobbying work demands careful thought about the best targets and the most suitable approach—practical and psychological. In the Commission's case, its main choice of target was the psychiatric profession, both in the USSR and abroad. We have of course seen how it understood the purely political or KGB dimension, but also how carefully this is disguised. Without hard evidence, therefore, putting effective pressure on the politicans or their immediate instrument, the KGB, would have been impossible, and also dangerous.

As we noted earlier, key targets were the doctors responsible for the treatment of dissenters, in particular mental hospital doctors, whom it sometimes tried to interview,[26] but mostly wrote to. Here the Commission's approach at first put the main emphasis on an appeal to their better instincts and honour. Thus, when it wrote to the head doctors of the SPHs in 1977, it commented:

We are sure that the outcome of the Sixth World Congress of Psychiatrists in Honolulu, which condemned the USSR for using psychiatry for political purposes, will not leave Soviet psychiatrists indifferent, at least not those to whom the humane ideals of medicine are dearer than mercenary considerations and political aims. We appeal to you not to forget your doctor's oath and not to take actions which might compromise you as a doctor and a human being.[27]

In early 1979 the Commission began the regular practice of sending relevant portions of the *Bulletin* to the same addressees, together with this covering letter:

We are sending you for your information some materials published in *Information Bulletin* no. . . . of the Working Commission . . . If it should be that inaccuracies appear in these reports, we ask you to let us know and to send appropriate corrections to the address below. Corrections and additions to published material are published by us in subsequent issues of the *Bulletin*.

The Commission also announced that it would in future do likewise for other relevant individuals and organizations: "We hope that this practice will help us to avoid possible errors and inaccuracies in the *Bulletin*'s reports."[28]

The Commission was always reluctant to accuse particular doctors directly of particular unethical acts. It did, however, join its parent body, the Moscow "Helsinki Group", in issuing a long statement in response to the examination of General Grigorenko in the US, which, in general terms, took a more judgemental position. The two groups argued that the "criminal system" of political psychiatry, "although to some extent undermined by the efforts of Bukovsky, Gluzman and Alexander Podrabinek . . . and by the widely based campaigns of protest in the West, still continues to function. . . . We consider that a careful and objective investigation not only of Grigorenko's case, but also of all other known cases of groundless internment of people in mental hospitals is necessary. Such an investigation should aim to have the guilty brought to justice, and should be conducted with the extensive participation of public groups and foreign psychiatrists."[29]

The Commission made this approach more specific by documenting the attempt by dissenter Evgeny Nikolayev, whose case we discuss below, to sue two psychiatrists for interning him without grounds and then treating him with cruelty in the OPH. The attempt not surprisingly proved fruitless: no official body would consider the evidence.[30]

Another of the Commission's approaches was to try to arouse humane instincts in those doctors and medical personnel who read the *Bulletin* or heard it on foreign radio-stations. This broad design concentrated on drawing attention both to examples of ethical conduct—thus stressing that this was at least feasible, if hazardous—and, by contrast, to cases of grossly unethical behaviour which might be expected to arouse revulsion.

In the Soviet context, ethical conduct is difficult to report directly unless the doctor in question is either dead, or prepared to serve a prison term. As the last condition applied, the Commission could report freely on Drs Voloshanovich and Koryagin,[31] after they went public, and on Dr Gluzman,[32] because his stand in defence of psychiatric ethics was well known in the past. It could also recount how Dr Vladimir Privalov revealed to a dissenter he had examined: "They're putting pressure on me, demanding that I rule you not responsible. But I'll tell you that I won't go against my conscience. I find no mental abnormalities in you." The dissenter was later ruled responsible and sent to a camp—saved, as he writes, "from the nightmare of a special psychiatric hospital". Privalov soon died, and so the man felt free to write a letter to the Commission about his "noble act", as the best memorial to him.[33]

Another psychiatrist with whom the KGB clearly had difficulty was Vladimir Moskalkov. First he is reported as being harassed by the authorities because of his refusal to co-operate with the KGB.[34] And then he turns up as a prosecution witness at the trial of Alexander Podrabinek, where he suddenly confirms the defendant's account of the death of an inmate, thus refuting a major charge of the prosecution and revealing a number of the other witnesses as perjurers.[35]

Dr Anatoly Barabanov is reported as being harassed in similar circumstances. And Alla Totenko resigned her post at the new Volgograd SPH after six months, "because of her disagreement with the severe conditions in which patients were kept in the SPH".[36]

Having implicitly held up such examples for emulation, the Commission doubtless felt there was some point in appealing to psychiatrists to mitigate the lot of dissenters kept on their local psychiatric register. Such people, it wrote:

> have to live in constant fear of new psychiatric oppression. On the eve of any important official event they have to wait for a ring at the door, and be ready to be seized on the street and interned in a mental hospital "as a preventive measure". The Commission considers that only the publicizing of every such case and a clear understanding of the dangers of the present system can decrease the number of victims of such psychiatric tyranny. We hope that this problem will attract the attention of psychiatrists of integrity, and that they will help in finding ways to resolve it.[37]

The Commission had no difficulty reporting material which might arouse revulsion in readers. There was far too much of it, and it could be printed without fear of causing anyone trouble with the KGB.

Nikolai Vetrov, for example, was an orphan who had been imprisoned for six years in the Dnepropetrovsk SPH for trying to escape abroad. He asked his doctor how much longer he would be held. "Another six to eight years," came the reply. He hanged himself in her office.[38]

In 1973 Raisa Ivanova, a teacher and an Orthodox Christian mother of two children, was arrested because of her non-recognition of the official Orthodox Church, and sentenced to a camp term. Later she was sent to the Serbsky Institute for assessment, but returned to the camp. Then a well-known informer among the prisoners fabricated, apparently, evidence against her suggesting mental illness. She was transferred to a psychiatric block and then to Kazan SPH. Here she was subjected to intensive drug treatment which had very painful effects on her. At the end of 1977 she hanged herself.[39]

Two further particularly tragic episodes came to light after the Commission was suppressed.[40] It had reported at length on the early stages of one of these cases, Nikolai Sorokin. He was a young, critically minded metal-worker who twice travelled to Moscow to talk to Dr Sakharov and foreign journalists. For this he was briefly interned and then, in 1978, arrested. The Commission informed the Ukrainian Supreme Court that in the event of a psychiatric commitment it would "regard this as a use of psychiatry for political purposes". Nonetheless he was dispatched to the Dnepropetrovsk SPH. Here intensive drug treatment resulted in a kidney disease, for which he was refused treatment. When the doctors saw that he was dying, they suggested his transfer to an OPH. This was forbidden by Colonel Kapustin of the regional KGB. During the month before his death in early 1980, aged twenty-seven, Sorokin was in agony. But those around him were not allowed to give him even water. After his death Dr Anatoly Kovunnikov, a psychiatrist, was made into a scapegoat and demoted.

Valery Zaks was a Ukrainian Jew born in 1956. He had applied several times to emigrate to Israel, but was always refused permission. In 1978 he tried to hi-jack a plane in a desperate attempt to get out of the Soviet Union. Shots were fired and he was arrested on board. Ruled not responsible, he was interned in the Dnepropetrovsk SPH. Here he was isolated from other inmates and subjected to intensive drug treatment. His psychiatrist regularly conducted "therapeutic" conversations with him about the harmfulness of thinking about emigration. Despite the drug treatment, in early summer 1980 he was forced to work on the construction of a new block for the SPH. According to the hospital rules, patients are strictly prohibited from ever climbing more than one metre above the ground. Nonetheless, Zaks was ordered to work on the roof of the six-storey block, from where he fell to his death, allegedly jumping deliberately. These two deaths led to extreme tension in the hospital and a brief revolt by inmates.

Lobbying of Foreign Organizations
The Commission lobbied not only domestically but also internationally. We describe most of the responses from psychiatric bodies in chapter five. The section which follows here aims to give a clear idea of what exactly the Commission requested, and when and why.

Not surprisingly, the Commission (supported by 39 co-signatories) addressed an appeal to the WPA's Honolulu Congress. After wishing the participants a fruitful scientific occasion, they continued:

> The history of human society shows clearly how closely interwoven, sometimes, are scientific and socio-political problems. And the science which you today represent is no exception. For this reason we hope you will not remain indifferent to the fact that in the USSR psychiatry is used not only to cure the mentally ill, but also as an instrument for suppressing civil rights. . . .
> We ask you to note that the establishment of agreed international norms for the handling of mentally ill people would in some degree inhibit the well-known abuses of psychiatry. . . .
> We call on you . . . in the name of human decency and humanitarian ideals to condemn the practice of using psychiatry for political purposes.[41]

After reporting what subsequently happened in Honolulu, the Commission referred to the outcome as "unprecedented". "For the first time such a large and representative organization as the WPA has directly and unambiguously indicated to the Soviet Union the impermissibility of using psychiatry for political purposes. The Commission welcomes the resolute and honest decisions of the congress, and is certain that many of the victims of psychiatric terror in the USSR join us in this welcome."[42]

In November 1977 the Commission sent the WPA an appeal entitled "Two Months after Honolulu". A note of concern creeps in:

> Two months have passed since the resolution condemning the Soviet Union . . . was passed at the Honolulu congress. However, the Commission cannot, unfortunately, report any apparent changes in the policy of punitive medicine.
> In the last two months the Commission has documented five new forcible commitments to mental hospitals. . . . [These are listed.] Under threat of reinternment in mental hospitals are Vyacheslav Igrunov in Odessa and Lev Konin in Leningrad. As before, political prisoners are held in severe conditions in special psychiatric hospitals . . . [six

examples listed] . . . Relatives of two political prisoners, Evdokimov and Zhikharev, have appealed for help to the recently formed special committee of the WPA.

We call on the association not to stop at the passing of resolutions, but to make every effort to implement them.[43]

In her appeal, the seventy-year-old mother of Mikhail Zhikharev, who had been interned for criticizing official corruption, wrote from the Black Sea town of Sochi:

> . . . I assert that my son is healthy, has never suffered from any mental illness, and needs no treatment. . . . All the appeals of my son's wife to various Soviet bodies have yielded no result. I ask the Committee to investigate my son's case and do everything possible to free him. . . .[44]

In April 1978 the Commission gave up on the WPA's discouraging silence in the face of these and other letters, and dispatched an "Appeal to Foreign Psychiatric Associations". The anxiety level was understandably rising:

> Seven months ago the Honolulu congress of psychiatrists passed a resolution which sharply condemned the abuse of psychiatry in the USSR. Nevertheless, the committee designated by another adopted resolution has still not been set up. We are very disappointed by this. For us, the urgent need for the committee is clear. We are already receiving letters and statements addressed to this still non-existent committee.
>
> We ask national psychiatric associations abroad to take the necessary steps to set up the WPA Committee to Review Abuse of Psychiatry as soon as possible. . . .
>
> We ask you not to forget that psychiatric oppression in the USSR is not slackening.[45]

In the same month the Commission received fresh support from abroad when Dr Low-Beer brought a letter of greetings to Moscow from the Royal College of Psychiatrists in London (see chapter five). In its reply the Commission thanked the College for its work on behalf of victims, and expressed the hope that mutual co-operation would continue.[46]

Such co-operation did continue. Indeed, it was widened to include, most notably, psychiatric bodies in the USA and France. The Commission's attention was naturally caught when it received copies of a lively debate in the paper of the American Psychiatric Association (APA) on how best to combat psychiatric abuse in the USSR. First Vyacheslav Bakhmin joined in, contributing a letter which expressed the Commission's views on this subject with clarity and succinctness: we include it as appendix II of this book. Then Dr Voloshanovich replied to a contribution from the APA's President-elect, Alan Stone, who had reported on a recent meeting with Professor Snezhnevsky in Moscow. Regarding Western criticism of abuse, Snezhnevsky had continued "to deny any guilt and to demand an apology". In answer to this, Voloshanovich wrote that his experiences as a hospital psychiatrist and a consultant to the Commission had convinced him that the abuses were real. Also he could not agree with Stone's view that they were declining in frequency.

Voloshanovich then explained how he felt that Western psychiatrists could influence the situation:

The leaders of Soviet psychiatry, like the Soviet government itself, strive in every way to achieve respectability and international recognition. In this connection the threat of the Soviet delegation in Honolulu about cutting of psychiatric co-operation was terrifying first and foremost to those who had to make it. Beyond this, one should also bear in mind that foreign trips and professional contacts with foreign colleagues are an exceptional privilege for Soviet psychiatrists, and this privilege is available only to a small élite. Such trips are literally used as a reward for those who have won the authorities' favour and readily perform what is asked of them. . . .

If Western colleagues were to reject Soviet psychiatrists who are found to have abused psychiatry to suppress dissent, or covered up for such abuses, this would significantly facilitate a "revision of values" among psychiatrists in this country. It is quite probable that an attitude of intolerance to abuses of psychiatry would significantly undermine the existing system of rewards and encourage psychiatrists to strive to carry out their doctor's duty with—on the moral and ethical side—integrity. To achieve this aim, the methods of "quiet diplomacy" may also be useful, but only as a supplementary means of pressure aimed at helping particular individuals.

Voloshanovich was alarmed by a situation in which political abuse had led to psychiatrists "losing the trust of their patients and the public". He therefore advocated vigorous international investigations of all cases of abuse, in all countries, and also strong campaigns to free imprisoned critics of abuse like Gluzman and Podrabinek.[47]

Later, Voloshanovich's successor, Dr Anatoly Koryagin, responded with alacrity when the French Association of Psychiatrists in Private Practice sent him its newly published code of psychiatric ethics, "A Charter for Psychiatry". He found it "an admirable document . . . I read it with enthusiasm and felt proud to be a psychiatrist". Testifying to his personal knowledge of sane people being interned and treated, "simply because they think for themselves", he urged that "we doctors . . . must as a matter of priority take steps to combat the dire consequences of this abuse of our science. . . . The simple fact that politicians are able to arrogate to themselves the right to exploit psychiatry for their own immediate interests, devalues, in the eyes of the man in the street, not only all moral ideals, but even life itself. This situation . . . throws a sinister shadow over our future."[48]

Quite apart from interchanges of this sort with foreign psychiatric bodies, the Commission made a strong and regular contribution to the work of Amnesty International and other humanitarian bodies by sending the *Bulletin* abroad. Here it was systematically processed by these groups, the information transmitted in various languages along their own networks and appropriate action taken to intervene for particular individuals faced with the fact or threat of psychiatric internment. In addition, Amnesty acknowledged its debt to the Commission regarding the section on political psychiatry in its report *Prisoners of Conscience in the USSR* (revised edition, 1980).

How Successful Were the Commission's Interventions?
We have looked at the Commission's work in supplying information, educating *Bulletin* readers and lobbying psychiat-

rists at home and abroad. But how successful was all this in terms of helping individual victims? To answer is not easy, as the authorities do not state their reasons either for releasing people or for abstaining from internment. And the Commission, with self-denying modesty, never claimed credit for anything. However, there were at least fifteen cases where the authorities were clearly preparing to intern a dissenter, where the Commission intervened (directly or by giving publicity) and where no internment subsequently took place.[49] There were also nine cases in which the following pattern obtained: a dissenter was arrested, charged, and sent for in-patient psychiatric diagnosis; the Commission intervened; the psychiatrists then found the individual responsible for his actions; and he was then sentenced to labour camp or exile rather than indefinite detention in an SPH.[50] There were also cases where the victim of a long-term internment believed that the Commission's intervention hastened his release,[51] and others where pressure put an end—temporarily if not permanently—to harrowing courses of drug treatment, and thus at least brought relief.[52]

Equally, though, there were cases where strong efforts by the Commission to prevent an impending internment failed, and others where interventions for long-term internees proved fruitless.

The averting of internment is illustrated by the case of a provincial telephone operator, Tamara Los. In 1977, aged twenty-two, she refused the KGB's demands to inform on some Iranian students, and as a result was dismissed. She appealed for reinstatement, then, when no response came, for permission to emigrate with her family. Soon she was summoned to various police bodies, told that emigration would be allowed, but first she must undergo a medical examination. She smelt a rat and refused. An official then told her it was obligatory, as she was mentally ill. At this point, in May 1978, she travelled to Moscow to seek out the Commission. Dr Voloshanovich examined her, and the conclusion of his report—that he found "no signs of mental illness" in her—was promptly quoted in the Bulletin, along with an account of her case. The authorities backed off, and in 1980 the family emigrated to West Germany.[53]

The case of Mikhail Kukobaka, a Belorussian worker,

demonstrates how persistent dissenters could sometimes be rescued from the toils of Soviet psychiatry, if only at the cost—unwelcome, but readily paid—of imprisonment in a labour camp. In the years 1970–77 he was held in SPHs and OPHs. When he was arrested again in 1978 and sent to the Serbsky Institute, the outlook thus seemed black. In the meanwhile, however, he had been examined by Voloshanovich, who could find no abnormalities in him. The Commission went into action, quoting Voloshanovich's report in a letter to Professor Morozov, the head of the Serbsky, appealing to Dr Low-Beer to intervene from London, and giving maximum coverage to the case in the *Bulletin*. As a result, no doubt, the Serbsky found that the schizophrenic process it had detected in Kukobaka in 1970 was in remission, and he was responsible. The outcome was three years of forced labour.[54] Later the *Bulletin* printed his account of the strange ways of the Serbsky psychiatrists,[55] which confirmed and updated the picture given by other first-hand witnesses like Viktor Nekipelov in his widely praised book *Institute of Fools*.[56]

A similar pattern obtained in the case of Vadim Konovalikhin, who was ultimately exiled for four years, and who described the sequence of events in his own words:

Fearing that the investigating organs would soon send me for psychiatric examination . . . I travelled to Moscow and visited . . . Vyacheslav Bakhmin, who organized an assessment of my mental state by psychiatrist Voloshanovich. . . . [Later] I was interned for a forensic-psychiatric examination. On 23 May 1978 the chairman of the commission of doctors read out their decision: "Found responsible." The head of the forensic department . . . then added, hinting at who had facilitated this outcome: "Remember, Konovalikhin, if you land up in hospital again, nothing will save you then from an SPH! You won't be rescued by any 'Working Commission' or BBC!" Later, when I was studying the case against me . . . I read the document which had saved me from an SPH. Its letter-head read: "Working Commission to Investigate the Use of Psychiatry for Political Purposes." At the bottom stood the signature of Vyacheslav Bakhmin.[57]

ft: Dr Eduard
ıbayan, leader of the
ıviet delegation, at
e world psychiatric
ngress in Honolulu,
•77

Below: Professor Georgy Morozov (*2nd from left*), the top administrator of Soviet psychiatry, with his Serbsky Institute colleague N. Zharikov (*right*) and two Finnish psychiatrists

Above: Dr Gery Low-Beer of London (*2nd from right*) with (*l. – r*). Alexander Podrabinek, Dr Alexander Voloshanovich and Vyacheslav Bakhmin, members of the Working Commission to Investigate the Use of Psychiatry for Political Purposes; Moscow, April 1978

Below: Alexander Podrabinek is detained by plain-clothes men in Moscow while attending a Baptist meeting on 3 April 1977. He was given two weeks in jail for "hooliganism"

Above: (l. – r.) Felix Serebrov, Irina Grivnina and Dr Leonard Ternovsky, members of the Moscow "Working Commission", 1980

Below: (l. – r.) Olga Ternovskaya (daughter of Dr Ternovsky) with F. Serebrov, Dr Anatoly Koryagin and I. Grivnina, 1980

Above: (*l. – r.*) Alexander Podrabinek, his fiancée Alla Khromova and Vyacheslav Bakhmin, at Podrabinek's Siberian place of exile, Chuna, February 1979

Below:(*l. – r., standing*) Galina Koryagin, her son Ivan, Dr Anatoly Koryagin; (*sitting*) Koryagin's son Alexander, Galina's parents, Koryagin's mother, his son Dmitry, *c.* 1979

Above: Alexander Shatravka, would-be emigrant, sitting outside a building of the Geikovka psychiatric hospital during one of his internments (see Appendix IV)

Below: Standing far left, Sergei Potylitsyn; *third from left,* Vyacheslav Bakhmin; *fourth from left,* Tamara Los; *sitting, far right,* Evgeny Nikolayev; 1979. Potylitsyn and Nikolayev had earlier been hospitalized for their dissent, and Los had been threatened

Left: Nikolai
Baranov,
technician,
prior to his first
arrest in 1963

Right: Nikolai
Baranov in
Kazan SPH,
1977

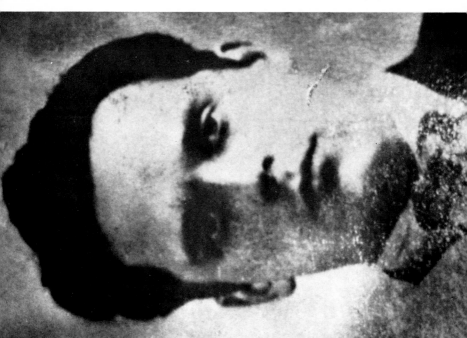

Left: Viktor Davydov, a student interned for his political dissent

Right: Aleksei Nikitin, a miner interned for fighting for workers' rights

Left: Nikolai Sorokin, a dissenter who died of deliberate official negligence in Dnepropetrovsk mental hospital aged 27

Right: Sergei Batovrin, unofficial peace-campaigner, in Moscow OPH No. 14, August 1982

An interesting example of how the Commission facilitated a release from hospital is the case of Evgeny Nikolayev. Since 1970 he had been a lone dissenter subject to occasional psychiatric internment. In 1977 he became an active dissenter and thus a more serious nuisance to the KGB. To put an end to his support for the Commission and for the newly emergent cause of free trade-unionism, the KGB had him interned in February 1978 in Moscow's Kashchenko OPH. Soon, however, he spirited out of the hospital an appeal to the WPA and detailed accounts of how his psychiatrist talked to him in the style of a secret police investigator. So the authorities went to great lengths to bar visitors from seeing him, including Dr Low-Beer of London (see chapter five). The Commission acted vigorously. It wrote letters to the Ministry of Health and the Chief Psychiatrist of Moscow, quoting Voloshanovich's earlier finding that he was not mentally ill. It also appealed to Professor Pichot, President of the WPA, calling for his intervention, as "in recent months the abuse of psychiatry in the USSR has taken on still greater dimensions". And it printed a whole series of Nikolayev's vivid reports of his interviews with his OPH psychiatrist.

In September, after a mere seven months of internment, Nikolayev was freed. Immediately he wrote to the Royal College of Psychiatrists: "I am profoundly grateful to all members of the College for their efforts to free me . . . I am sending you a copy of my letter to the WPA, so that you can get an idea of what I've had to experience during the last seven months."[58]

Even though Nikolayev resumed his vigorous activity as a dissenter, the authorities hesitated to touch him after his case had aroused so much publicity, and in 1980 they allowed him to emigrate to West Germany. His book about his psychiatric odyssey was published there in 1983.[59]

Of those dissenters who have expressed views on what helped or hindered their release, most have stressed the beneficial, even decisive effect of domestic and foreign lobbying. By contrast, none have felt that such lobbying was a hindrance. Arvydas Čekanavičius, for example, wrote as follows in a letter of thanks to friends, to the Commission and, especially, to foreigners: "My sincere thanks to the Western public and all my Western friends, who did much for my release. I want to emphasize the important role of those honourable Western psychiatrists who are active in publicizing political abuses of psychiatry. Their work is very important. . . . In our country there are still many innocent people suffering in mental hospitals."[60]

Yury Belov wrote in like vein in 1977:

> I express my thanks and gratitude to all the people and organizations (both known and unknown to me) who have extracted me from the abominable dungeons which are Soviet psychiatric prisons. I thank them in the name of hundreds of thousands of my fellow countrymen who have experienced the horror of the worst of all mockeries of a human being . . . [and] also in the name of those who, while still held in those monstrous jails, now have a hope of rescue. I warmly thank in particular: The Working Commission . . . Nobel Prize winner Amnesty International, the European Society for the Defence of Human Rights, the Swiss Committee to Combat the Abuse of Psychiatry for Political Purposes [etc.].[61]

In contrast to all this, stand the Commission's disappointments. Its greatest sense of failure probably concerned the case of Vladimir Rozhdestvov, an engineer. It fought tenaciously to prevent his internment, interviewing the psychiatrists who examined him, attending his trial, obtaining a lawyer who brilliantly exposed in court the fraudulence of the psychiatrists' report, appealing to Soviet bodies and the WPA, and publicizing the case in a 40-page special issue of the *Bulletin*. When all this failed, it continued to press for his release. But again to no avail. Six years after his arrest for "slandering the Soviet system" in 1977—an offence with a maximum camp term of only three years—Rozhdestvov was still immured in the Tashkent SPH.[62] Probably the decisive factors were his determination not to recant and the failure of foreign groups to capitalize on the Commission's efforts and organize a powerful campaign for his release.

Humanization of Conditions, Regulations and Laws
Although the demands made by "consumers" on its limited resources were always excessive, the Commission nonetheless

managed to devote some of its time to lobbying for the humanization of the conditions, regulations and laws which were most relevant to its clients' problems. It printed, for example, a lengthy analysis of the Rozhdestvov case by its legal consultant, who pointed to weaknesses in the system of criminal procedure in such cases.[63] And when the WPA's Declaration of Hawaii (see appendix I) was published in the USSR, the *Bulletin* provided a thoughtful analysis of how Soviet psychiatric regulations violate some of its provisions. To make this clear, the Commission published the text of the standard form used in the Moscow region for ordering an administrative (or civil) commitment. This states, for example, that "It is categorically forbidden to show this order to the patient, his relatives or other persons, and also to convey to them any of the information contained in this order" (e.g. the patient's alleged mental condition). This, the Commission showed, contradicted point four of the Declaration, which requires psychiatrists to give patients maximum information and the chance to choose between possible alternative treatments.[64]

The Commission also campaigned for an end to the illegal barring of mail addressed to inmates of the SPHs. It printed a letter by Yury Belov in which he reported that the doctors of three SPHs "did not hand over to the addressees a single one of my letters to prisoners Demyanov, Čekanavičius and Evdokimov, and also failed to give them four parcels and two small packets". The Commission confirmed such practices from its own experience, adding that "inmates of some SPHs are often subjected to threats and pressure by the administration in an effort to force them to refuse to accept parcels". The Commission sent letters protesting against this abuse to the worst offender, the Kazan SPH, and to the Kazan Procurator, whose duty it was to enforce legality in the hospital.[65] But with no apparent result.

The Commission did, however, score a minor victory over the Serbsky Institute. When it complained that the Serbsky was operating an illegal bar on detainees under examination receiving parcels from anyone but close relatives, the bar was acknowledged to be illegal and removed.[66]

The Commission protested too, apparently without success, about a curious practice which it viewed as unconstitutional.

Reporting that a steady stream of people who had simulated mental illness to avoid doing military service were seeking its help, it explained that many of them had later realized their mistake and sought a psychiatric assessment in order to be removed from their local psychiatric register. They were ready to accept punishment for their offence. In all cases, however, "the official organs refuse to re-examine such people." This, the Commission said, constituted "a limitation on citizens' exercise of their constitutional rights and duties."[67]

The Authorities' Hesitant Toleration, then Suppression of the Commission

Now that our survey of the Commission's main types of activity is complete, we can turn to the ways in which the authorities responded to its very existence and to its members as individuals. The first member to receive unwelcome attention, three months after the Commission's formation, was Alexander Podrabinek, who was given two weeks' administrative detention. This was in April 1977, soon after the KGB had confiscated a copy of his book *Punitive Medicine*, which we discussed above.[68] Although he refused to be intimidated, the favourable publicity the book attracted abroad inhibited the KGB from arresting him. So it backed off and arrested instead, in August, the middle-aged Felix Serebrov, who it probably thought was the brains behind the group. As, however, the Commission's appeal to the WPA Honolulu congress on his behalf received mention in the press, and as, more importantly, the outcome of the congress was such a sharp blow to Soviet prestige, he was later sentenced to no more than one year in a camp.[69]

The congress, in fact, forced a careful reappraisal of Soviet policy. As the new situation was ambiguous, so too was the emergent policy on political psychiatry. On the one hand the WPA failed to follow up quickly on the congress resolutions (see chapter four), but, on the other, bodies like the Royal College of Psychiatrists had become active and soon made direct contact with the Commission. Thus the Kremlin's policy was to retain the official psychiatric leaders and continue political internments, but, at the same time, to release quietly a number of long-term internees,[70] and—so as not to inflame the delicately poised international situation—grudgingly tolerate the Commission's existence.

But grudging toleration did not mean acceptance. All members were subject to intimidation through flat searches,[71] and soon Podrabinek was singled out as the most active member whose removal from the scene might deprive the group of its momentum. A further reason for homing in on him was that he also played a bold and vigorous part in other dissenting circles apart from the Commission. Thus, in December 1977 he was told to emigrate—or face a ten-year sentence. He declined to go, even when faced by the black-mailing threat that in this case his innocent brother would be arrested—a threat that was carried out. So his own arrest soon followed in May 1978.[72]

To see why, at Podrabinek's trial in August, the promised ten-year sentence became in fact a mere five years of exile, we must briefly note a number of points. First, he was immediately replaced in the Commission by Dr Leonard Ternovsky, a radiologist at Moscow's prestigious Medical Institute No. 1 and a longstanding dissenter. This showed that the Commission would not easily be persuaded to shut up shop. Second, the President of the Royal College of Psychiatrists and other foreigners of standing wrote letters to Soviet authorities on Podrabinek's behalf. Third, an International Committee to Defend the Podrabinek Brothers was formed and became active. Fourth, Podrabinek appointed a well-known British lawyer, Louis Blom-Cooper, to act in his defence. And fifth, on 13 July in London, Blom-Cooper and his colleague Brian Wrobel conducted public hearings on the defence case.[73] Among the nine witnesses were several, including Dr Low-Beer, who knew Podrabinek personally. Another witness was Dr Yury Novikov, who until his defection in June 1977 had been head of the Serbsky Institute's Information Department and also one of the two secretaries of the Soviet Society of Psychiatrists. Although Novikov had had almost no personal involvement in political psychiatry, he was well informed about the practice because of his close association with Morozov and other Serbsky colleagues. Five long interviews with him had recently been published in the German press, and both these and his London testimony must have caused Morozov acute unease.[74]

The witnesses were cross-examined by Blom-Cooper in front of the press. At the end he concluded that no case existed for Podrabinek's arrest, and also that serious abuses of the Soviet legal codes had been committed in the case by the authorities. The testimony and conclusions were then compiled into a dossier and mailed to the court which was due to try Podrabinek. This court had the legal duty to take the foreign evidence fully into account.

The detailed transcript of the trial compiled by Podrabinek's friends shows that in fact the court violated the law by failing to take any account of this evidence at all. Nor was Blom-Cooper given a visa to take part in the trial,[75] the nature of which is well conveyed in the Commission's appeal of the following day "To the Psychiatric Associations of the World":

> Podrabinek . . . was tried for his book *Punitive Medicine*. . . .
> He was not given the chance to defend himself. All of his 27
> petitions [for materials and witnesses necessary to his
> defence] were rejected by the court. He then dismissed his
> [Soviet] lawyer and refused to take part in the trial, as the
> court and the investigators had done everything possible to
> prevent him defending himself against the false and hypo-
> critical charges. . . . Even the materials produced by such a
> tendentiously conducted investigation enabled Podrabinek
> to confirm the accuracy of most of the episodes in his book,
> and disprove the claims of the indictment. . . .
>
> Attempts by us to send material aid to the political
> prisoners in various SPHs prove the falsity of the court's
> assertion that there are no limitations on the receipt of
> parcels in such hospitals.

The Commission concluded by calling on the associations to unite and organize a "public, objective investigation of the known cases of psychiatric abuse".[76]

The same day, as we noted earlier, Dr Voloshanovich "went public" by telling a press conference about the examinations of dissenters which he had been conducting on the Commission's behalf.[77] This further gesture of defiance by the Commission, and the strong response it elicited from foreign psychiatrists (see chapter five), helped to keep the KGB on the defensive. Clearly the latter could not hope to crush the

Commission without arresting several people with substantial foreign support, and thus probably provoking an upsurge of protest abroad.

So the Soviet Society of Psychiatrists set up—presumably on the KGB's instructions—a special commission to investigate the cases of psychiatric abuse mentioned by Voloshanovich at his press conference. Its chairman was a deputy-president of the Society, Vladimir Kovalëv, and the other members were also senior psychiatrists. On 19 October they met Voloshanovich at his hospital. He informed them of the names and addresses of his examinees, the hospitals where they had been held, and his conclusions regarding their mental health. The Working Commission then issued a statement welcoming the formation of the Special Commission, but expressing the fear that its real aim might be "to discredit the findings of the examinations."

On 28 October a second meeting was held to discuss a case of political abuse in which Voloshanovich had been personally involved in 1976. In the *Bulletin*'s words, "The Commission studied the materials of the case, but did not allow Voloshanovich to do likewise. All his references to specific violations of the Directives of the Ministry of Health [on involuntary hospitalization] and the groundlessness of the diagnosis were ignored. The Commission's approach to the case gave Voloshanovich reason to conclude that its real aim was not an objective investigation and clarification of the violations committed, but the professional discrediting of both himself and the findings of his examinations." As a result he wrote to the Society to say that he would continue to collaborate with the Commission only if an observer from the WPA were allowed to be present. No reply came, and the Commission soon fizzled out.[78]

For the next year the Working Commission was paid little overt attention by the authorities,[79] and its work steadily developed. A key explanation for this may be the fact that the WPA was gradually setting up its Review Committee in the face of the Soviet Society's vehement objections and threats (see chapter four), and the KGB did not want to make the Society's job any harder by provoking undesirable publicity in the West.

In October 1979, however, official policy began to change.

Voloshanovich, who had been forced to leave his hospital job, was detained while visiting Gorky,[80] and then on 18 October Bakhmin was summoned to the KGB. Here an officer calling himself Sokolov explained that the KGB was conducting an "administrative inquiry"—apparently into the Commission. Their conversation went in part as follows:

S: I have here some extracts from your *Bulletins*. You mention, for example, a certain Yanin.

B: Yes, that's right, but we published information about him in a special section entitled "More Information Wanted", where we stated that our facts may be incorrect and asked for any available information about the fate of these people . . .

S: Then you mention the fact that someone was transferred from the Leningrad SPH to another hospital. But we know that he was discharged from the Leningrad hospital because his health improved.

B: What is the man's name?

S: Chernyshov.

B: Very well, I'll make a note of it and we'll check it out. Read out all you have, it's very important to us. Whenever we make a mistake we always issue corrections and addenda in subsequent issues.

S: No, I won't read it out to you. It's a fine state of affairs for *me* to be giving *you* information! . . .

S: Doesn't it disturb you that your information is used by anti-Soviet centres—Radio Liberty is always broadcasting your *Bulletins*, and the Possev publishing-house has published them in a booklet. . . . All this information is used to undermine our authority. How do you react to this?

B: It's unimportant to me who uses the information, as long as I'm convinced that it is true and necessary. The same anti-Soviet centres use information published in the Soviet press for the same purpose. What is written is the important thing, not how and by whom it is used.

S: No. Possev does not publish, and Radio Liberty does not broadcast, information from the Soviet press.

B: Yes they do. They often publish it and comment on it. Don't you remember when the communist newspaper in

Britain reprinted an article about Fainberg in *Literaturka (Literary Gazette)* and was then fined for libel?

S: How readily you remember this example. Yes, I remember the incident. We did not interfere, so as not to discredit the English psychiatrist who examined Fainberg.

B: How noble. You mean you didn't want to discredit a British psychiatrist, so you calmly discredited the whole British Communist Party. Strange. . . . If you object to our information and find the *Bulletins* slanderous, then publish the facts openly in the press and give me, for example, the opportunity to reply. . . .

S: It would be a great deal better for you if you stopped concerning yourself with matters that are none of your business. You're not a psychiatrist. I strongly urge you to do this.

B: I would very much like to stop concerning myself with all this—I have many other things to do. But before I can do this, the misuse of psychiatry must stop; people must stop coming to us every day asking for help, telling us about horrific illegality and injustice.

S: I am not bringing charges against you at the moment . . . I am simply telling you that your activities are illegal. . . . I hope that you will draw the appropriate conclusions.[81]

Four months later, with the Commission highly active (though with Voloshanovich having suddenly been allowed to emigrate); with the pre-Olympic Games purge of dissenters moving into top gear (Sakharov had just been exiled to Gorky); with the West too focused on the Iranian revolution and the invasion of Afghanistan to protest much about the purge; and with Soviet international prestige so battered in the wake of the Afghan adventure that the political price to be paid for conducting the purge had suddenly gone down—Bakhmin was arrested. Soon he was followed into prison by Ternovsky. Developments then ensued which were similar to those precipitated by Podrabinek's trial. For example, Irina Grivnina, a computer specialist, defiantly joined the Commission. And Blom-Cooper and Wrobel conducted new defence hearings in London. These concerned the two arrested men and also their jailed associate Viktor Nekipelov.[82]

By now, however, the Politbureau had ordered the KGB to suppress, if possible, all organized dissenting groups. So hearings and protests could only hope to mitigate sentences, not prevent further arrests. Arrest followed for Grivnina in September, for Serebrov in January 1981 and for Koryagin a month later.

The impact of the Honolulu congress and the follow-up actions by psychiatric and other bodies had allowed the Commission to function for four years, despite the authorities' hostility. But now Mr Brezhnev and his colleagues had radically changed tack on dissent. A heroically determined and disciplined humanitarian enterprise was, from early 1980 on, irredeemably doomed.

Bakhmin's trial was the occasion when the authorities tried hardest to discredit the Commission. Psychiatric witnesses were assembled, and in various ways the judge made it impossible for him to conduct a proper defence. The main charge concerned his editing and circulation of 22 issues of the *Bulletin*. Of the roughly 1,000 "episodes" in these issues, however, only fourteen were held to "defame the Soviet social and political system". In his final speech Bakhmin said that only two of these fourteen episodes "contain inaccuracies. The evidence in the case file on the other twelve either confirms the accuracy of our accounts, or contains internal contradictions." Bakhmin continued:

How was the pre-trial investigation conducted? Those officials whom we know to have been responsible for violations of the law were, on each investigated episode, sent such questions as: "Please tell us what you know about this or that incident concerning the criminal case against V. I. Bakhmin, who is charged under article 190–1 with circulating deliberately false fabrications. . . ." What could these people reply when asked such a question? . . . They said that everything was fine, that there were no violations of the law, either in hospital procedures or over hospitaliza- tions. . . .

In her speech the Procurator often said that all the persons referred to in the *Bulletins* were ill. But the Commis- sion never tried to debate this point. The real point is that a sick person has certain rights, just as any other one does, and these rights are firmly stated in the "Directives on the urgent hospitalization of mentally ill persons", which are very often violated. For example, Sebelev, mentioned by witness Koltsova, was forcibly hospitalized in a state of alcoholic intoxication by the police, who removed him from his own flat. He was shortly afterwards discharged, since it was considered that he did not require in-patient treatment. This was an example of flagrant violation of the Directives, as a state of alcoholic intoxication does not constitute one of the stated grounds for forcible hospitalization. More than this, in many cases even the psychiatrists themselves do not know the Directives. They are not only unfamiliar with their provisions; they do not even know of their existence. This was highlighted when it was discovered that among the members of the Commission charged with checking the medical reports of Voloshanovich, not one of them had even heard of the Directives. . . . In her speech the Procurator referred to the secrecy of our activities, yet the activities of the Working Commission were absolutely legal. We do not hide from anyone, something which cannot be said about this trial, which is being conducted virtually behind closed doors. . . . Issues of the *Bulletin* were regularly sent by me to the USSR Procuracy and the Ministry of Health. I enclosed letters requesting that if any inaccuracies or incorrect information were discovered, corrections should be sent to the members of the Working Commission, so that they could be included in the next issue. However, the Procuracy, which is supposed to ensure that the law is observed, would, the very next day, send the *Bulletin* to that organization so endearingly referred to by the Procurator as "the committee", namely the KGB. The same happened to the issues of the *Bulletin* sent to the Ministry of Health. Evidently the KGB is more competent in matters of psychiatry. . . .[83]

After the trial the Moscow "Helsinki Group" commented as follows:

It would be ridiculous to imagine that witnesses so directly interested in the outcome of the case would corroborate statements about their own unlawful actions. However, none of the evidence given by these witnesses proves the existence of deliberate falsehood in the specific reports in the *Information Bulletin* which were cited against Bakhmin. Those witnesses who could have objectively confirmed the accuracy of these statements were not called, either during the pre-trial investigation or at the trial. . . .[84]

Bakhmin's sentence of three years in camps was later matched by Ternovsky's,[85] and Grivnina received five years of exile.[86] Serebrov, as a third-time defendant and, in addition, a member of the Helsinki Group, got four years of camp, plus five of exile.[87] The trials followed a roughly similar pattern, with the loyal psychiatrists who were the main witnesses in most of them being shielded for various reasons from any probing cross-examination. Only Serebrov could be induced, by formidable psychological pressure, to make a recantation. But it was hesitant, generalized, and far from what the KGB wanted.

Ternovsky's final speech was notable for its simple dignity:

As a doctor I felt particularly responsible for what was being done in the name of medicine. . . . I would prefer there to be no need for my activities. Defending human rights and the rule of law should really be done by the Procuracy and the legal institutions. If they did their job properly, there would be no need for amateur defenders of the rule of law. I anticipated my arrest and this trial. That doesn't mean, of course, that I was seeking to be imprisoned. I am nearly fifty, not fifteen, and have no need of romantic gestures. I'd have preferred to avoid years of imprisonment. But to do that, I would have had to shirk what I considered my duty, and that would have been unworthy. . . . My juridical exculpation some time in the future is as inevitable as my conviction is today. . . .

The trial of Dr Koryagin stood out from those just mentioned, because of the severity of the sentence: seven years of camp, plus five of exile. We can only assume that the key factor in this was the KGB's desire to intimidate future would-be imitators of him among Soviet psychiatrists. For brave and honest psychiatrists—as we have seen since Dr Gluzman led the way in 1971—pose the greatest threat of all to political psychiatry's defences.

In any case, Koryagin somehow resisted a gamut of psychological tortures and beating while under investigation, and made a long, stirring speech at his trial. A short extract follows:

> I have sat here for a long time and reflected. I have analysed my actions and do not consider myself guilty—I have in no way gone against my conscience or my duty as a psychiatrist. . . .
>
> My investigation and trial do not constitute an act of justice, but a means of suppressing me for my views. I know that the sentence will be harsh. I do not ask anything of this court. Regardless of the sentence imposed on me, I state that I will never accept the situation which exists in our country, where mentally healthy people are imprisoned in psychiatric hospitals for trying to think independently. I know that long years of physical imprisonment, humiliation and mockery await me. Fully aware of this, I embark on it in the hope that it will increase the chances for others to live in freedom. I know that a hard life, full of material deprivation, bitterness and perhaps direct persecution by the authorities, awaits my family.[88]

Domestic Opposition Continues

In April 1981 the Moscow "Helsinki Group" wrote: "The arrest of Koryagin puts a definite end to the humane and legal activity of the Working Commission . . . and gives rise to the fear that the authorities are planning to increase their use of psychiatric persecution for political purposes."[89] That this fear proved unfounded—at least up to the time of writing—may be attributed first of all to the continuance of domestic opposition to psychiatric abuse, despite the Commission's demise. From early 1981 on, such activities as the *Bulletin*, open domestic lobbying and the psychiatric assessment service organized by the Commission naturally ceased. But the flow of information about long-interned dissenters and new cases continued to reach the West along the networks of the—by now—largely underground human rights movement. This meant that well-informed foreign lobbying was maintained.

A case of special interest from the "transitional" period of the Commission's gradual destruction, which serves well to round off this chapter, is that of the miner Aleksei Nikitin. The *Bulletin* had reported on his history of psychiatric internments since 1972 for leading workers' protests, seeking reinstatement in his job, and enquiring about emigration at the Norwegian Embassy. When released in 1980, he soon sought an assessment from Koryagin, who could find no trace of mental illness in him. He then started forming a free trade union group in his home city of Donetsk; and also invited two foreign journalists, David Satter and Kevin Klose, to visit him there. In December 1980 he spent three days showing them round Donetsk, drawing attention to the miners' poor living conditions and lack of civil rights. After their departure, he was arrested, reinterned in Dnepropetrovsk SPH and given intensive drug treatment. In January Koryagin stated publicly he was sane. Then, to separate him by 2,000 miles from his bravely supportive sister in the Ukraine, he was transferred to the SPH at Talgar, near Alma-Ata, on the Chinese border.[90]

Nikitin's case aroused worldwide concern, and was soon referred by several psychiatric associations to the WPA Review Committee. As we shall see, it was the gradual development of this Committee and other Western lobbying efforts which provided the essential complement to the dedicated information-gathering of the Soviet human rights movement. All this prevented a sudden escalation of psychiatric repression when the Commission was crushed by *force majeure*. In chapters four and five, therefore, we turn our attention to these notable advances in the West.

CHAPTER FOUR

THE REVIEW COMMITTEE:
AN ATTEMPT TO INVESTIGATE

WITH THE APPOINTMENT of Peter Berner as the new secretary-general, Vienna replaced Honolulu as the chief site of activity for the enactment of the decisions taken at the WPA's General Assembly.

Establishing the Committee to Review the Abuse of Psychiatry for Political Reasons was a foremost priority for him. A logical first step was the request to member societies for suggestions regarding the committee's membership and working procedure. A fly in the ointment promptly appeared: a Soviet note protesting against the creation of the committee on the grounds that it was entirely illegal.[1] Berner's assignment was clearly not going to be straightforward: a minefield of legal and bureaucratic snares lay before him.

The decision taken by the Executive at its first meeting after Honolulu, held in January 1978 in New Delhi, to set up a Legal Sub-Committee was eminently sensible and proper. Designated as an interim working group, it was charged with the task of formulating procedural guidelines for the Review Committee. With the first legalistic salvo already fired by the Russians, and with the waters completely uncharted by the psychiatrist office-bearers of the WPA, a working group composed of lawyers familiar with the intricate field of human rights in an international context was absolutely crucial.

Anthony McNulty, an experienced British legal expert then working as director of the British Institute of Human Rights, was appointed chairman. Dr K. A. Norgaard of Denmark and Mr B. Kiernan of Ireland, both former members of the European Commission of Human Rights, were additional appointees. The trio of jurists was asked to submit proposals within twelve months.

A second interim working group—the *ad hoc* Sub-Committee of Psychiatrists—was also set up, to receive complaints of abuse pending the formation of the Review Committee itself. This sub-committee would have no executive power but would document complaints and report them to the Executive. Professor Jean-Yves Gosselin from Ottawa was appointed chairman. He would prove an admirable choice for an awesome task—his sense of responsibility, indefatigableness and probity would serve him well for the tricky and thankless work ahead of him.

Thus, the first phase in the establishment of the Review Committee was under way. The second phase was scheduled to begin about a year later, in December 1978, at the meeting of the Executive that was to be held in Cairo.

Soviet opposition to these developments was inevitable in the light of objections raised at Honolulu and in the weeks that followed the congress. In a spate of letters to the WPA, leading Soviet psychiatrists made a concerted effort to prevent the setting up of the Review Committee. The first of these came from Professors Vartanian and Zharikov, who had both attended the Executive meeting in New Delhi.[2] They concentrated on alleged procedural irregularities. To their knowledge no formal decision had been taken then to form an *ad hoc* Sub-Committee of Psychiatrists (they made no mention of the Legal Sub-Committee). Instead, they claimed, it had been arranged "to hold a number of consultations with jurists and individual psychiatrists in order to elucidate the possible working conditions and powers of the sub-committee". The formation of the sub-committee was therefore not justified, and neither were the actions generally of the Executive. This communication, some ten months after the New Delhi events, was decidedly curious, seemingly reflecting more a strategy to delay the birth of the definitive Review Committee than an authentic grievance.

In another letter a month later,[3] the president of the Soviet Society, Georgy Morozov, not only reiterated the procedural objections but also declared his basic opposition to the principle of a Review Committee: its existence would politicize psychiatry and the WPA, and also violate international law and the "professional sovereignty of psychiatrists from different countries"; furthermore, there were neither agreed diagnostic criteria nor a juridical basis to enable such a committee to function.

In an apparent effort to maintain pressure on the leadership, Vartanian dispatched yet another letter,[4] similar in content to Morozov's but also employing another tack—the inclusion of a personal appeal to WPA leaders—". . . I call upon you, Professor Pichot and Professor Berner . . ."—to take the necessary steps to prevent the Association from losing its scientific purpose and becoming a political body instead. Recently-held conferences in psychopharmacology and biological psychiatry (see chapter 5), he added, demonstrated the great benefits that accrued from genuine scientific contacts between psychiatrists from different countries. The Honolulu congress, by contrast, was the victim of "political manipulation"—a wholly undesirable development.

This comparison was drawn in order to unsettle Pichot and Berner: the Review Committee was unquestionably a distraction from the conventional activities of the WPA, namely, arranging the World Congress and regional symposia—and constituted a distinct "political" dimension. They must have felt deep concern at this stage that Vartanian and Morozov were perhaps in a sense correct—the Association was vulnerable and could all too easily be derailed from its fundamental purpose. The Executive might then preside over the demise of the WPA as it had always functioned. They may also of course have looked deeper and noted that it was the Soviet psychiatrists who had introduced politics into psychiatry, thereby giving the WPA the headache of trying to take it out. In any case, Vartanian's tactic was bound to fail. As "civil servants" of the organization, Pichot and Berner were obliged to carry out the mandate of its governing body; a U-turn was inconceivable. Like good civil servants, they would have to soldier on in the hope that their approach would be sufficiently diplomatic and proper to spare any member offence.

A more trenchant communication, sent off at the same time as Vartanian's letter, and with him as a signatory together with Babayan and Zharikov (the Soviet Society seemed to be playing a variant of "musical chairs"!), reminded the WPA yet again that the Review Committee was unacceptable both on legal and ethical (sic) grounds, and the Soviet Society resolutely opposed the Association's intrusion into political

matters: "The Review Committee represented a political body
since one of the main criteria for accepting a complaint for
investigation would be the presence of political motives."
Moreover, the practical problems associated with such a
committee were described as "insurmountable", "insoluble",
and "well-known".[5]

But, probably accepting the unavoidable, the signatories
declared: "If the Review Committee is indeed established . . .
[its] activities will not be recognized by the All-Union Society." Furthermore, "The society reserves its rights to take any
necessary steps." Despite Vartanian's more conciliatory sentiments in the letter under his name alone, the Russian
representatives had finally placed their cards on the table: the
Review Committee might go ahead, but Soviet co-operation
would not accompany it. Indeed the society might even be
forced to withdraw from the WPA. We hypothesize that at
this stage the ultimatum was probably bluff, merely a further
tactic amid a series devised to thwart the Executive from
carrying out its task. Threat, ultimatum, admonition,
appeal—all stops were being pulled in a last bid to stave off a
development which for the Russians must have by then
assumed the unwelcome form of the completely inevitable.

The inevitable in fact took place at a session of the
Executive held in December 1978 in Cairo, despite a last ditch
stand by a team of Soviet psychiatrists (about which more
momentarily), and written support for their viewpoint, from
Hungary and East Germany.[1] A report presented by the
Legal Sub-Committee was accepted as satisfactory, which led
to its immediate dissolution together with that of the *ad hoc*
Sub-Committee of Psychiatrists, and the formal setting up of
the definitive Review Committee. This was to consist of six
psychiatrists representing the six geographical groupings of
member societies in the organization. Financial support
would come from WPA central funds rather than from a
special budget, as had been voted through at Honolulu. An
instrument for the "composition, election and operation of the
Committee to Review the Abuse of Psychiatry" had been
prepared by the Legal Sub-Committee and was in a sufficiently advanced form to serve as guidelines to an embryonic
committee of four psychiatrists, under the continuing chairmanship of Professor Gosselin. Although the committee was

empowered to proceed, its procedure was still subject to possible change in that it had to be circulated among member societies for comment. Only in November 1979 did the committee, with the filling of the last two places, move from a provisional to a permanent footing.

In a rearguard action in February 1979, yet another communication was sent by the Soviet Society in which surprise was expressed at the Review Committee's formation. After all, the discussions in Cairo "had shown the existence of insurmountable difficulties of a professional and juridical nature" in setting it up. Furthermore, the "juridical foundations of such a body were not in keeping with elementary norms of international law and professional ethics".[6] The four signatories, who had been present in Cairo as observers, were the familiar figures of Babayan, Vartanian and Zharikov, joined on this occasion by a young psychiatrist, Dr G. Gause. They asked that their letter be published in the next WPA newsletter, presumably with the aim of seeking publicity for their case and in the hope that other societies might impede the Review Committee's progress by refusing to co-operate with it. Their hopes were not realized. Other WPA members remained entirely passive with regard both to potential opposition and to submitting ideas on the Legal Sub-Committee's draft document of procedure.

Perhaps inured by then to repeated Soviet criticism, in great part levelled against his own handling of the Review Committee matter, Berner replied in courteous but firm manner to all the points raised by Babayan and his associates.[7] Yes, differences of opinion concerning the Review Committee had emerged in Cairo, but its formalization had been decided upon by five votes to one* and this justified pressing on with its creation. The sole opposing voice had come from Ivan Temkov of Bulgaria—whether out of personal conviction or out of "loyalty" to his East-bloc neighbour is pure guesswork. In any event, at the Executive's following meeting he would proclaim that the formation of the Review

---

* The Executive consists of a president, a vice-president, secretary-general, treasurer and two associate secretaries; these positions had been held since Honolulu by Pichot, Shervert Frazier from the United States, Berner, K. Kryspin-Exner from Austria, W. Lo from Hong Kong and Ivan Temkov from Bulgaria, respectively.

Committee was a "mistake", and although irrevocable, measures should still be taken to remedy what he regarded as its glaring flaws.

With regard to the central complaint about the lack of a proper legal basis for the committee's work, Berner wished to "remind" the Russians of the discussion in Cairo to the effect that the committee was to be set up as a "working group" of the WPA, "created in order to assist the Executive", and with no inherent power. Anthony McNulty, the legal adviser present, had elaborated further on this issue: ". . . the Review Committee would be a private organization, not subject to the legislation of any given country . . .".[1] Berner dealt just as bluntly with a Soviet query about funding. Finally, the request by the Soviet correspondents that their letter should be published in the WPA newsletter could definitely not be met. Here Berner revealed a more snappish tone, a reflection of his impatience with a member stubbornly erecting one hurdle after the other. No, the letter would not be included in the newsletter, which was designed to contain "mainly scientific and professional items." Since the entire correspondence would in any case be circulated to all member societies, he held that the request would in essence be complied with.

If Berner then believed that his firm handling of the Russians would enable his Executive to proceed unhindered with setting up the Review Committee, he was much mistaken. At the Executive's next meeting, in May 1979, held ironically in Moscow, Babayan, Vartanian and Zharikov bounced back into action.[8] Attending by invitation (the Executive had no choice—out of convention and courtesy—but to welcome local psychiatric leaders), they promptly launched forth with well-rehearsed objections. Berner's letter of a mere six weeks earlier was like water off a duck's back.

Berner first reported on progress made. Four psychiatrists from Canada, Norway, Czechoslovakia and Brazil had been officially appointed to sit on the Review Committee whilst nominations were still being sought to fill the remaining two vacancies. An attempt to select legal advisers was also continuing. The "Instrument for the composition, election and operation of the Committee to Review the Abuse of Psychiatry" had been amended in the light of discussions at the meeting in Cairo. The treasurer, reporting on the question of funding, indicated that societies had been requested to suggest the size of contribution they might be willing to make. He had prepared the minimum annual budget necessary (in fact, $30,000, which would cover two meetings and clerical assistance).

With the reports tabled, the Russian observers, as if orchestrated, jumped into the spotlight. Oddly, they put aside the legalistic objections they had formerly stressed, and concentrated on the question of the committee's viability. In Babayan's view, financial resources were entirely lacking and implementation was therefore impossible. The matter should be deferred for reconsideration by the Assembly—that is, at the next World Congress four years hence! There were precedents for this arrangement: some past assignments which had proved impossible to implement had been taken back to the Assembly for reappraisal. This was news to Pichot—undoubtedly to Babayan as well: the wily Russian had resorted to a ploy he believed he might just get away with. His next tactic was even more outlandish. The Executive would have to bear responsibility for the predictable failure of their "venture". Pichot rapidly squashed Babayan's assertion— the Executive were simply office-bearers carrying out a mandate voted on by the governing body. Vartanian, perhaps in an effort to bail out his colleague, returned to the concrete issue of funding. The treasurer's budget estimate of the Review Committee was extremely costly, especially in view of the WPA's poor financial state. In any event, the organization should allocate resources to its real purpose, the scientific advancement of psychiatry.

All these points were by then more than familiar, indeed somewhat worn. A relatively new issue raised at this meeting, however, was the Review Committee's remit (it had been briefly brought up at the Executive's meeting six months earlier by Professor T. Helgason of Iceland[1]). Ivan Temkov, the Bulgarian we mentioned earlier, suggested an extension of the remit beyond abuse of a political nature alone. All cases of the abuse of psychiatric practice should be open to investigation. He would push this notion again but be overruled on the grounds that the Honolulu resolution cited specifically the *political* misuse of psychiatry. The name of the committee was, however, altered, in deference to Temkov, to the "Committee to Review the Abuse of Psychiatry" and the phrase "for political purposes" deleted. Was Temkov's recommendation a move to get the Soviet Union off the hook? After all, with a wide remit, all manner of abuse taking place in a large number of countries would potentially serve as the subject of complaint. Whatever was his motivation, the idea did not find favour with Babayan. A mere change of name would not help. The committee's purpose—to harry his Society—was well-known and would remain the same.

With this exchange the sparring was over. The Russians, Babayan declared, would simply not co-operate with the Review Committee. There was nothing more to say. Pichot brought the discussion to an end but invited the Soviet representatives to submit their objections in writing. Their statement would be included in the Executive's minutes. The statement, however, never arrived.

Pichot and Berner left Moscow in a dispirited mood. Apart from persistent Soviet intransigence and Professor Temkov's failure or reluctance—whichever it was—to appreciate the bald fact that as a member of the Executive it was his task to carry out the Assembly's decisions, not to formulate policy himself, the job of formalizing the Review Committee was proving exceedingly tortuous and complicated. Much of this was attributable to inertia on the part of the WPA membership. Repeated efforts to obtain nominations for the two outstanding vacancies on the committee, to receive suggestions for improving the "operational instrument", and to gain agreement for punctual and full payment of subscriptions were meagrely rewarded. Perhaps this tardiness was typical of a large international organization, many of whose 76 member societies were small, had never had a close liaison with their office-bearers, and were lacking in financial resources. Yet nearly two years had elapsed since the passage of the resolution proposing a Review Committee. The leadership might again be accused of foot dragging or worse. Any further delay would seriously threaten the Association's credibility.

These factors may have served as the necessary spur to speed matters up. Also of crucial import was the first submission of an alleged case of abuse by the Royal College of Psychiatrists on 15 August 1979. The Review Committee had no choice other than to rid itself of its provisional character and buckle down to its investigatory assignment. Thus, when the Executive met in November 1979 in London, then 27 months after Honolulu, a commitment to tie all remaining loose ends was evident.[9] The surprising absence of Soviet observers (did they consider it futile to attend on this occasion?) may well have helped, although the redoubtable Dr Temkov could be expected to maintain his campaign of opposition, ostensibly out of personal conviction but possibly as Soviet surrogate. He did indeed raise a series of objections, including his opposition to on-site investigations, and reiterated his view that the Review Committee was too limited in its scope.

There had certainly been behind-the-scenes activity since the Moscow meeting. Gosselin had been in close touch with Berner, McNulty and the three co-members on his own committee. The "operational instrument" had been a chief focus of correspondence, alongside its pilot implementation upon the Royal College's submission. This spadework made for a more business-like session in London compared to previous meetings in New Delhi, Cairo and Moscow. The committee's membership* was finally completed with the addition of a psychiatrist from Egypt and another from India. The "operational instrument" was examined in the light of suggestions made by Gosselin, with McNulty offering legal advice. Reminded by Pichot that a further delay in finalizing the document was most undesirable, the Executive reached agreement on a number of amendments and accepted the instrument as satisfactory.

Because of the instrument's importance, we now summarize its chief features. The document comprises thirteen "basic factors" and eighteen "provisions". The former reveal clearly the hand of a legal expert knowledgeable in the field of human rights and the investigation of their violation. The committee is set up in accordance with the terms of the Honolulu resolution. Reference can be made to the Declaration of Hawaii (the WPA's own code of ethics) and to two indirect

---

* The committee comprised J. Y. Gosselin from Canada, L. Eitinger from Norway, J. Pogady from Czechoslovakia, R. de Pinho from Brazil, O. Shaheen from Egypt and S. Sharma from India.

sources: the Declaration of Helsinki of the World Medical Association (a code of ethics concerned with proper professional conduct in biomedical research) and a recommendation on the mentally ill by the Council of Europe.[10] It is conceded that the investigation of a complaint is complicated by differences in diagnostic theory and the possible unavailability of the "patient" to present his case adequately. The committee should be small but represent fairly the six geographical groupings within the WPA. It should work expeditiously and impose a time limit to avoid repeated submission of an old complaint. Societies involved in an investigation should do so on behalf of the WPA, and not as "opposing parties in a dispute". Only the four official languages of the WPA should be used. Although the procedure should not be unduly legalistic, legal experts should be available for consultation.

The provisions concern practical issues of membership and procedure. Noteworthy among them are the following: the committee's decisions are reached by majority vote; a complaint must be submitted by the president of a member society; the committee only deals with a complaint sent to it within eighteen months of the termination of the episode; and the complaint must concern *political* misuse of psychiatry. The actual procedure on receipt of a complaint is explicitly spelled out: if competent to deal with it, the committee requests the local society to investigate it and forward written comments within a specified period; these comments are then sent to the society which originated the complaint and its written reaction is sought; this reaction is sent to the local society for information only; the committee may request further comment from either society, which it transmits to the other.

In addition to this series of steps, the committee can invite any person to provide oral testimony, or "take any other action in order to carry out its investigations". This last provision seems to be intentionally vague to allow wide latitude in the course of an investigation and one assumes that among these actions is an on-site inspection, as specified in the original Honolulu resolution. With the investigation completed, a full report is prepared for the Executive containing the "facts established", the comments received, and an "opinion" on whether the case is one of political abuse. All proceedings are confidential but the Executive may issue "communiqués" about the "factual nature" of the complaint, and the "state of its proceedings".

The meticulous quality of the instrument is obvious—the guidelines are unambiguous, the basis for them informed and judicious. Nonetheless, some aspects are shaky. Consider the last provision, concerning the media. That the Executive is charged with the delicate task of issuing press releases is no doubt preferable to distorted media reporting, the result of leaks and speculations. Yet the principle of confidentiality seems in severe jeopardy. What is meant by "the factual nature" of the complaint? Can the name of the "patient" be cited?

It would also have been highly desirable to include a specific provision relating to funding, so that adequate sums would be available for clerical support and to convene at least one annual meeting; it should not be an arbitrary matter for the Executive to decide upon. A group faced with as intricate a task as the Review Committee's cannot possibly be expected to function on a series of financial handouts or to conduct its business through the mail alone.

A third point, of great significance, concerns the implications of a judgement that a case of political abuse has occurred. In the original American proposal the committee's job was envisaged as double-barrelled—the investigation of complaints *and* the recommendation of "corrective actions which seem appropriate to the Executive Committee".[11] Provision 17/vii avoids mention of the latter—only an investigatory report is required. As we have already noted, reports to the media are concerned solely with factual matters and presumably do not cover suggestions for "corrective actions". Frustratingly, the document methodically details all the appropriate procedural steps required, but stops short of what should be done in the case of a person judged to be the subject of politically-motivated psychiatric repression. How can we account for this clear discrepancy between the original proposal and the final operational instrument?

The answer can be found elsewhere in the document: ". . . the two member societies concerned in the investigation of a complaint [that is the society from which the complaint originates and the society in whose country the case occurs], shall be regarded as acting on behalf of the WPA for the investigation and not as being opposing parties in a dispute". Underlying this statement is the notion that all psychiatrists involved in a case would wish to ensure that the investigation was carried out optimally, and that in the event of unwarranted hospitalization the detained person would be released promptly. In so doing they would respect the guideline in the Declaration of Hawaii which states that: "The psychiatrist must not participate in compulsory psychiatric treatment in the absence of psychiatric illness" (See Appendix I).

Had the legal framers of the "operational instrument" been too idealistic? Or perhaps just the opposite—coldly realistic? Idealistic, if they genuinely believed societies could be relied upon to give priority to a person's civil rights above any other consideration. Realistic, if they were somewhat discouraged by the self-protective, virtually cynical stance displayed by members of international forums such as the United Nations Commission on Human Rights, whose credibility is strained and standing low in the eyes of many informed observers. Clearly it was accepted, following the counsel of an experienced human rights expert lawyer such as McNulty, that the Review Committee, like the United Nations Commission, could never have the power to impose legal sanctions. This point, plus the omission from the instrument of any reference to the recommending of actions, leads us to infer that the Executive wished to reserve maximum freedom for itself, and that such actions (e.g. publication of the Review Committee's reports) would aim for moral, not legal effects.

The Review Committee in Practice

The question of whether our criticisms are valid or not is of course best left to the empirical test; and we must concede that we have made them with the advantage of hindsight. In November 1979, the committee was still basically a theoretical concept, despite ten months of "provisional" existence. We would then have supported Mr McNulty's reaction to Professor Temkov's expression of doubt—at the eleventh hour—that the committee could possibly function in the light of its total lack of experience and practice. McNulty's response was commendably to the point. Both experience and practice would provide the committee with the basis for necessary amendments and improvements of the "operational instrument". Let us now turn to this experience and practice as they evolved during the three and a half year period until the World Congress in Vienna.

As we mentioned earlier, the committee received its first complaint for investigation in August 1979. The Special Committee on Political Abuse of the Royal College of Psychiatrists (which we describe in chapter five), specifically set up in the wake of the Honolulu resolutions to examine the field of political misuse and to liaise with the impending Review Committee, had sought information in January 1979 about the procedure to be pursued in the submission of cases.[12] At the same time it furnished documents on four Soviet dissenters who were then compulsorily hospitalized and judged to be victims of abuse. Professor Gosselin had indicated in reply[13] that the provisional nature of his committee precluded definitive action; procedural rules had not yet been completely formulated. Within three months, however, the machinery was sufficiently intact for the first formal submission. Following the procedure scrupulously, the Royal College's president Desmond Pond, wrote to Pichot:

> I enclose documents relating to the plight of Iosyp Terelya, a Ukrainian Catholic dissenter who according to our latest information is still confined in Dnepropetrovsk Special Hospital, though members of the Moscow Working Commission for the Investigation of the Abuse of Psychiatry for Political Purposes, who know him, have no doubt that he does not suffer from a mental disorder let alone of so threatening a nature that he requires treatment in a Special Hospital.
>
> I am sending this letter . . . with the request that if you are satisfied that our documents offer grounds for further enquiry, the case of Iosyp Terelya be sent to the WPA Committee to Review the Abuse of Psychiatry.[14]

Although Pond's letter was couched in diplomatic language, the College was itself convinced that Terelya was a *bona fide* case, and confident that further investigation was warranted. Indeed, a better pilot case could not have been chosen. We digress briefly at this point to paint a portrait of

Terelya, in many ways typical of the Soviet dissenter repressed by means of psychiatry.

Iosyp Mikhailovich Terelya was born in 1943 in the Ukraine.[15] Although reared in a Communist family, his loyalty to the Ukraine and to the Catholic Church was evident at an early age. When only nineteen he was sentenced for a non-political offence to four years in a labour camp. Since then, his life was characterized by a long struggle—the authorities on one side determined to crush what they saw as a relentless, tiresome troublemaker, and Terelya on the other side, unwilling to recant, unshakeable in his convictions, both nationalist and religious. In 1967, while still serving his first sentence, he was given eight years in a severe-regime labour camp for his Ukrainian nationalist activity. During this period of imprisonment, a new charge was laid—one of anti-Soviet agitation (this action is permissible in Soviet law, and is based on the rationale that one can commit an offence as readily in a Soviet prison or labour camp as anywhere else, even of a political nature).

The year was 1972—ten years had passed since his first sentence. But a novel phase was about to begin in Terelya's experience of Soviet penology, the use of a psychiatric hospital as prison. He was ruled not responsible by the Serbsky Institute for his anti-Soviet activity and sent for "treatment" to the prison psychiatric hospital in Sychyovka. Terelya's *Notes from a Madhouse*,[16] in the form of an open letter to Yuri Andropov, then head of the KGB, reveals the horror of his experience there, and that of his fellow inmates. "What is Sychyovka?" he asks. "It is what would have been the envy of Dante for characters and descriptions of scenes from hell. . . ."

On his release in 1976, Terelya married, was ruled fit for work and for army service, and took a job as a joiner. But his psychiatric ordeal soon resumed, following the circulation of his *Notes from a Madhouse*. First, he was detained in the Beregovo Psychiatric Hospital, from which he escaped a month later. Promptly apprehended he was sent by the court, which tried him *in absentia*, without defence counsel, to the Dnepropetrovsk SPH in June 1977. There he began to receive continuous "treatment" with major tranquillizers, which seriously affected his health, both mental and physical. The unceasing efforts of his wife, a medical doctor herself, to secure his release came to nought. Her frustration and despair were captured in an appeal she made only weeks before the Honolulu congress:

My husband is well, but in that setting [psychiatric hospital] and with that diagnosis anything he says verbally or in letters, in his own defence or in defence of his comrades, is looked on as a worsening of his illness. I cannot entrust the fate of my husband to people in white coats who are subservient to secret organizations [a reference to the KGB, presumably] and who prescribe treatment according to court decisions and not according to state of health. The story of my husband's illness is an example of the use of psychiatry in the struggle against dissidents. I am powerless to help him.

A few months later she wrote a letter direct to the WPA Review Committee, which she imagined to be already functioning:

The terrible conditions in this hospital are well-known from the testimony of L. Plyushch. My conversation with psychiatrist Nelly M. Butkevich made a dispiriting impression on me. The only syndrome she could formulate was my husband's desire to emigrate from the USSR. I am a doctor, and I state that my husband does not need treatment in a mental hospital. I appeal to you to help my husband. I ask you to help him because you, as psychiatrists, are in a position to help him. . . . My husband and I trust you to investigate his case and, if this proves possible, to examine him. For my part . . . I am ready to answer all your questions.[17]

At the point of the Royal College's submission of his case, Terelya had been hospitalized for 26 months in Dnepropetrovsk whilst his psychiatric saga had lasted seven years.

His case was a forerunner of 28 others that were submitted to the Review Committee during the period up to the Vienna congress. The procedure followed and the progress achieved in his case well exemplifies the whole series. If we recall, documentation about Terelya and a request for an investigation were sent by the Royal College on 15 August 1979. On their receipt Berner immediately forwarded a copy of the material to Pichot and Gosselin. The latter then informed the College that "immediate attention is [being] given to this request" and that an opinion and recommendation from his committee would be delivered as soon as possible.[18] So far, so good—within a fortnight the Review Committee had committed itself to speedy action. Alas, such an effective start was not to be matched by the events that followed—or, to be more accurate, the events that did *not* follow.

On 10 September 1979, Gosselin sent a letter of enquiry about Terelya to Professor Morozov in his capacity as president of the society involved. No reply was received. Meanwhile, the committee's membership was completed. At their first meeting held in February 1980 Gosselin and his colleagues confirmed their competence to deal with the case. On 13 April—after seven months of silence—a second letter of enquiry was mailed to the Russians. Again, silence. In the midst of the procedure, on 29 July 1980, the Netherlands Psychiatric Association joined the Royal College in its request for an investigation of the Terelya case. On 9 August 1980 Gosselin cabled Morozov requesting a reply to his previous two letters. Again, the communication produced no result. By then, one year had passed since the College's initiative. Gosselin's original hope to expedite the matter rapidly was severely dashed.

A personal approach two months later to Vartanian—then representing the Soviet Society at the Executive half-yearly meeting in Madrid—was no more fruitful.[19] He acknowledged the failure of his society to collaborate, explaining that it still did not recognize the Review Committee. This pronouncement should not have occasioned surprise. After all, the Executive had been warned in forthright terms by Babayan as early as May 1979 that Soviet co-operation would not be forthcoming.

In an effort to fend off the complete disruption of a dialogue with the Russians, the Executive compromised to the extent of usurping in part the functions of Gosselin and his colleagues. He was instructed to suspend his pursuit of Soviet co-operation, and to prepare "concluding reports" on those cases about which the Russians had failed to respond. The president and the secretary-general would then be equipped to approach Morozov directly on behalf of the Executive. Although the Review Committee had been established as a working group under the Executive, the Russians could at least argue that it had no independent authority or power. But even if the Executive's compromise was constitutionally dubious, it was nonetheless expedient.

With little room for manoeuvre, the Review Committee thereupon prepared its first concluding report, on Iosyp Terelya. It consisted of a catalogue of steps that had been taken to obtain clinical data about him from the Russians. As no evaluation of the case was included, the document was neutral in tone and comparatively innocuous. On receiving the report on 27 January 1981, Pichot and Berner acted promptly. They forwarded the material in March to the Soviet Society together with a request for information about Terelya's psychiatric history, and more pointedly perhaps, the reasons for his compulsory treatment in a prison psychiatric hospital.

Up to this point of a partial "takeover" by the Executive, a period of some eighteen months, the activities of the Review Committee were not confined to the Terelya case alone. Once the operational procedure had become better known to member societies, other complaints were lodged—eleven during 1980 by five societies covering seven cases, all Soviet. The West German and Swedish Psychiatric Associations submitted one case each in February, the Royal College four further cases in March, the American Psychiatric Association three in December and the Australasians one in November and one in December. During the course of the next year, 1981, six further requests for investigation, from the British, the Americans, the French Association of Private Psychiatrists, and the Norwegians—raised the number of cases dealt with by the Committee to eleven (some societies lodged the same complaint).

When Gosselin tabled a report on his committee's progress at an Executive meeting in October 1981 in New York, he expressed his sense of frustration over the immense difficulties he had encountered.[20] Communication between members had been slow and cumbersome because of their worldwide distribution; limited funding had impeded their task; and above all

else, no response had been elicited from the Soviet Society
about a single case. The last was obviously particularly vexing
considering that all the complaints concerned "patients"
interned in the USSR. In one sense, the committee was at a
complete standstill. Although it had much to investigate, and
concluding reports on four cases had been submitted to the
Executive, little if anything could be accomplished without
some measure of Soviet co-operation. At this session it was
revealed that Pichot and Temkov had, following the concluding report on Terelya, written personal letters to Morozov,
urging him to collaborate. The customary silence had ensued.
Vartanian, again in attendance as observer (he must be the
most widely travelled psychiatrist of all time!), pointed
out—probably quite disingenuously—that the lack of a
response might be attributable to Morozov's belief that the
Russians had provided a satisfactory response to the allegations at the Honolulu congress (he was referring to the dossier,
containing case reports on ten dissenters, distributed at the
General Assembly).

Observers representing the Royal College and the American Psychiatric Association reacted strongly to this explanation. Sydney Levine of the College's Committee on Abuse
suggested that sanctions should be imposed if the Russians
failed to co-operate, while Mel Sabshin, the American observer, insisted that Pichot should ask the USSR Society for a
response one way or the other, even if it were only a letter
clarifying the reason for the non-response. Any answer
received could be discussed at the next Executive meeting in
Kyoto in April 1982. If no reply arrived the Russians should
be told that further action would be taken against them.

In the light of the obvious Soviet stone-walling, and the
pressure applied by two influential member societies, Pichot
and his colleagues were left with no choice but to act more
decisively than heretofore. It was agreed that the absence of a
response was unacceptable, that a reply would be demanded,
and that the Review Committee would consider what further
steps could be taken in the event of an unsatisfactory reply. At
the same time the Executive stressed that it would not
contemplate the withdrawal of Soviet membership. Although
they had the statutory power to take such steps, the issue was
far too important; it would have to await the next meeting of

the General Assembly, the WPA's governing body, which was scheduled to meet in July 1983.

Alongside the demand for Soviet co-operation emanating from the meeting in New York, the Review Committee pursued its customary procedure: submitting a complaint deemed to be legitimate to the Russians for comment, initially by letter, followed by a second letter two months later, and finally by a telegram two months after that. Of foremost concern, however, was how Morozov and his colleagues would react to the blunt message brought home by Vartanian. With the Royal College raising the spectre of sanctions and the American Psychiatric Association firmly resolved not to tolerate further procrastination, the Russians must have felt themselves to be under considerable pressure. This sense became even more pronounced in the next few months, and for two main reasons: (a) they received in February 1982 a further communication from the WPA Secretariat about Terelya (needless to say, the first intervention of a year earlier had proved fruitless), and about another case, Anatoly Ponomaryov, on whom a concluding report had been prepared; and (b) the Royal College had in November 1981 passed a resolution, with a large majority, calling on the WPA to expel the Soviet Society from the organization because of its lack of co-operation. We discuss the latter development in chapter six. Suffice to say at this point, the chances of being ignominiously booted out were probably rated by the Russians as frighteningly real.

Such relentless pressure ultimately provoked a response. The WPA Secretariat must have blinked incredulously when they opened their mail in late March 1982 (only a week or so before the Executive meeting in Kyoto, which had been agreed in New York would mark the deadline for a Soviet response). Before them lay partial case histories of Terelya and Ponomaryov plus a promise to submit information on four other cases and also on any others which might be referred in future. This co-operation would, however, be extended to the Executive only. Gosselin remained *persona non grata*, his committee unrecognized. Moreover, the Russians pointed out that problems were likely in providing clinical data in future since the Executive's enquiries had hitherto not been specific enough. Any durable sense of achievement was soon shattered by the realization that the material had been sent in Russian only. This was despite the provision in the "operational instrument" that all communications should be in one of the WPA's official languages.

That this was an oversight was most unlikely. More tenable is the notion that the Russians knew the lapse would need to be rectified, thus producing a welcome delay and the squandering of more time. We must recall that this first response had taken 30 months to materialize. If the Russians could prevent any action being taken against them before the next World Congress in July 1983—only fifteen months away—they stood a fighting chance of persuading the WPA's Assembly to consider a radical reappraisal of the Review Committee, and thus of achieving its emasculation or even dissolution. In any event, by appearing to co-operate they probably hoped to cause enough hesitation and uncertainty in the West so that the General Assembly would at the 1983 congress end up by taking little or no action with respect to the British resolution on expulsion. If that were the outcome Morozov and his fellow leaders would be able to breathe a huge sigh of relief and to relax in the knowledge that the next congress was not due until 1989. But, as we shall see in chapter six, this desired scenario did not ensue.

The problem of language was resolved surprisingly quickly, at least in the context of the overall Russian tardiness. A response to the request for an English translation was met within a mere three months! A call for information about the treatment given to Terelya and Ponomaryov was by contrast ignored. The timing of the documentary submissions seemed to spare the Soviet Society any new difficulties arising at the Executive's April session in Kyoto. Since co-operation had finally been extended, albeit in embryonic form, it would hardly be fair to issue new demands or to set further deadlines. Consequently, the Kyoto meeting was a relatively tame affair with the Soviet problem for the moment *in suspenso*.[21] One noteworthy development did, however, take place. At the suggestion of the representative of the American Psychiatric Association, the "operational instrument" was modified with respect to the time period permitted for submitting a complaint, from 18 to 36 months dating from the "termination of the incident or situation concerned". This extension had become necessary, it was argued, because of lengthy delays in obtaining up-to-date information about the fate of Soviet dissenters in mental hospitals. The reason for these delays was blatantly obvious: the chief source of information, the Moscow Working Commission, had by then been virtually destroyed by the KGB (see chapter three).

The American representative also featured in another episode which followed hard on the heels of Kyoto. Dr Sabshin wrote to Professor Berner after the Executive meeting to ask for a copy of the Soviet material which had been provided on Terelya and Ponomaryov. Berner refused this request, stressing the incompleteness and confidentiality of the documents thus far received. The Review Committee would use the material, when it was all available, in compiling a report on each case; these reports would be studied by the Executive; and only then would they be forwarded to the relevant originating societies (the Americans would therefore have been entitled to receive Ponomaryov's report in due course, but not that on Terelya since he had not been referred by them). One could interpret Berner's response in one of two ways: he was either acting in a decidedly bureaucratic fashion, intent on submitting reports which were tidy and complete, or something more intriguing was afoot, namely, a strategy to drag out the procedure as long as possible. The need for the latter stemmed from the rapidly-growing movement to suspend or expel the Russians. The Royal College had by then been joined by Denmark (in February 1982) and the United States (in June 1982), and several other societies were in the midst of debating the question, some of them poised to support the trio. The threat to the integrity of the WPA was thus escalating by the month. Berner might have felt it imperative to pursue his correspondence with the Russians in order to play for time. Perhaps he subscribed to the view that a lack of time before the Vienna congress would prevent the compilation of a full and complete report on all the cases under investigation, in which event no action could justifiably be taken to expel the Russians—the whole issue would be *sub judice*. Was it not a fact that Soviet psychiatrists had begun to co-operate? What was needed then was gentle diplomacy, not confrontation.

Meanwhile Berner continued his liaison with Morozov with

the dispatch on 11 August 1982 of two new concluding reports prepared by the Review Committee. In mid-October another pair of cases was forwarded, bringing the total number of Executive enquiries to six. The new year saw progress in obtaining material from the Russians—brief clinical reports on five cases. The commitment to co-operate expressed nine months earlier, and reiterated subsequently in telephone contacts with the WPA Secretariat, was finally being honoured. Then, quite out of the blue, on 31 January 1983 came the Soviet Society's dramatic resignation from the WPA, and with it the irreversible termination of all further co-operation. A report prepared by Pichot and Berner on "The Issue of Abuse 1970–1983" had been distributed earlier in the same month; its conclusion, ironically, contained the following paragraph:

The Executive Committee has been successful in obtaining from that member society [the Soviet] assurance of imminent, active co-operation in any stipulated form i.e. provision of medical records as well as on-site examination—and all possible avenues will be explored during the months still remaining until the Association's General Assembly convenes its next meetings [in July 1983 in Vienna], in order to employ the co-operation the Executive Committee has thus been assured of, in clarification of the circumstances that have occasioned the allegations of professional abuse in reference to the complaint cases submitted to the Association by several of its member Societies.[22]

Clearly the Secretariat had been completely misled or the Russians themselves had done an abrupt *volte-face*. We take up this question and the whole subject of their resignation in chapters six and seven.

Up to the point of the resignation, complaints about 27 cases, all Soviet, had been submitted by nine societies—in Britain, the United States, Japan, Holland, Australasia, Norway, France, West Germany and Sweden.[23] (A 28th case had been turned down because of lack of documentation.) An appendix in the Secretariat's report on abuse demonstrated the arduous work that had been performed by the Review Committee over the preceding three and a half years. Gosselin (as chairman, he had done the bulk of it) had methodically and painstakingly adhered to the procedure laid down in the "operational instrument". He had written innumerable letters, sent off telegrams, prepared concluding reports, and liaised with member societies, the WPA Secretariat and various human rights organizations such as Amnesty International. Although the results of this gargantuan effort had been meagre in terms of the committee's fundamental purpose— the elucidation of a complaint and the release of the person involved in the event of confirmation of psychiatric abuse—Gosselin and his colleagues could, in our view, take satisfaction from having carried out their difficult assignment impeccably and with total impartiality, being committed to the scientific examination of the evidence.

CHAPTER FIVE

HONOLULU TO VIENNA:
THE OPPOSITION INTENSIFIES

WE SAW IN chapter two how Honolulu spawned an initiative on the part of several national psychiatric associations to work within the framework of the newly established Review Committee in order to press their Soviet counterpart to refrain from applying psychiatry for political purposes. Although much of their effort was devoted to the investigation and submission of cases to the committee, campaigns were also conducted in other spheres, all directed to the goal of abolishing political psychiatry. In this chapter we provide an account of these campaigns, together with the Soviet reaction to them. Rather than catalogue chronologically every event that took place between the congresses at Honolulu and Vienna, we have opted to cover the ground thematically, concentrating on major episodes, and, where appropriate, adding a footnote to record lesser, related developments. A small group of active national psychiatric bodies is our chief focus but we also consider, although more briefly, the role of a variety of independent pressure groups. Inevitably there will be some overlap with the previous chapter and with chapter three, which dealt with the Working Commission.

The months succeeding Honolulu were comparatively quiet in the international psychiatric arena. A lull replaced the feverish, hectic and at times tumultuous atmosphere which immediately preceded and then endured through the fateful days of the World Congress. Representatives of the member societies returned home in a state of some perplexity about the likely implications of the events they had recently witnessed: the forthright condemnation of the world's second-largest psychiatric society and the decision to establish a monitoring committee to investigate unethical practices. Evidently, a pause was necessary to absorb the experience at Honolulu—both to mull over what had taken place there, and to try to imagine what the repercussions would be for international psychiatry. One thing, however, was certain— the profession had undergone a radical and irrevocable trans- formation. The latter's denouement, by contrast, was shrouded with ambiguity and unpredictability.

The new year of 1978 marked an end of this reflective phase and ushered in a period of continuing endeavour by a small number of psychiatric associations, especially the Royal Col- lege of Psychiatrists and the American Psychiatric Associa- tion, to bring political psychiatry to an end. A key decision taken by both organizations was to set up special committees to liaise with the Review Committee and to attend more generally to abuses of psychiatry. In June 1978 the Royal College established a Special Committee on the Political Abuse of Psychiatry with the remit to keep abreast of develop- ments in this area by "[considering] all reports of the political abuse of psychiatry wherever it might occur" and to make suitable recommendations to the governing council.[1]

We consider here only the committee's activities relevant to the Soviet issue, but note in passing that it also studied reports of alleged abuse taking place in other Eastern European countries, South Africa and Argentina.

Although the remit was couched in general terms, political abuse of psychiatry was soon defined as the "[use of] psychiat- ric skills and knowledge to serve political ends rather than the true purpose for which they were intended, namely the treatment of mentally ill people".[2] Malpractice in the sense of professional incompetence, and politically-motivated discri- mination in the provision of care and facilities for the mentally ill, were recognized as related phenomena but beyond the committee's scope.

The importance attached to the committee's work was immediately obvious from its composition. Included among its ranks were Desmond Pond, the president, and two senior fellows, Peter Sainsbury (who became chairman) and Ken- neth Rawnsley (who was destined to succeed to the presidency before long). The comparable group in the United States, the Committee on International Abuse of Psychiatry and Psychiatrists was somewhat longer in gestation, and became established in 1979 under the chairmanship of Harold Visotsky. Its remit was more explicit than that of its British counterpart: "This Committee will review complaints of abuse and misuse anywhere in the world [except the United States—another committee was formed at the same time to deal with domestic abuses] and will set up a mechanism for referral of those cases deemed appropriate to be sent on to the World Psychiatric Association's Committee to Review Alleged Abuses of Psychiatry."[3] The remit was also set wider in the sense of including psychiatrists who might themselves be mistreated as a consequence of political psychiatry. In practice, however, the College's committee would expend considerable effort in support of Soviet psychiatrists who were punished for their open criticism of the perversion of their profession.

Let us now examine the range of activities undertaken by British and American psychiatrists, as well as by psychiatric bodies in other countries, during the period between the two world congresses. Putting aside the task of liaison with the Review Committee (which we dealt with in chapter four), their programme entailed: support of the victims of psychiatric abuse, together with opponents of this abuse and—in both cases—their families; applying pressure on the Soviet psychiatric establishment and the regime generally to dispense with the psychiatric "gambit"; attempts to establish contact with ordinary Russian psychiatrists; and steps to sever links with those in the top echelons regarded as culpable.

Support of the Victims of Psychiatric Abuse

Western support of dissenters suffering psychiatric repression took many forms. Perhaps the most extraordinary was their direct clinical examination, that is, the provision of a second professional opinion in the hope that this might, as was the aim with the independent assessments carried out by the Working Commission's consultants, spare the examinee subsequent harassment by "official" psychiatry. Dr Gerard Low-Beer, a member of the College's Special Committee, pioneered this programme when he set out in April 1978 for Moscow with official blessing and a request for a first-hand report. A fluent Russian speaker and an expert on the Soviet abuses, Low-Beer was particularly well qualified for the assignment. He was able through his contact with the Working Commission to interview nine dissenters, many of whom had been detained in the past, allegedly for political reasons; the others had reason to believe they were ear-marked for a similar fate. All were eager to take the "preventive measure"—to have themselves certified sane by a Western psychiatrist. Low-Beer's report vividly reveals the difficulties and hazards such an investigative visit entails. The fact that he left his psychiatric reports—the chief purpose of his trip— in Moscow lest they be confiscated on his departure, testifies to the problems he faced. Even then, he did not leave unscathed. At the airport he was searched by two officials, obviously KGB men, and deprived of his diary-notebook. Low-Beer attributes this relatively "benign" send-off from Moscow to a letter he had received from the president of the College wishing him a successful trip, and which the officials had found and read. The letter demonstrated that Low-Beer was no lone adventurer but represented an influential Western organization, a fact necessitating his delicate handling.

Although he had not set out to study the question of whether the abuse of psychiatry occurred or not (the voluminous evidence, including testimony of émigré victims and psychiatrists, over the preceding seven years made this quite superfluous), Low-Beer's clinical findings are of interest. Five of the nine dissenters could be considered "completely normal using very strict and narrow criteria of normality not usually applied in medical practice, and four had abnormalities of one sort or another. These abnormalities [however] were used as excuses for making people disappear into mental hospitals with the minimum of publicity."[4] Yuri Shikhanovich was one of the examinees. He had been forcibly interned in 1973–1974, diagnosed as a psychopath with a possible "sluggish schizophrenic development".[5] Low-Beer's comments on his clinical state echo one of the author's (SB) own impressions gained on meeting him in Moscow two years earlier: "It was really quite embarrassing for me to interview such a completely sane and normal man, who manifested no psychiatric abnormalities . . . it is difficult to see how any unprejudiced psychiatrist could have put his pen to a compulsory treatment order. This impression was confirmed to me by various people who have known him over many years, including Dr and Mrs Sakharov."[4]

Low-Beer's visit also illuminates dramatically another facet of Soviet psychiatry—the threat felt by psychiatrists from any extraordinary event in their professional work. At the request of the wife of another dissenter, Evgeny Nikolayev,[6] who was then detained in the Kashchenko Mental Hospital (he had been forcibly hospitalized for political reasons on several occasions during the previous eight years), Low-Beer approached the consultant involved and sought his permission to provide a second opinion. Dr Morkovkin's encounter with his unwelcome visitor was tense and acrimonious. No, Low-Beer could not visit his patient. As a foreigner he required special permission from the Ministry of Health. "Why not phone the Ministry there and then?" Low-Beer suggested. Predictably, the authorities refused to grant permission and Low-Beer and Mrs Nikolayev departed. Morkovkin no doubt heaved a huge sigh of relief. As was to be expected (and as we discussed in chapter one), he had resorted to the customary strategy of any Soviet psychiatrist facing a tricky, ambiguous situation. First, try to eradicate the source of the uncertainty ("Soviet law does not permit you to examine my patient"); and failing that, pass the buck and let a higher authority grapple with the problem (such as the Ministry of Health).

Low-Beer's mission was an exceptional one for a psychiatrist: to examine people at their own request in order that they might obtain protection against possible compulsory admission to hospital in the future. It was therefore important for his examinees that his report achieved maximum coverage in the Western media. They derived great comfort and reassurance from the keen attention displayed by journalists when Low-Beer held a press conference on his return to London.[7] Apart from this, though, how much protection did Dr Low-Beer's visit afford his examinees in the longer term? Quite a lot, it would seem. Over the five years since his trip only one of the nine has been psychiatrically interned—Vladimir Gershuni, and he (excepting a brief internment during the Olympic Games in 1980) only in 1983. The others apparently gained considerable immunity from the publication of his findings.

Low-Beer's task in Moscow was handicapped by the brevity of the visit, the pressure of the KGB on his tail, the associated hazards attendant on conducting an assignment without official Soviet backing, and the absence of colleagues to conduct special clinical investigations. None of these constraints applied to the examination of General Pyotr Grigorenko, carried out by a team of American clinicians in December 1978. Earlier a psychiatrist from Washington D.C., Walter Reich, had been approached by Grigorenko, who had come to New York on a temporary visit from the USSR to receive medical treatment and see his émigré son, but then been deprived of his citizenship. He wished to undergo a psychiatric assessment. He believed he stood a good chance of being repressed by psychiatric means if he should ever achieve his ardent wish of returning to Moscow. He had reason to be afraid. In 1964–1965 and again in 1969–1974 he had been interned in psychiatric hospitals because of his dissenting activities.[8] Notwithstanding these harrowing experiences, which we documented in detail in *Russia's Political Hospitals*, he had—undeterred—continued to express his political views. Further punishment was very much on the cards if he should ever return.

Reich first sought Grigorenko's informed consent. He explained that there were potential dangers for Grigorenko. But the Russian was firmly decided—he was confident of the outcome, and anyway, in view of his previous diagnoses of mental illness (chronic paranoid reaction) he had nothing to lose.

With the utmost care to maintain objectivity, Reich proceeded with the evaluation. Two distinguished and experienced psychiatrists—Alan Stone and Lawrence Kolb, joined him to conduct the examination, but their interviews were carried out independently of one another. Two of the three interviews were videotaped, and the tapes shown to a panel of research psychiatrists. In addition, consultants from the Harvard Medical School conducted three separate, special investigations—psychological, neuropsychological and neurological in type. A more elaborate and comprehensive psychiatric examination is difficult to imagine.

We quote the team's unambiguous conclusions:

In reviewing our tests, interviews and other examinations, we could find no evidence of mental illness in Grigorenko, a conclusion confirmed independently by the Biometrics Research Staff of the New York State Psychiatric Institute on the basis of their standardized evaluation of our videotaped interviews. Nor could we find evidence in Grigorenko's history consistent with mental illness in the past. In particular, there is no evidence of any mental illness in the paranoid range, even of the mildest sort. While there is evidence, on the basis of history and physical findings, of arteriosclerotic disease, there is no sign that this condition has significantly compromised Grigorenko's intellectual or emotional capacities, or that it has in any way formed or determined his behaviour or mood.[9]

How could the gross discrepancy between American and Soviet findings be explained? Reich clarified this in part. He and his colleagues had found in Grigorenko qualities that reminded them of the Soviet clinical reports, but—and this is a crucial difference—the Soviet version of Grigorenko was "consistently skewed": "for where they claimed obsessions, we found perseverance; where they cited delusions, we found rationality; where they identified psychotic recklessness, we found committed devotion; and where they diagnosed pathology we found health".[9]

It could be argued that the composition of the examining team precluded a totally objective and impartial evaluation. Short of an international panel, such as the WPA Review Committee, the Reich initiative was an impressive substitute. Impeccably thorough in its work, and with the advantage of videotaped material for observations by independent judges using a standardized diagnostic questionnaire, the investigation is difficult to fault. Only one aspect might have been improved, the addition to the interviewing team of psychiatrists from countries besides the United States. But we remain confident that the conclusions reached would still have been similar.

We might add at this point that members of the Special Committee of the Royal College had also had an opportunity to gain an impression of Grigorenko at a meeting with him in London in May 1980. We were struck by his lucidity, engaging sense of humour, and warmth. We found it virtually impossible to conceive that he could have shown paranoid traits in his personality in the past.

Interestingly, Professor Stone had raised the issue of Grigorenko's request for a second opinion with Andrei Snezhnevsky during a visit to Moscow in the summer of 1978. This doyen of Soviet psychiatry had agreed that an examination should be performed and, moreover, psychiatrists of Stone's calibre and standing should participate as assessors. But, notwithstanding the result of the examination, statements were still periodically made by the Soviet psychiatric leadership to the effect that Western physicians had been given the opportunity to examine ill dissenters and always concurred with the Soviet diagnoses. In a communication of 1983, for example, the Soviet Society proclaimed that: "Many outstanding psychiatrists from Western countries . . . during their visit to the USSR . . . had the opportunity to examine the corresponding patients in whom they were interested, and no one expressed any doubts as to the correctness of the diagnoses of the mental diseases in these individuals."[10] This completely groundless ploy had been resorted to regularly since 1973 (as documented by us in chapter ten of *Russia's Political Hospitals*), despite rebuttals by those Western psychiatrists allegedly involved. Its re-employment as late as 1983 is quite staggering.

Dr Reich was in a position to tackle Professor Snezhnevsky, together with Marat Vartanian, about the discrepant judgement on Grigorenko's psychiatric state between American and Russian psychiatrists during a visit he made to Moscow in April 1982. The Russians knew of the assessment conducted in New York. Its finding of normality was readily explicable: in the USSR Grigorenko was mentally ill as a result of his fixation on the Crimean Tatars and "a few other causes", whereas in the United States he was "away from that setting and that stress, and he was OK".[11] Clinically, this was a feeble explanation and one promptly criticized by Reich. If Grigorenko had actually suffered from a paranoid illness and cerebral arteriosclerosis, some evidence of these maladies would surely have still been recognizable despite the passage of time and the change in his social environment. Vartanian had, reluctantly, popped up with a novel defence against the Western criticism, but a defence out of keeping with another standard Soviet claim made repeatedly over the previous decade, to wit, that many dissenter-patients who had emigrated to the West were still ill and in receipt of treatment—"such facts [however] are being hushed up . . ."[10] The meeting ultimately revealed the discomfiture of the Soviet hosts: an authoritative and responsible diagnostic assessment such as had been performed by Reich and his colleagues could not be summarily dismissed and efforts to wriggle away from Reich's penetrating probe had proved tricky and embarrassing failures.

Contact with Ordinary Soviet Psychiatrists

Low-Beer's report and the American findings on Grigorenko not only had direct effects on the dissenters concerned but also on other victims of political psychiatry insofar as the ensuing publicity was a source of considerable embarrassment to the Soviet psychiatric establishment.[12] Whether ordinary psychiatrists were influenced by the results of these examinations, which so contradicted Soviet diagnoses, let alone learned that the examinations had taken place, we can only surmise. But it seems likely that a "preventive" effect did obtain. Certainly a proportion of them experienced the same embarrassment on receiving regular communications of enquiry about specific dissenters under their care from national psychiatric associations (as well as from human rights organizations such as Amnesty International and independent pressure groups).

Through the diligent work of pressure research groups like the London-based Working Group on the Internment of Dissenters in Mental Hospitals,[13] the names and addresses of psychiatrists treating particular dissenters became widely known, facilitating direct contact by letter, telegram or telephone. The Special Committee of the Royal College, for example, early in its existence determined that "nudging" individual psychiatrists was an important strategy in the campaign to abolish psychiatric abuse. Moreover, it incorporated an obvious humanitarian dimension: the treating psychiatrist was in a sense in the public gaze, his decisions and actions under surveillance. Although he might be spared the criticism of colleagues, distinguished members of a body like the College were by implication standing in judgement of him. A mere enquiry about the welfare of a dissenter-patient was tantamount to disapprobation. The Soviet psychiatrists could also be informed about any procedural irregularity involved in a case, or, more explicitly, about a strong suspicion that a patient was detained on political and not medical grounds.

A letter sent in October 1979 by the College to Dr A. Tobak, the psychiatrist treating Anatoly Ponomaryov in a Leningrad mental hospital, illustrates this "nudging" approach (the submission of his case had been made to the Review Committee earlier in the year). It read:

The purpose of my letter is to enquire about Mr Anatoly Dmitrievich Ponomaryov who was admitted ... under your care and to ask your opinion about the nature of the psychiatric disorder he is suffering from. ... my other reason for writing ... is because we have well documented grounds for believing that Anatoly Ponomaryov was forcibly detained in your hospital on 14 December 1978 without any preliminary examination by a psychiatrist, which is, I believe, in violation of the Soviet Instructions on Urgent Hospital Admission. Further, my understanding is that he has been admitted to psychiatric hospitals previously and prescribed powerful neuroleptic drugs, but his "mental disorder" appears to amount to no more than refusing to be a compulsory outpatient on one occasion, seeking authority to emigrate on another, and making critical comments on the government's policies on several occasions. These latter acts appear to be no more than exercising his legitimate rights according to the Soviet Constitution and to the International Declaration of Human Rights.[14]

Dozens of letters of this sort were sent during the six years following the Honolulu congress by Western psychiatric bodies and human rights groups. On occasion a highly specific request was made. For instance, the American Committee on Abuse, having lost contact with a particular dissenter-patient wrote to the director of the Tashkent SPH in February 1983 enquiring "as to the whereabouts and condition of Vera Lipinskaya, who we understand may have been transferred from your hospital . . . We are very concerned about Ms Lipinskaya's condition and hope that the news of her transfer means that she has been released."[15] (Her case had been submitted by the Americans a year before to the Review Committee.) In another letter from the Royal College, Colonel Babenko, the director of the Dnepropetrovsk SPH, was asked why a particular dissenter had been admitted to his hospital when a psychiatric commission had recommended treatment in an ordinary psychiatric hospital.[16]

A further use of this policy of direct communication with Soviet psychiatrists treating dissenters went beyond the level of "nudging" and amounted to more aggressive "shoving". The following paragraph, contained in a letter to Dr Porodnov of the Talgar Psychiatric Hospital, the physician in overall charge of Nikolai Baranov (another case submitted to the Review Committee) reflects this more critical stance:

> As you know it has now been established that people who oppose the political structure of the Soviet Union are frequently treated as mentally disturbed and treated in special hospitals such as yours. The Royal College of Psychiatrists has examined such people who have reached the West, and former inmates of Soviet special hospitals were also examined by a Russian-speaking member of our College when he was in the Soviet Union. The conclusion is always the same. No justification has ever been found for compulsory detention in mental hospitals in any of the subjects studied and it is therefore our inescapable conclusion that in the Soviet Union psychiatry is used as a means of enforcing political uniformity and repressing dissent.[17]

On occasion, a specific enquiry or request was addressed to a higher authority, not necessarily in the hope that a response would be elicited, but because the recipient might be provoked to reconsider the whole policy of political psychiatry. Thus the Royal College sought the co-operation of Dr S. Burenkov, the Minister of Health, in March 1982, following a request from the same Nikolai Baranov for a second psychiatric opinion by a member of the College. The letter indicated the willingness of the College to accede to Baranov's request on the grounds that ". . . it is the fundamental right of every patient to have access to a second opinion".[18] While no connection with this British pressure can be proved, Baranov's transfer to an OPH in his home city of Leningrad in May 1983 may well have resulted from it.

Not unexpectedly, all these variations of correspondence with Soviet psychiatrists and officials failed to elicit a single direct reply. It was fanciful to anticipate that ordinary psychiatrists in particular, exceedingly uneasy and uncertain about their role in treating a person tainted with the "mark of dissent", would wish to become further entangled in such a hazardous occupation as a correspondence with a foreign, critical colleague. We surmise however that their silence constituted a kind of communication and amounted to a tacit admission of their personal impotence to effect any change in the system of abuse out of fear and conformism. They were in effect saying: "We have forwarded your letters to Moscow, because we leave the whole messy business to our psychiatric leadership. Let the likes of Babayan, Snezhnevsky, Vartanian, Morozov and Zharikov grapple with our critics; we shall maintain a safe distance." The nihilist might regard the letter-writing campaign as having little or no effect. We believe otherwise. Even if nothing else was achieved by it, the recipients were pressed to reflect on the relationship between psychiatry and dissent, and between psychiatry and the State. Further, they could not possibly be so inured that their moral consciousness was not activated, even if covertly and minimally.

Correspondence with dissenters themselves and their families was another feature of Western psychiatric activity, although the volume in this sphere was relatively slender. Perhaps out of a sense of professionalism, national psychiatric associations regarded it as more appropriate to contact members of their Soviet counterpart who supposedly would be expected to act in the best interests of their patients. The contact with dissenter-patients however became more acceptable in recent years. The Royal College, for example, wrote in 1979 to Evgeny Nikolayev (whom Dr Low-Beer had attempted to examine in the Kashchenko Hospital in 1978), expressing satisfaction at the news of his release from hospital, and assuring him of its intention to act swiftly in the event of any further psychiatric victimization.[19] That this support was helpful seems virtually certain. Nikolayev continued to be an active dissenter, but instead of hospitalization for the sixth time, in 1980 the authorities gave him permission to emigrate. He now lives in Munich where we (PR) had the opportunity to meet him, and the German psychiatric society conducted a formal examination of him and found him to be in no need of treatment. His autobiography was published in 1983.

Sensitive to the distress of the families of dissenters forcibly hospitalized, the Committees on Abuse in Britain and the United States broke with longstanding custom and also began to write them letters of support and comfort. Among the many contacted by the Americans was the tragic case of the Khailo family. Vladimir Khailo had been interned in the Dnepropetrovsk SPH since early 1981 because of his religious practices. A devout Christian, he had adhered since the 1960s to the "reform Baptist" Council of Churches which rejected the tight State controls imposed on the Baptists in 1960. He was severely harassed by the authorities, especially through pressure on his children. His eldest son was imprisoned in 1973, when aged eighteen, for eight years. Later, two sons were forcibly taken from home and placed in a special boarding school. In 1977 the authorities asked a court to deprive the Khailos of parental rights over all their children. The couple resisted, obtaining public support from the Moscow Helsinki Monitoring Group and from President Carter's family, and the case was eventually dropped. Khailo was himself first interned in a mental hospital in September 1980. Subsequently arrested, he was ruled not responsible and shunted off to Dnepropetrovsk.[20] In a letter to his wife, the American Psychiatric Association expressed concern and distress about Khailo's position adding: "We want you to know that many individuals and organizations worldwide are concerned about you, your husband and your family and we are trying to be of assistance."[21]

The Royal College "adopted"—in much the same way that Amnesty International adopts "prisoners of conscience"—the above-mentioned case of Nikolai Baranov. In April 1981 the College wrote to his sister, expressing support and requesting her "to convey to your brother [then hospitalized in the Talgar Psychiatric Hospital] the sympathy which is felt by members of the Royal College for the suffering which has been inflicted on him and to express to him the general indignation on the part of the members of the Royal College that such practices should be used in order to ensure political uniformity".[22]

Throughout this correspondence, the College collaborated closely with an Amnesty International group in England, which had adopted Baranov as one of its "prisoners of conscience". This link, between a professional psychiatric association and an independent human rights organization proved productive, with Amnesty often obtaining valuable information about the dissenter's circumstances through its well-informed research department, and the Royal College applying its prestige and influence in order to press Soviet colleagues and the Soviet authorities to act more humanely and justly towards a particular dissenter. Indeed, the liaison between the two bodies grew to a point where great mutual respect was felt for the contribution each made to their common purpose. This culminated in the president of the College agreeing in March 1982 to participate in Amnesty International's Urgent Action Scheme (provided that the cases involved were connected with psychiatrists or psychiatry).[23] The scheme facilitates maximum pressure being applied on relevant authorities in cases of prisoners of conscience who are in dire or precarious straits.

Western Support of Soviet Resisters of the Abuse

Support was not confined to the victims of psychiatric abuse alone. The realization by Western psychiatrists that Soviet colleagues who spoke out against the practices were taking an enormous risk, not only jeopardizing their careers but also making themselves vulnerable to the State's harsh retribution, became strikingly obvious with the ten-year sentence given to Semyon Gluzman in 1972 (see chapter eight of *Russia's Political Hospitals*). Several Western psychiatric associations had campaigned on his behalf then, and continued to press for his release in subsequent years.

The advent of other "dissenting" psychiatrists during the 1970s—Marina Voikhanskaya, Alexander Voloshanovich and Anatoly Koryagin—and the formation of the Working Commission in January 1977 (see chapter three), composed of both psychiatrists (Voloshanovich and Koryagin) and lay people, attracted considerable Western psychiatric attention (and that of Western human rights organizations) during the period between the Honolulu and Vienna congresses. A reflection of this interest is seen in a resolution passed unanimously by the Royal College in July 1979 which asked the WPA to extend the resolution adopted at Honolulu "to include not only those suffering the abuse of psychiatry, but also people being persecuted for bringing this abuse to the attention of the world".[24] An identical resolution was subsequently passed by the Royal Australian and New Zealand College of Psychiatrists.[25] As we shall see in chapter eight, this addendum was debated by the General Assembly in Vienna in July 1983.

Another indication of Western psychiatrists' concern for Soviet colleagues was the title chosen for the American Psychiatric Association's Committee on Abuse—the Committee on International Abuse of Psychiatry *and Psychiatrists*, upon which we commented earlier in this chapter.

The activities undertaken by psychiatric associations in the West—the Royal College, French societies and the American Psychiatric Association foremost among them—on behalf of Soviet psychiatrists and other critics threatened or actually punished by the authorities were multifarious and extensive. Here we describe some of the more noteworthy of them.

Semyon Gluzman had served half of his sentence at the time of Honolulu and his plight was already well recognized in the West. Vigorous campaigns on his behalf had continued during his five years of imprisonment. He became a top priority for the Royal College's new Committee on Abuse. In a letter to him in October 1978, the College applauded his fortitude: "We remain acutely aware not only of what we owe to you and your courageous stand against the political abuses of psychiatry, but also of our responsibility to take such action as is open to us to press for your release and that of other psychiatric colleagues."[26] A letter requesting his release was also dispatched to various Soviet authorities.[27] Some months later, the presidents of the American, British and Swiss psychiatric associations jointly cabled Leonid Brezhnev with a similar appeal.[28] Also, the Japanese Society of Psychiatrists was particularly active at this time, 189 members submitting an appeal to the Soviet authorities for Gluzman's prompt release together with a protest about the political abuse of psychiatry.[29] One year later, a similar protest carried 232 signatures.[30] None of the signatories of these various appeals were naïve enough to expect immediate Soviet compliance, but they hoped that their display of concern and commitment might save Gluzman from an even harsher regime than the one to which he had been subjected hitherto.

Another form of recognition of Gluzman's ordeal, but more so of his exceptional moral courage, was the honour conferred on him by both the Americans and the British. The former made him a Distinguished Fellow, the Association's highest honour, in December 1979,[31] whilst the latter welcomed him as an Honorary Member a year later.[32] International psychiatric pressure continued, indeed mounted, as Gluzman approached the end of his ten-year sentence, in May 1982, particularly when it was feared that he might be charged afresh. He had been far from a "model" prisoner in the eyes of the KGB, regularly criticizing violations of prisoners' rights and audaciously co-authoring with Vladimir Bukovsky the now classic *Manual on Psychiatry for Dissidents*.[33] Notwithstanding his expressed desire to emigrate, the authorities had presumably calculated that the risk of "recidivism", namely his vocal criticism of psychiatric abuse, was high. Protests by Swedish and Norwegian psychiatrists in early 1982 were therefore timely,[34] as were appeals by the Swiss and Australasian psychiatric societies for permission to be granted to Gluzman to leave the USSR.[35] The response at first was slight. Though spared rearrest, he lived precariously in Kiev, unable to obtain employment, and he was refused a visa to emigrate. In 1983 his situation improved when he was at least allowed to resume work as a general doctor, though not as a psychiatrist.

Alexander Voloshanovich was more fortunate than Gluzman but no less courageous. We have discussed his remarkable role as consultant to the Working Commission in chapter three. When he gave his press conference in Moscow in August 1978 he well knew that hazardous repercussions would automatically follow. Immediately, however, he was "adopted" by several Western psychiatric organizations. In November 1978 the Royal College unanimously passed a resolution expressing its admiration and support for him:

his "clinical reports have been invaluable for the brave work in Moscow of the Working Commission to Investigate the Abuse of Psychiatry for Political Purposes".[36]

To further enhance his security, Western psychiatrists from various countries sent him invitations to give lectures or conduct research with them. Among these invitations was one from the president of the Royal College to visit his own department. In a letter of April 1979 Voloshanovich wrote that he had received these invitations, for which he was most grateful, but—and this was to be expected—he was unable to "give any definite answers . . . as the official bodies did not consider such invitations to be a sufficient basis for granting exit permits" (they normally require the invitee to have the full backing for his trip of both his employer and the KGB—Voloshanovich had neither. In a subsequent letter he described how hard it was "for a rank-and-file physician to obtain permission to travel abroad upon invitation from foreign colleagues".[37] We focus on this issue later in the chapter.

Although he was not succeeding in obtaining the travel permit, the existence of the invitation did serve to protect him from arrest. As he himself would later comment with hindsight: "I am certain that this support protected me from serious persecution and possible arrest."[38]

The protection was not, however, sufficient to prevent the humiliation and harassment he suffered at his hospital, where he was treated by his colleagues as a pariah. The ostracism ultimately forced him to resign. Then, on 7 February 1980, after suddenly receiving permission, he emigrated from the USSR. Given that the Soviet regime rarely explains its actions, we can only speculate along with Voloshanovich that the "authorities considered it in their interests to get rid of [him]" and thus weaken the Working Commission. If they had a second Gluzman to contend with—and this young psychiatrist shared many of Gluzman's qualities, especially his unwavering commitment to professional ethics—the adverse publicity which would ensue from his arrest and sentence was at the time too costly a price to pay. His emigration would of course bring in its wake an embarrassing denunciation of Soviet psychiatry, but the spotlight would then dim and Voloshanovich sink into obscurity. The outcome was not entirely as predicted. Following a widely reported press conference on his arrival in Britain,[38] Voloshanovich maintained close liaison with the Royal College and the independent Working Group on the Internment of Dissenters in Mental Hospitals, and proved in both forums to be a source of valuable information on Soviet psychiatry and an astute adviser.

While the decision by the Soviet authorities to deal with Voloshanovich through emigration is explicable in the above terms, their very different method of dealing with the psychiatrist who took over as consultant to the Working Commission, Anatoly Koryagin, clearly needs another explanation. We have already discussed the role of this remarkable man and the harsh retribution exacted on him by the regime in chapter three. Here we examine the reactions of Western psychiatrists to his tragic fate. Following the news of his arrest in February 1981, protests were lodged by the American Psychiatric Association, and groups of French and Swiss psychiatrists,[39] but all to no avail. His harsh twelve-year sentence was a clear signal from the KGB that internal criticism of Soviet psychiatry was to be quashed once and for all, and foreigners convinced that their criticism was futile. Koryagin's manuscript "Unwilling Patients", an indictment of colleagues who had compromised their professional integrity, and which was smuggled out of the Soviet Union and published in the West just two months before he came to trial, probably provoked the KGB further and contributed to the severity of his sentence.

For the publication of "Unwilling Patients" in the reputable journal of medical science, The Lancet,[40] was altogether an exceptional event—the presence of a medico-political article amid scientific papers pointed to the clinical credibility of the consultative role played by Dr Koryagin and his predecessor Dr Voloshanovich. It also pointed to the esteem in which Koryagin was already held by British medical circles. An editor's note in a subsequent edition further reflected this respect. A report on Koryagin's prison ordeal began thus: "Lancet readers will be saddened by the latest news of Dr Anatoly Koryagin."[41] Respect for his professional integrity and moral prowess also came from his colleagues in the American, British and French psychiatric societies. The

American Psychiatric Association made him a Corresponding Fellow in 1981[42] and the Royal College admitted him as an honorary member in early 1983.[43] More recognition came when the American Academy of Psychiatry and the Law awarded its highest annual honour to him in October 1981,[44] and the American Association for the Advancement of Science gave him its Scientific Freedom and Responsibility Award in 1983.[45]

In the citation supporting the proposal to elect Koryagin to membership of the College, his nominators highlighted his qualities in these terms:

> Dr Koryagin is thus a psychiatrist who has reached a secure senior position in the psychiatric establishment of his country [prior to his arrest he was a consultant at the Kharkov Regional Psychiatric Clinic]. Conscious of the need for the highest professional integrity he chose not to remain silent in the face of gross violation of professional ethics, knowing full well that he and his family might pay a heavy price for his attempt to save his country's and his profession's sense of decency and honour. His published work shows that he is an extremely competent psychiatrist, fully equivalent to what is expected of senior psychiatrists who are members of the Royal College.[46]

This citation pinpointed Koryagin's sensitivity to unethical conduct. He had revealed this quality earlier in eloquent communications to Western colleagues. In one letter addressed to French psychiatrists in early 1981, only weeks prior to his arrest, he referred to the misuse of psychiatry as "abominations" which should "rend our hearts and sound an alarm for the fate of the whole of humanity . . . this situation does nothing for the development of man's moral conscience and throws a sinister shadow over our future".[47] In a later communication, smuggled out of his labour camp, Koryagin appealed to psychiatrists throughout the world to examine the moral implications and to act accordingly (see appendix IV for full text). The fate of dissenters forcibly treated in mental hospitals was a "reproach to our conscience, a challenge to our honour, a test of our commitment to compassion". Western psychiatrists, furthermore, should "brand with shame those who out of self-interest or anti-humanitarian motives trample on the ideals of justice and on the doctor's sacred oath".[48]

These were stirring words and, in some quarters, they fell on receptive ears. As we shall see in the next chapter, Koryagin's moral challenge together with his personal sacrifice exerted a marked effect on Western psychiatrists at a time when some of them were veering to a position of despair about the efficacy of any further dialogue and diplomatic exchange with the Soviet psychiatric leadership. The passage of a resolution by an overwhelming majority of British psychiatrists on 20 November 1981 calling for the expulsion of the Soviet Society from the WPA was influenced by this appeal from Koryagin which had appeared in the press one week earlier.

In France, where several psychiatric associations had joined together to give a widely reported press conference in May 1981, no less than 400 psychiatrists signed a petition on Koryagin's behalf to the Soviet authorities.[49]

But not all psychiatrists were sensitive to Koryagin's ghastly situation. A lack of appreciation was specially evident at the World Congress of Biological Psychiatry held in mid-1981 in Stockholm.[50] On the first day of the conference, hundreds of leaflets were distributed containing information about Koryagin with an invitation to a public meeting in his support. This action provoked the ire of the congress secretariat who threatened to call the police if the demonstrators did not move away from the congress building! On their refusal, the police were called but did not intervene after it was argued that the entrance was public ground.

Amnesty International had been granted permission to use a table for distribution of its material, but psychiatrists representing the International Association on the Political Use of Psychiatry (IAPUP)[51] were refused a similar facility on the grounds that unlike Amnesty it had not applied weeks in advance. A commitment to raise the matter at a meeting of the board of the World Federation of Biological Psychiatry the following day was not honoured. Despite this setback, IAPUP proceeded with its plans to publicize Koryagin's plight. A press conference it convened was attended by the major Swedish media and resulted in extensive coverage, and a public meeting it held in support of Koryagin dispatched cables to President Brezhnev and Professor Snezhnevsky, calling for his release. Further efforts were made to distribute material including copies of Koryagin's "Unwilling Patients" and of an open letter from Grigorenko to the congress secretariat.

The secretariat then decided at the eleventh hour to allow Amnesty to organize a session on abuse of psychiatry, but the decision was made known only the evening before. Thus there was almost no time to prepare or publicize the symposium, and attendance was limited.

The behaviour of the conference organizers makes us doubt whether they had any genuine wish to permit consideration of the abuse of psychiatry, or to enable support for Koryagin to be mobilized. By their actions they showed a disregard for the fate of a colleague who less than a month before had been given a terrible punishment. Koryagin settling into labour camp number 37 in the Urals would no doubt have been dismayed at such a shabby expression of moral conscience. He could take some comfort, on the other hand, from the efforts on his behalf of a minority of participants and, ironically, from the last minute absence of a *bête noire*, Marat Vartanian, who had been due to chair a symposium but telephoned on the eve of the conference to indicate that he was unable to come. Another irony involving Vartanian was his comment in a letter to the WPA leadership a year later that the WPA would be wise to avoid politicizing its forthcoming World Congress and instead use the Stockholm conference as a model of a genuine scientific encounter between psychiatrists from many countries.[52]

The Stockholm episode stands in sharp contrast to the vigorous worldwide campaign waged on behalf of Koryagin during his imprisonment, especially following his transfer in July 1982 from his labour camp to Chistopol Prison, an ill-famed top-security facility for political prisoners. His move there was almost certainly precipitated by the determination of the authorities, in the face of Koryagin's outstanding courage in his labour camp, to break his spirit and so obtain a recantation.[53] Protests and appeals were lodged by, *inter alia*, the French Association of Psychiatrists in Private Practice,[49] the American Psychiatric Association,[54] the Swedish

Psychiatric Association,[44] the Norwegian Psychiatric Association,[44] and the Royal College of Psychiatrists.[55] Complementing this activity, various human rights groups concerned with psychiatric abuse maintained pressure on the Soviet authorities and Amnesty International adopted Dr Koryagin as a "prisoner of conscience".

We have mentioned the honorary memberships conferred upon Semyon Gluzman and Anatoly Koryagin by the Royal College in recognition of their commitment to ethical psychiatry. The flouting of such a commitment led the College to deal in just the opposite way with another Soviet psychiatrist, Andrei Snezhnevsky. We noted in chapter one his pivotal role in changing the face of Soviet psychiatry during the 1950s and 1960s until his theories came to dominate the entire profession. With this ascendancy was associated the attainment of enormous power and influence. One of a minuscule group of psychiatrists who has received the prestigious Soviet title of Academician he had also been given honorary membership of both the American Psychiatric Association and the Royal College.

Dr Snezhnevsky was approached by the College in October 1978 in his capacity as director of the Moscow Institute of Psychiatry and as doyen of his profession, with regard to the use of psychiatry for political purposes.[56] His reply was an echo of his many previous rejoinders to criticism of Soviet psychiatric practice.[57] The allegations were unfounded and emanated from unnamed, well-funded sources, the testimony of émigré psychiatrists was pseudological, and the material in our *Russia's Political Hospitals* was "detective stories". Snezhnevsky expressed his appreciation of the College's wish that its Corresponding Fellows should be duty-bound to "spread accurate scientific and professional information", but it was the College which had compromised itself in this regard with a lack of objectivity and professionalism. A summary of the high qualities of Soviet forensic psychiatry took up the rest of the letter.

The Committee on Abuse considered Snezhnevsky's reply, and the broader question of his role in the history of political psychiatry. The Committee had been persuaded for some time that he had played a key role. Not only had he repeatedly repudiated Western criticism, he had been the principal defender of Soviet psychiatry until replaced at Honolulu by Eduard Babayan, and he had also participated in the abuse itself. The committee was aware of at least two cases in which there was good evidence that Snezhnevsky had been involved with the unjustified psychiatric internment of dissenters.

In the hospitalization of the scientist Zhores Medvedev in 1970 he had played a crucial "behind-the scenes" role.[58] Soon after Medvedev's detention, a friend of the family managed to see Snezhnevsky and was informed by him that the "patient" was a psychopathic personality with an exaggerated opinion of himself, but that this diagnosis did not warrant compulsory treatment, only his supervision in an out-patient clinic. The following day Andrei Sakharov met with a group of doctors at the Ministry of Health, including Snezhnevsky. On this occasion, Snezhnevsky conceded that mistakes were made; if Medvedev's psychiatrists had erred, this could be rectified by a directive from the Health Ministry. Several days earlier, however, Snezhnevsky had participated in a meeting of high-ranking functionaries at the Ministry to discuss Medvedev's case. By then international protests were pouring in against his commitment. Snezhnevsky pointed out that continuation of the internment would embarrass the Soviet delegation attending the WPA congress in Mexico in a year's time. Thus, on this occasion he apparently argued for Medvedev's release. Senior officials, however, opposed his advice and decided that Medvedev should remain in hospital. This episode reveals the political nature of the case: although Snezhnevsky was aware that Medvedev had been committed inappropriately, his concern was for his profession's image abroad rather than for the patient's welfare. Nonetheless he acquiesced to his political superiors.

Three years later, at a meeting where Snezhnevsky was a host to a visiting Western psychiatric group, he and his colleagues explained the reasons for Medvedev's detention. The psychiatrists had wanted to determine the suitability of providing Medvedev with an invalid pension in the light of his unemployment (he had been sacked for his human rights activities). According to Snezhnevsky, his stubborn refusal to co-operate had made compulsory hospitalization necessary. He did, however, concede that the doctors involved had made a mistake and should have acted more cautiously. This explanation is unconvincing when placed alongside the account provided by the Medvedev family, the truth of which there is no reason to doubt and which no Soviet authority has ever publicly questioned. It seems that Snezhnevsky was participating in a cover-up of the original miscalculation in detaining Medvedev, which showed up Soviet psychiatry in such a poor light. Why was it necessary to commit Medvedev merely to assess the question of an invalid pension? Why had the psychiatrists not released him immediately (instead of nineteen days later) when it became obvious that commitment was inappropriate? Why the need for a commission of visiting forensic psychiatrists from Moscow in such a routine case?

As regards the second case, Snezhnevsky participated directly *qua* psychiatrist in that he was chairman of a panel which examined Leonid Plyushch (see chapter one). Plyushch had worked as a mathematician until July 1968 when he was dismissed after his criticism of the newspaper coverage of a political trial. A year later he became a founder-member of a human rights group. His arrest came in January 1972. After eighteen months of detention he was placed in a special psychiatric hospital. He spent two and a half years there, "treated" in the most inhumane fashion. His release and forced emigration followed because of the continuing swell of international protest. During Plyushch's investigation, he was examined by three psychiatric commissions. The first in Kiev found him responsible whereas the other two, both conducted in Moscow, came to the opposite conclusion. Snezhnevsky chaired the second of the Moscow commissions, which diagnosed Plyushch as a schizophrenic and recommended compulsory hospitalization. After two years of "treatment" and of marked deterioration in Plyushch's health, his wife, in the company of a family friend, managed to visit Snezhnevsky in his home. Professor Yury Orlov, the friend, has described the tense conversation they had with him and their astonishment at hearing him pose the presumably hypocritical question: "Would it really have been better for him to have got seven years in strict regime camps?"[59]

Three years later Snezhnevsky cited the case of Plyushch in his letter to the Royal College: he and others had committed crimes against the State and been exempted from punishment because of their psychiatric illness. They had undergone compulsory treatment, been discharged from hospital, and then emigrated to the West. Impartial Western psychiatrists had the opportunity, in case of doubt, to examine these cases. This indeed happened with Plyushch. Soon after his arrival in the West, he was interviewed by three leading members of the Royal College and although this was not a formal psychiatric examination, they concluded that he was free of any mental illness. We would readily concur: in several meetings with him we (SB) have not been able to detect any psychiatric symptoms.

After considerable reflection and debate, the College's Committee on Abuse arrived at the following judgement and associated recommendation:

> The evidence is now sufficient to conclude that Professor Snezhnevsky has acted unethically and no longer warrants a place of honour in the Royal College of Psychiatrists. This judgement is not an indictment of Soviet psychiatry overall; the vast majority of Russian psychiatrists probably react as critically about the misuse of their profession as do members of the Royal College and other Western psychiatric associations which have passed resolutions condemning the abuse. The issue at hand concerns Professor Snezhnevsky alone as he is the psychiatrist who has been accorded the privilege of being admitted to the College membership. His direct involvement in the misuse of Soviet psychiatry seems incompatible with this privilege.[60]

Expulsion of an honorary member was an extraordinary decision to take. Although the evidence was overwhelming that Snezhnevsky had acted unethically and unprofessionally, he had the right to defend himself against the charge. Accordingly, he was notified in December 1979 that "the Council of this College has received a report [from the Special Committee on Political Abuse] from which it appears that you, as an Associate with the College, have acted in certain respects in a dishonourable or unprofessional manner or in a manner calculated to bring discredit to the College or to render you unfit to remain an Associate with the College".[61] Snezhnevsky was invited to appear before the Court of Electors on 14 April 1980. He had the right to be represented by a lawyer or any other person, and to call and cross-examine witnesses. In the event of his failure to attend, the court would hear and judge the issue in his absence, and would consider any representations made in writing or by an authorized representative. If the court found the report to be true, it might take certain steps including the removal of Snezhnevsky's name from the College's Register. This radical measure would only be resorted to with the aid of a legally qualified assessor.

In the event, the College was not required to conduct these proceedings, which would have been without precedent. A letter of resignation soon arrived from Snezhnevsky. This led to no particular satisfaction on the part of the College, not even of justice having been done, although the resignation was regarded as an admission of unprofessional conduct. The sense felt was one of sadness that such a procedure had been necessary in the first place.

The possible expulsion of Snezhnevsky (as well as Drs Zoya Serebryakova and Boris Lebedev—all three Honorary Members of the American Psychiatric Association) was also duly considered by the American Psychiatric Association, in June 1982. Its Committee on Abuse decided as a first step to gather information about his role in the practice of unethical psychiatry. Also, two other relevant committees, on ethics and on membership, would have to be consulted.[62] Despite this initiative, the committee was ambivalent about expelling Snezhnevsky, and contrary opinions were expressed. Some believed it was an inappropriate step to take at that particular time, for strategic reasons—the expulsion of the entire Soviet psychiatric profession from the WPA was then a topical issue and delving into the complex issues surrounding Snezhnevsky's future membership would only act as a distraction. Any definite decision about his fate was temporarily shelved.

In welcoming Gluzman and Koryagin to the membership and initiating proceedings to expel Snezhnevsky, the Royal College was heeding the advice of Vladimir Bukovsky. Among the recommendations he had conveyed to the College leadership at a specially convened meeting after his arrival in the West was that the latter should differentiate between various categories of Soviet psychiatrists and relate to each of them differently. Thus links with psychiatrists who were obvious perpetrators of psychiatric misuse should be severed completely. Critics of this position, who argued for the maintenance of bridges with the Soviet Union were misguided; diplomatically-toned dialogue had achieved virtually nothing over the preceding seven years since the abuse had become known in the West. On the other hand, open resisters of the abuse deserved maximum support. These two categories were relatively small. Between them sat a large anonymous group of ordinary psychiatrists who belonged to neither camp. Ties with them were crucially important since they should realize that it was not the Soviet profession *en bloc* that was being black-balled but only its offenders against ethical practice.

The great snag in following this advice involved the third group. Its members, with few exceptions, were virtually inaccessible to Western colleagues. Professional visits by them to foreign countries, their free reception of Western visitors, their access to Western journals (only one copy of the prestigious *British Journal of Psychiatry* is ordered by the entire psychiatric profession in the Soviet Union), and their correspondence with foreign scientists, have always been firmly controlled by the Soviet bureaucracy as part of the State's omnipresent hold over its citizenry. Indeed, it was Medvedev's critique of this interference with the professional life of scientists that so irked the authorities and led to his suppression by means of psychiatry in 1970. The views he had expressed then were still applicable a decade later.

One striking and recurrent demonstration of the limitations imposed on psychiatrists is seen in the nature of their representation at international congresses. At Honolulu, for example, the Soviet delegation comprised a mere 29 members, a minute proportion of the second-largest psychiatric body in the world, numbering well over 20,000. Among the 29 were figures familiar to Western psychiatrists: Marat Vartanian, Andrei Snezhnevsky, Ruben Nadzharov, Georgy Morozov and Nikolai Zharikov. They were complemented by a contingent of senior government officials: Eduard Babayan, Dmitri Venediktov (a Deputy-Minister of Health) and his aide, Yevgeny Kuritsyn. Most of the remainder occupied senior posts and represented various geographical regions of the USSR. The ordinary psychiatrist was conspicuously

The Serbsky Institute of General and Forensic Psychiatry, 23 Kropotkin Lane, Moscow: view of the main building, which contains Section 4 for political cases (second storey from top, far right). Two nurses and two ambulances can be seen in the yard. Most of the building is occupied by Section 1 (ground floor), Section 2 (first floor), Female Section (second floor) and Section 3 (third floor)

The Lenin-
grad SPH

Above: The Kashchenko OPH in Moscow, to which a
visiting British psychiatrist was refused access

Below: The SPH in Dnepropetrovsk, south-east Ukraine, which
has a well-founded reputation for special brutality

absent from Honolulu, his chances of participating there, or indeed in any other meeting abroad, virtually nil.

Mindful of this state of affairs and of Bukovsky's advice to establish ties with the rank and file of Soviet psychiatry, the Royal College grabbed the opportunity to invite a representative of this group in 1981. We use the word "grab" intentionally. In the normal course of events, the step of identifying a Soviet psychiatrist who might be able to contribute a useful paper to a conference has posed a major problem. Soviet psychiatrists rarely publish their work abroad and only a minute number of Western psychiatrists read Russian. The gulf between the Soviet and Western professions is huge. The circumstances surrounding the invitation were therefore unusual. The College noted an interesting article in a respected Western psychiatric journal in mid-1979, written by a previously unknown Moscow psychiatrist, Dr Etely Kazanetz.[63] Especially intriguing with regard to this publication were three features: Kazanetz was a research worker at the Serbsky Institute, the premier centre of forensic psychiatry but also the "headquarters" of the abuse of psychiatry (see chapter one). Second, his article entitled "Differentiating Exogenous Psychiatric Illness from Schizophrenia", though a strictly scientific contribution involving the follow-up of over 300 patients originally diagnosed as schizophrenic, could clearly be construed as a veiled critique of Professor Snezhnevsky's theories—these, as we saw in chapter one, had incorporated a substantial broadening of the concept of schizophrenia, and predominated throughout the Soviet profession; and third, under ordinary circumstances the article would have been submitted to the sole journal of psychiatry in the Soviet Union and published therein, assuming the editor would have accepted it (Kazanetz's previous writings had always been published locally). Instead, Kazanetz had gone to exceptional lengths, with the assistance of two American colleagues who served as translators, to submit his work to a Western journal. He presumably anticipated that a research study which demonstrated the over-diagnosis of schizophrenia and pointed to the need to revise many longstanding diagnoses of the condition would be viewed by Snezhnevsky as tantamount to a repudiation of his own theories—no less than heresy since it is no exaggeration to depict the Snezhnevsky approach as doctrinal.

The College considered the question of inviting Kazanetz to present his work at its annual conference. But a number of questions immediately arose. Would it be risky for him to receive such an invitation? Would Kazanetz welcome the opportunity? Might there be awkward repercussions on his return to the Soviet Union? These questions were complex, the matter not at all eased by any obvious precedent. The concern of College members escalated with the news that Kazanetz had encountered professional difficulties since publication of his article, culminating in the loss of his position at the Serbsky. Reassurance soon came from a Western friend of Kazanetz (who wishes to remain anonymous)—an invitation would do no harm "and might do him a lot of good" but, the correspondent added, the chances that he would be permitted to travel were "very thin". After further deliberation, the College decided to go ahead; it would be honoured if Kazanetz accepted its invitation to present his paper on schizophrenia at the annual meeting.[64] A phone call from Kazanetz soon followed accepting with pleasure the opportunity to participate. But the matter was not entirely straightforward—would the College cable the Soviet Minister of Health requesting permission for the trip?[65]

A cable was duly dispatched, but with disappointing results. A matter of days before Kazanetz was scheduled to read his paper, the College received the following letter:

I am extremely grateful for your efforts in organizing my trip to England for the meeting of the Royal College of Psychiatrists. In particular I received a copy of your telegram to the Minister of Health, Mr Burenkov, about my invitation to the meeting. For my part I have also done as much as possible to ensure that my trip to England should take place. In particular I wrote a letter to Mr Burenkov in which I detailed reasons why my journey to the conference was essential—I asked the Minister to facilitate my trip. My letter to the Minister was sent at the end of April [that is, several weeks earlier] but so far I have not received a reply. Thus, my possible absence from the meeting should in no way be taken as an indication of my disrespect to the Members of the Royal College of Psychiatrists, nor as a lack of concern for the interests of science and of patients. In order that there should be no doubt on this matter, I am sending you with this letter the text of the communication I had intended to give at the meeting of the College. With deepest respects, E. P. Kazanetz.[66]

Kazanetz's friend had been proved correct when he had referred to the chance of his being granted permission to attend the conference as "very thin". The episode had also confirmed Medvedev's views about the constraints imposed on scientists by the Soviet bureaucracy.

Mr Burenkov had not only failed to deal with Kazanetz's request but also snubbed the College by ignoring its telegram. There was little more the College could do to salvage its original intentions other than to record the explanation for Kazanetz's absence. His letter and a summary of his manuscript were read out to the conference and a news item about the unsavoury episode appeared in the College's bulletin.[67] The College also expressed in a letter to Kazanetz its regret that he had been unable to attend the meeting, and its gratitude that he had taken the trouble to send his manuscript. Were it to become possible in the future for him to visit Britain, the College would be delighted to welcome him at one of its scientific meetings.[68]

A decision was also taken to broach with the Soviet Minister of Health the whole issue of inviting psychiatrists from the USSR to attend scientific meetings. Following Kazanetz's inability to obtain permission, the College asked Mr Burenkov what the precise procedure was, should the College wish to invite a Soviet psychiatrist in the future.[69] The Minister should understand that the College was referring to meetings "purely devoted to scientific research and . . . devoid of any political content". No word from Burenkov followed. A second letter a few months later met with the same fate. Thus was the College's attempt to establish a bridge with "ordinary" Soviet psychiatrists frustrated: Kazanetz eager to attend the British meeting, sacked from his post for obscure reasons though probably because of the publication in the West, without official permission, of a paper obliquely critical of the official line on schizophrenia; and the deafening silence of the Minister of Health—these were the main threads of a dismal tale. Given the exceptional hierarchical nature of the psychiatric profession in the USSR and the complete dominance over it of the State bureaucracy, the outlook for achieving liaison with the bulk of the Soviet psychiatric profession appeared very bleak indeed.

Equally bleak in mid-1981, when the Kazanetz initiative had failed, was the prognosis for a reasonable resolution of the heightened tension that prevailed then in international psychiatric circles. That the Soviet psychiatric establishment would co-operate with colleagues elsewhere in investigating complaints of psychiatric abuse in the USSR looked increasingly unlikely. As the new year approached, world psychiatry arrived at a crossroads, one sign pointing to co-operation and dialogue, the other to dissension and schism. For the Royal College, the realization was growing that genuine communication with the Russians was impossible to achieve, and the belief was reluctantly evolving that any further effort to influence Soviet colleagues by persuasion was bound to fail. Diplomatic language had to be replaced by some other method. Confrontation seemed the only alternative, and that could easily lead to the ostracism of Soviet psychiatry. We deal with the bitter struggle that developed, unparallelled in the annals of psychiatry, in the next chapter.

CHAPTER SIX

DIALOGUE OR CONFRONTATION?—
THE MOVEMENT TO EXPEL

DIALOGUE OR CONFRONTATION with Soviet psychiatry? This question became controversial in international psychiatry during 1981. True, it had been debated in earlier years, but it had remained in a hypothetical realm.

The prospect of confrontation was not appealing to many members of a profession supposedly adept at dealing with tensions between groups and expert in the art of constructive communication. Moreover, an influential body of opinion held that some form of contact, however flawed, was more satisfactory than none at all. Once the door was bolted in the wake of confrontation, and in particular in conjunction with the Iron Curtain, any further opportunity to influence Soviet psychiatrists would be ineluctably shattered. Furthermore, collaborative scientific research would be placed in jeopardy. Notwithstanding the manifestly inexorable Soviet position, continuous unremitting pressure, albeit discreetly applied, stood a greater chance of success than all-out war. A further argument for restraint was based on the premise that "people in glass houses should not throw stones". Psychiatrists should hesitate to act precipitously against their Russian colleagues as long as they had not inspected their own backyards, where some form of unethical practice might well be lurking. All these factors pointed to the only appropriate and reasonable course of action—quiet diplomacy and gentle persuasion.

A foremost proponent of this position was the Swedish Psychiatric Association. Perhaps matching Sweden's long-established status of neutrality in world politics, and with an eye on avoiding the alienation of the Soviet *force majeure*, the association had taken a consistent "softly-softly" line towards the Soviet abuses. In Honolulu, for instance, the Swedes (along with other Scandinavians) had opposed the motion condemning Soviet practices (see chapter two), a stand reinforced at their annual meeting a year later when a similar resolution was heavily defeated. The argument was advanced that it would be illogical to pronounce on a specific country before the findings of the WPA Review Committee were known. Sweden should co-operate with this committee and submit cases of abuse if satisfied that they were *bona fide* (the case of Vladimir Rozhdestvov was in fact forwarded for investigation in February 1980), but also preserve its unique diplomatic role.[1] However, by the time of the annual meeting in January 1981, Swedish attitudes had altered somewhat, to the extent that the association reversed its 1978 decision and openly criticized the Soviet abuse. The change was evidently spawned by new, compelling evidence that had emerged since Honolulu and by the persistent Soviet refusal to assist the Review Committee. The association's board was assigned the task of choosing from several proposals designed to apply pressure on the Russians.[2] One action taken was a protest at the imprisonment of Gluzman and Koryagin.[3] In another, the Swedish Foreign Ministry was requested to raise the Soviet problem at the European Security Conference then in session in Madrid, and duly obliged.[4]

Despite these steps and what seemed to be the evolution of a tougher stance, the Swedes still adhered by and large to their original policy of keeping lines of communication with the Russians open. Soviet recognition of this moderate position (moderate by comparison with those of other national associations discussed above) probably contributed to an invitation to Swedish psychiatrists to participate in a symposium in May 1981 in Moscow. A nine-man delegation, including the association's president, Göran Eberhard, and other notable figures in Swedish psychiatry, not only attended the scientific sessions but also took the opportunity to meet with "some influential colleagues for informal talks to convey our worry as concerns the abuse of psychiatry in the Soviet Union."[5] The delegation's leaders also had a special meeting with Eduard Babayan at which they presented documents from Amnesty International on Gluzman, Koryagin, and others. The material had been sent to them by Amnesty a few weeks before with an accompanying letter pointing out the potential hazards and pitfalls attached to a visit of the kind they were to embark on. In particular they were advised to avoid examining any cases other than those "about whom there is sufficient evidence showing unequivocally that they are prisoners of conscience"; to arrange for the attendance of an independent interpreter, and of relatives who could identify the examinee; and to seek permission to inspect specific psychiatric institutions, especially those in Dnepropetrovsk and Chernyakhovsk.

In the event this advice proved superfluous. Though Babayan indicated that the Swedes "would be afforded full facilities to examine any patients they liked" the invitation was not taken up on that occasion, evidently because they wanted to establish dialogue and felt that examining patients might threaten that aim.[5] Eberhard subsequently reported that he and his colleagues would in future seek a way to carry out examinations but further reflection on their part appeared to lead to diminished interest in such a scheme. A suggestion from the Royal College's Committee on Abuse in May 1982 that the Swedes consider taking up Babayan's offer in order to examine Nikolai Baranov, whose family had requested an independent second opinion, met with no response.[6] To our knowledge, the possibility of a Swedish *in situ* investigation evaporated. What had been a good opportunity to try to assess the allegations of abuse first-hand was lost, probably irretrievably.

A full explanation for this turn of events is not readily at hand but evidently the Swedes, cherishing their customary custodianship of a diplomatic role, opted to avoid what they feared might become a complicated entanglement in Soviet internal affairs. They apparently concluded that the Review Committee was better placed—because of its official, impartial status—to examine dissenter-patients, and that the delicate task should thus be left in its hands.[2] They were probably also concerned about the possibility of being manipulated, as the Austrians had been four years earlier (see chapter two). A further reflection of Swedish caution was later to be seen in their decision of January 1983 not to support the expulsion of the Soviet Society from the WPA—an issue we take up later in this chapter.

Another pointer to the Swedes' attitude was their refusal of a second invitation to visit the USSR. In 1982, at short notice, the Soviet Society invited Sweden, along with Norway and Denmark, to the fifth Soviet-Finnish Symposium on Psychiatry. The Danes too refused, concerned that their participation might be exploited politically by the Russians. The Norwegian Psychiatric Association decided, by contrast, to use the invitation to gather first-hand information. Its representatives decided not to examine any patients, but to confine themselves instead to discussing with their hosts the abuse of psychiatry generally. They would also inform them of the decision taken by Norwegian psychiatrists on 29 October 1982 to support other societies calling for the exclusion of the Soviet Society from the WPA if it failed to co-operate with the Review Committee.[7] At the same time the delegation planned to "be open to signs for willingness to find solutions".

Prior to passing the resolution for expulsion the Norwegians had adopted a cautious position *vis-à-vis* their Soviet colleagues. This had entailed the submission of a case—Alexei Nikitin on 1 July 1981—to the Review Committee, and the occasional protest to the Soviet authorities.[8] Thus, when Drs Ekern, Lystrup and Magnussen landed in Tallinn, Estonia, on 15 November 1982 they were essentially at a watershed between dialogue and confrontation. The response of Professor Morozov and his colleagues to this approach would not only be illuminating in itself but might also serve as a pointer to their likely behaviour in the crucial remaining eight months before the World Congress in Vienna.

Soviet-Norwegian differences emerged dramatically on the visitors' arrival in Tallinn, when Dr Ekern was detained for three hours and books and papers—including material from Amnesty International—which he had brought to refer to in discussion with his hosts, were confiscated. This was a highly unusual experience, to say the least, for an invited professional guest, but not without precedent in a state threatened more by ideas than by weapons. The visitors' reception thereafter by Morozov and his colleagues was cordial and polite, an attitude attributed by the Norwegians themselves to the fact that they had emphasized at the outset their intention to clarify differences between the two parties and not to level charges.

At the first of three major sessions—there were several informal meetings too—it became obvious that the Russians had expected the visitors to raise the issue of abuse. Morozov launched the discussion with a long "monologue as a defence". He cited the visit to Grigorenko in 1973 by Professor Carlo Perris (an eminent Swedish psychiatrist)[9] and the visit of the Austrian psychiatric delegation in 1977 as evidence to contradict allegations of abuse. Both citations must have been made with tongue in cheek. Perris reported that Grigorenko had declined to be interviewed in the absence of an independent interpreter, and that obviously this had precluded the possibility of making any clinical judgement. Morozov was perpetuating the fabrication originated by the Soviet press at the time to the effect that Perris had found Grigorenko to be "really ill". Intriguingly, several years were to elapse before Perris issued a denial of this untruth. Morozov would also have been aware of the clean bill of health given to Grigorenko by Reich and his colleagues in the United States four years earlier.[10] Thus, to deploy the Perris-Grigorenko episode with the Norwegians was guileful in the extreme. Equally so was the use of the Austrians' visit. As we noted in chapter two they had been tight-lipped about the abuse issue during and after their tour in the knowledge that the imagination of Soviet journalists was exceedingly vivid and liable to border on outright mendacity. In a further distortion involving the WPA Executive, Morozov claimed that the latter was satisfied with the clinical reports the Russians had submitted. In fact, only two reports had been forwarded by the time of the Norwegians' visit and their quality had not been pronounced upon.

Morozov then invited questions but the Norwegians preferred to discuss the abuse more generally in an effort to establish whether the different social and political features of various societies might lead to different concepts of normality and mental illness. They obviously had in mind the relative ease with which even the mildest unconventional behaviour was labelled as abnormal in the USSR, as the result of a basic conformism which permeated Soviet life. Within that context it was reasonable to hypothesize that certain patterns of non-conformist, "socio-political" behaviour might be interpreted as the product of a disturbed, rather than of an original, mind.

The Russians displayed marked reluctance to tackle this sort of subject. Further attempts to discuss the links between social forces and the psychiatrist's theoretical position came to nought. Similarly, more specific enquiries about concepts such as "reformist delusions", "emigrational delusions" and "metaphysical intoxication"[11] were brushed aside with a comment that these clinical features were never used in any exclusive way in making a diagnosis of mental illness. The visitors were however left with an impression that the Russians were "not very sensitive to the possibility of abuse which is implied in the use of such concepts", nor to the misunderstandings which the concepts could easily produce. They were puzzled about the origins of this insensitivity and about the broader question of their hosts' reluctance to enter into discussion about social aspects of psychiatry. Was it lack of insight? or realistic "political self-censorship"? or an entrenched biological orientation towards mental illness? In one of their conclusions, the Norwegians appeared to regard the Soviet attitude as stemming from a combination of all three factors, but in fact, as they themselves noted, their discussions "brought no new information about the reality of political abuse of psychiatry in the USSR". The inner thoughts and motives of their Russian colleagues remained carefully concealed.

What about their attitude to the prospect of further disruption in relations with foreign colleagues and to the possibility of being ousted from the WPA? The Norwegian delegation sensed concern about this prospect, demonstrated in the Russians' request for suggestions as to how the deadlock might be resolved. They were also eager to identify strategies to avoid being kicked out. As for the Norwegians, despite their Society's resolution to expel the Soviet Society, they expressed the belief that regardless of the fate of this resolution, further long-term professional contact was essential if the abuses were to be combated. But the responsibility for this contact lay especially on Soviet shoulders, since it was Soviet participation in international psychiatric gatherings that was traditionally so limited. Western psychiatrists could, however, they concluded (perhaps ignorant of the Kazanetz affair), be more active in extending invitations.

Soviet Expulsion? A Problem for World Psychiatry
We must now backtrack in order to trace the origins of the movement to remove the Russians from the WPA. Early 1981

witnessed a confluence of developments in the Soviet Union which provided fertile soil for the seed of expulsion to germinate in. Psychiatric misuse showed no sign of abatement. The inaugural bulletin of the International Association on the Political Use of Psychiatry, published in May 1981, reported the current state of no fewer than 30 well-authenticated dissenters then interned in mental hospitals, and the list was highly selective.

Among those listed were cases which had been submitted to the Review Committee—Vladimir Klebanov, Valeria Makeyeva, Alexei Nikitin, Iosyp Terelya and Anatoly Ponomaryov. The absence of any Soviet response, especially regarding the last two, about whom complaints had been lodged as long ago as August 1979 and March 1980 respectively, began to provoke frustration and irritation among members of the Royal College's Committee on Abuse. They had originally submitted these cases in anticipation of some investigatory action, but the Russians were evidently adhering to their oft-repeated declaration that the Review Committee was not legally constituted and would therefore remain unrecognized. The chances of the Review Committee operating with even a minimal level of effectiveness looked increasingly remote.

The third development in early 1981 concerned the Moscow Working Commission. In January and February its last two members were arrested and the group destroyed. For many Western psychiatrists the arrest of Dr Koryagin was the last straw. Although expected, it signified the Soviet authorities' resolve to crush all sources of domestic criticism.

This unflinching repression of the Commission, when taken in conjunction with the lack of Soviet co-operation with the Review Committee and the continuing use of psychiatry as a tool against dissent, combined to create a sense of futility in the Committee on Abuse. At its meeting on 18 February 1981 the news of Koryagin's arrest five days earlier reverberated around the room. One member raised for the first time the probable need for a firm resolution to take to the 1983 World Congress. "The Soviet Society must be challenged even more resolutely than hitherto," he argued. "Although the conference seems a long way off, it is not too soon to start considering a resolution."[12] He was asked to prepare a draft for consideration. A related decision was for the chairman, Peter Sainsbury, to contact the WPA Secretariat informally and to indicate: ". . . that there is likely to be considerable pressure from the Royal College if there is no satisfactory response from the Russians, which might result in a resolution calling for [their] expulsion . . . at the World Congress . . . in 1983". The idea of expulsion had thus crystallized as an option in the face of Soviet intransigence.

This option was to prevail despite the response of Professor Berner, who felt it would be wiser to defer such radical action until the autumn, by which time Soviet co-operation might have been secured. One of the committee members had gained the impression during a visit to Vienna that Berner was concerned about the "long term effects" on the WPA of a resolution calling for Soviet expulsion. Presumably this phrase was a euphemism for the WPA's potential disintegration.

At the committee's next meeting in May 1981 it was unanimously agreed that a draft resolution should be submitted to the College's governing council with a recommendation that it be debated at the annual meeting two months later. The recommendation was accepted, but in view of Berner's attendance at this meeting as an honoured guest, it was felt the matter should be deferred.

Thus it was only on 20 November 1981—with the Soviet Society still showing no co-operation—that the following resolution was proposed by one of the authors (SB) and seconded by Peter Sainsbury:

It is resolved that the Royal College of Psychiatrists requests that the General Assembly of the World Psychiatric Association at its meeting in Vienna in 1983 considers the following resolution:
'In view of (a) well-documented evidence of the continuing, systematic abuse of psychiatry for political purposes in the Soviet Union since the General Assembly's resolution of September 1977 to "renounce and expunge these practices",

and (b) the failure of the All-Union Society of Neuropathologists and Psychiatrists to co-operate at all with the WPA's Review Committee on Political Abuse of Psychiatry

in its investigation of various complaints by the Royal
College of Psychiatrists and other WPA member societies,

this General Assembly resolves that the All-Union Society
should now be expelled from the WPA until such time as
the All-Union Society can show that the political abuse of
psychiatry has been brought to an end.'

The resolution spoke for itself. That psychiatric abuse had
continued unremittingly since the Honolulu congress was
incontrovertible; so was the lack of any Soviet co-operation in
attempting to investigate the matter. Three additional factors
went into the thinking of the Committee on Abuse, all of
which we have alluded to earlier.

First, the evidence was abundantly clear that quiet
diplomacy over the previous eleven years had been largely
ineffectual. The Soviet Society had not budged from its
original position. While the gentle approach had possibly
helped in freeing a few victims of political psychiatry (strong
public protests appeared to be the key factor in these succes-
ses), and had given moral support to many others and to their
families, and while it had offered the Moscow Working
Commission the chance to function with remarkable effectiveness for four years, the overall result had been meagre. The
Commission had finally been crushed, and the psychiatric
internment of dissenters had continued at a steady pace. One
would have to conclude that quiet diplomacy had proved too
weak. It may have helped to prevent a sharp deterioration in
the situation, but it had certainly not produced a notable
improvement. This is not in fact surprising, as it was precisely
the quiet approach which was insisted on by the Soviet
psychiatric leaders, when pressed; these men had, as we shall
see in a moment, an overwhelming interest in maintaining the
status quo. In sum, dialogue with those psychiatrists who had
monopolized contacts with the West had proved next to
useless.

Secondly, the argument advanced by the "keep bridges
open at all costs" lobby had been wearing thin in recent years.
Since the 1970s when the abuses had become known in the
West, contact with ordinary Soviet psychiatrists had been
virtually non-existent. At conference after conference Russian

participation had been sparse. Moreover, delegations usually comprised the same faces whatever the subject covered. Opportunities for contact inside the USSR between ordinary Soviet psychiatrists and foreign colleagues were limited by the rarity with which international conferences were held there and the difficulties facing an individual Western psychiatrist wishing to visit the country and to contact colleagues of his own choice. The experience of the College in attempting to invite Dr Kazanetz to its annual meeting in 1981 (see chapter five) had demonstrated the almost insurmountable hurdles confronting it long before any bridge had been sighted let alone crossed. Expulsion of the official Soviet psychiatric body could not therefore hamper fruitful contacts, as these hardly existed.

The third factor influencing the committee concerned the Soviet psychiatric establishment. Was it tenable to continue liaison with those very psychiatrists who, as occupants of senior academic and administrative positions, represented the profession in the USSR in international forums and at the same time actually organized or participated in the unethical practices (such as Andrei Snezhnevsky, Georgy Morozov and Ruben Nadzharov), or were the most vocal apologists for these practices (such as Eduard Babayan and Marat Vartanian)? The question was obviously rhetorical. The committee were wholly persuaded by the sort of argument advanced by Koryagin in his above-mentioned appeal, that Soviet psychiatric leaders used their ties with international psychiatry "as a means to rehabilitate themselves" and to convey the sense that "they are accepted internationally, not as violators of medical ethics and norms but as colleagues and equal partners". Koryagin himself then posed a rhetorical question: "Is it ethical to have any professional contacts with the official psychiatric representatives of ... countries ... where psychiatry is assigned punitive functions?"[13]

The issue, however, was not only how ethical it might be to maintain liaison with offending psychiatrists, but also what "political" repercussions might follow the cessation of contact with them, and the implications for the employment of psychiatry in the State's war against dissent. In other words, might the expulsion of Soviet psychiatry lead to the necessary political changes in whose wake the policy of psychiatrically-based repression could be ditched?

At this point we need to analyse the political dimension of the potential expulsion of the Russians from an international organization like the WPA. A useful starting point is to recall the intimate ties that exist between the professions and the Communist Party, upon which we commented in chapter one. In this context psychiatry is no exception. Moreover, the policy of political psychiatry involves close co-operation between the Party and a psychiatric establishment whose power and prestige stem from, and continue to rely upon, the Party's favourable disposition.

Let us consider now how strongly committed to the *status quo* in political psychiatry the two partners to the co-operation probably have been. The psychiatrists, we can assume, have been wholly committed. To appreciate why, it is helpful to compare them to the charlatan Lysenko and his followers, whom the Party installed in the key posts in Soviet biology in the late 1930s.[14] The Party helped them to establish a monopolistic dictatorship in this field based on Lysenko's bogus theories. All biologists who opposed them were removed from their posts, disgraced, and, in some cases arrested and brought to an early death in prison. Only in 1964 was the dictatorship ended, when the politicians finally responded to the criticism and ridicule of the scientific world, and grasped the enormity of the damage done to Soviet science and, indirectly, the economy. While the surviving biologists of integrity were then rehabilitated, the opposite fate struck the Lysenkoists. They lost their high posts, their honours, their material privileges, the chance to travel abroad. And they were subjected to a measure of public disgrace.

It is not hard to see that Professor Snezhnevsky and his associates would have a similar amount to lose from any reform of the *status quo* in psychiatry. Inevitably, therefore, they would continue to resist any change and deny all charges, just as they consistenly had for more than a decade. They would also conceal as far as possible from their political masters, both the criticism and ridicule of the outside world, and the damage they had wrought to Soviet psychiatry.

The politicians, by contrast, would not be much threatened, as individuals, if political psychiatry were to be abolished. The whole practice has been organized in such a way that, to outward appearances, they have not been involved. The psychiatrists' role has been clear enough, their own has not.

But perhaps the regime *as a whole* has regarded the practice as fundamental to its political interests? If that situation obtained—as it did in the possibly analogous contexts of the "Prague Spring" of 1968 and the "Polish renewal" of 1980–81—the regime would certainly dig in its heels, crush accessible "troublemakers", and reject all pressures for reform.

However, in the case of political psychiatry fundamental interests are not involved. The regime has plenty of other ways of suppressing dissent—imprisonment, exile, physical intimidation, deportation abroad, and so on. And the psychiatric establishment is just as expendable as the Lysenkoists were in 1964.

True, it has been useful to have a device (political psychiatry) for explaining away the ideologically impermissible persistence of dissent and opposition. True, it has been convenient to have a way of discrediting dissenters' ideas, avoiding the nuisance of staging political trials, and forcing the victims into recantation—in the awful conditions of a prison mental hospital.

But none of these conveniences are part of the essential defences of the regime's fundamental interests. A range of alternative options have always been available.

Indeed, going further, perceptive politicians might, once they were fully informed, find it quite easy to see that important interests of the regime might gradually be damaged by a rigid preservation of the *status quo*. Could the frequent criticism of foreign medical and lay bodies be explained away to the Soviet people indefinitely? Would the task not become impossible if Soviet psychiatry were gradually excluded from all international forums? And what if such a fateful precedent were possibly to lead on to Soviet expulsion from other world bodies concerned with, say, health, science, religion and culture?

Why, in short, damage both internal legitimacy and a much-prized international prestige when no fundamental interests are at stake? Why not end such a damaging process by radically reforming Soviet psychiatry, just as biology was reformed in the 1960s? Why not, by the same token, gain the bonus of better psychiatric theories, more respected psychiatrists, better treatment of patients, a healthier work force, and a less alienated population?

The problem, then, for bodies like the Royal College, was how to convince the Soviet political leadership of the force of the above arguments. The threat of expulsion from the WPA would be an especially promising line, because such a threat—potentially damaging to the USSR's international prestige—would lift the whole issue from the professional to the political plane.

Moreover, if other societies in the WPA joined the College and passed similar motions, so that the danger of expulsion became real, then the Kremlin might be induced to undertake quiet but radical reforms: interned dissenters gradually released from mental hospitals, the Working Commission freed from labour camps, the psychiatric establishment discreetly retired or demoted and new, more acceptable leaders installed in its place; the new leadership might even make lightly-veiled criticisms of its predecessors.

If all this were to occur—and there were many "ifs" involved—then, the College Committee felt, the British resolution could be happily withdrawn in Vienna in July 1983. If, however, nothing of substance had happened by then the Assembly would be urged to proceed with expulsion. The actual trauma of expulsion, with the attendant international publicity, would stand a chance of inducing reforms in the post-Vienna period, as the Soviet aim would probably be to seek readmittance to the WPA at a later stage. Even in the worst case of this not happening, nothing of value would have been lost (the "dialogue" with the official psychiatrists having proved fruitless) and some important things would have been gained: moral support for Soviet psychiatrists who had resisted the abuse, and for victims and their supporters; a warning to other countries already embarked on the Soviet path; and heightened world respect for psychiatry as a profession.

Having discussed the various factors which contributed to the judgement of the Committee on Abuse and paved the way for the resolution on expulsion, let us now return to the College's business meeting. Members attending appeared to appreciate the Committee's thinking. There was overwhelming support for the proposal although the opinion was voiced by some that "suspension" would be more appropriate than "expulsion". This ostensibly less severe sanction would later be pursued by the Americans and the Swiss but in the College debate the obvious point was made that the wording of the resolution was tantamount to suspension: ". . . expelled *until such time* as the [Soviet] Society can show that the political abuse of psychiatry has been brought to an end". Those who had drafted the resolution entertained the hope that expulsion would be temporary and the Russians reinstated following the accomplishment of basic reforms. The resolution went to the vote and was passed by a large majority.

The passage of the resolution was unprecedented in the history of the College, and probably in the history of psychiatry. Never before had a national association adopted such an extreme measure as censuring a fellow society in this way. The implications were unforeseeable. Would psychiatric bodies elsewhere follow suit? Or would they recoil from taking such drastic action? How would the Russians respond? In the light of Berner's previous caution to the College regarding expulsion, what attitude would the WPA Executive have? All these questions remained to be answered, but one did not need to be a seer to foretell that the resolution would send a seismic shock through world psychiatry. Two developments occurred within days. Firstly, Professor Rawnsley, the College's president, dispatched copies of the motion to 25 other member societies of the WPA, including the Russians. Copies were also sent to other medical bodies in Britain, to the press, and of course to Professor Berner.

The last, accepting the resolution as a *fait accompli* and therefore as an item for the agenda of the Assembly in Vienna, expressed displeasure that the College had proceeded to publicize the event "so far ahead" (in fact twenty months) of the World Congress. His task of organizing the congress would be made all the more difficult because of this, although just why and how remained unclear.[15] Underlying his pique, perhaps, was his sense of frustration that the College had undermined his own policy of applying quiet diplomacy, a policy which he hoped might yet bring about Soviet co-operation and a defusing of the situation.

Secondly, to the utter astonishment of the Committee on Abuse, a diplomat from the Soviet Embassy in London telephoned the College: he would be pleased to welcome representatives to the Embassy to talk about the resolution. For several years the College, and other British groups, had been trying to communicate with the Ambassador—in vain. The door was always closed. The call for Soviet expulsion had dramatically produced the opposite effect—no less than a cordial invitation to discuss the whole issue! The Soviet move was so entirely unparalleled that for a moment the College was nonplussed. Quick consultations with the Foreign Office and with Amnesty International confirmed the lack of precedent. No advice could be offered beyond speculating about the Embassy's motives. At a practical level, however, it was suggested that a pair of psychiatrists should participate to ensure an accurate record of the proceedings. Thus on 9 December Peter Sainsbury and Sidney Levine (members of the Committee on Abuse) found themselves at the portals of the Embassy. Getting past the doorkeeper was problematic, but once within they were welcomed courteously by Sergei Ivanov, a second secretary and the Soviet Union's scientific attaché.[16]

Ivanov indicated at the outset that he had been instructed (presumably—as he was ejected from Britain in 1983 for "impermissible activities"—by the KGB!) to report on the factors that had led the College to propose Soviet expulsion. He issued the customary denial that abuses had occurred and questioned the validity of the College's information. Almost to the point of total naïveté, at least ostensibly, he pointed out that his wife was a doctor and he would have been aware of unethical practices if they had taken place. His chief defence was that at the time of the Review Committee's establishment, Soviet psychiatrists had staunchly repudiated allegations of abuse and it was therefore pointless for the WPA to persist in its accusations; the Russians would "have no truck with the Review Committee". Neither would the visit of a Western psychiatrist to examine patients in the USSR be countenanced—in blatant contradiction of Dr Babayan's invitation first extended at Honolulu, and repeated on several occasions since). Ivanov likened such a proposal to a team of Soviet educationalists conducting an inspection of British schools. On the other hand he was eager for Soviet psychiatrists to be invited to Britain to address scientific meetings, but inferred hastily that they would be selected at home and could not therefore necessarily be the specific invitees of the College. These points reflected a firm stance, but were made politely and amiably.

Sainsbury and Levine were equally firm. Irrespective of Ivanov's opinion about the accuracy of the College's information, he and his superiors should note that the College was convinced (as were several other national associations) that the allegations of abuse were well-founded, and accordingly it would continue to act on that view until the Soviet Society responded adequately to the request of the Review Committee for information about the cases under investigation.

So ended a two-hour discussion, with both sides sticking fast to their positions and with little sign of room for compromise. That Ivanov could offer nothing new was obvious from his brief, which was to obtain information about the British development and presumably to ascertain with what degree of solidity the College held to its position on expulsion. But should the College now grab what was on offer, namely the chance to confer with Soviet psychiatric visitors, albeit not of its own choice? This question, as well as the broader issue of whether further contact with Soviet officialdom would be productive, was thrashed out at the next meeting of the Committee on Abuse.[17] A clear consensus emerged. The contact with Ivanov was of great significance since it was highly improbable that Soviet psychiatrists themselves would change policy—any decision to do so would be made by political authorities. A letter to him couched in a cordial yet firm tone was the result.[18] Exchanges like the one in December were "of considerable value and indeed essential to an increasing understanding of our differing points of view". But, and here the tone hardened, "It seems inevitable that the College's resolution will be put to the WPA in Vienna unless there is some definite response from the Soviet authorities and evidence that things will change." Finally, an olive branch was offered, or perhaps it was a carrot—the wording was intentionally ambiguous—". . . we would warmly welcome any informal contact in order to see if there are ways in which such a step could be avoided". Whichever way it was interpreted, the letter led to a second meeting, again at the request of Mr Ivanov.

On this occasion he came with a specific recommendation.

The College should invite two senior Soviet psychiatrists to address British colleagues. The psychiatrists suggested were Nadzharov and the peripatetic Vartanian. The selection could not have been more inappropriate. By now we have repeatedly come across Vartanian in his role as chief international apologist for Soviet psychiatry. Nadzharov, deputy to Snezhnevsky at the Moscow Institute of Psychiatry, had participated in several commissions which had diagnosed dissenters as mentally ill, including Zhores Medvedev. The reputation of both psychiatrists proposed was unquestionably tarnished. Nonetheless, the College representatives heard Ivanov out. His reasons for suggesting such a visit were two-fold: (a) the links between British and Soviet psychiatrists had steadily deteriorated over the preceding six years and relations needed to be improved; and (b) as the College had listened only to the views held by critics of the Soviet system, would it not be reasonable to hear those of Soviet psychiatrists as well? The projected meeting, Ivanov felt, should be confined to psychiatrists, so as to avoid a confrontation with the likes of Bukovsky and one of the present authors (PR)(!), and be arranged through the Embassy rather than through direct invitation. Were the meeting to prove successful, Ivanov implied, a reciprocal invitation would be extended to the College to visit the USSR, and out of this continuing dialogue, he hinted, a possible change in policy might ensue. Was this a veiled acceptance of the allegations of abuse or merely a manoeuvre to gain time and to lessen the College's resolve to press ahead with expulsion? We suspect the latter in the light of several previous episodes in which meetings between Soviet and foreign psychiatrists had been exploited for political purposes.

Ivanov had obviously done his homework after the first meeting—reporting to his superiors in the Embassy and thence to Moscow. There consultation with the psychiatric establishment must have ensued, leading to his package of recommendations and the conditions surrounding them.

It was now the turn of the College to do its homework. The Soviet offer was discussed at length. All members of the Committee on Abuse were convinced that a meeting with Nadzharov and Vartanian would not contribute anything new;[19] as they pointed out subsequently in a letter to Ivanov:

"We have read and listened carefully to the official explanation given by Drs Babayan, Morozov and Nadzharov [Vartanian's name could readily have been added here] on many occasions, and we do not feel that a fresh meeting now would be helpful."[20] Instead, a counter-suggestion was made—a wish to take up Dr Babayan's oft-expressed preparedness to make any Soviet hospital accessible to visiting colleagues for the purpose of examining specific cases. The committee, like Ivanov, attached a condition to its suggestion: to meet Soviet psychiatrists of its choice, without official interference.

The committee was sufficiently sceptical of Babayan's open invitation—despite his repeated offers since Honolulu, not a single Western psychiatrist had to our knowledge penetrated a Soviet SPH—to add a note that in the event of the College's request being turned down, it would have no choice but to conclude that "no change in Soviet practice is anticipated and that, therefore, there exists a gulf so wide in our respective understanding of medical ethics that it would not be possible to work together in the World Psychiatric Association." Once again the gauntlet was thrown down. Although the letter ended with an expression of hope that eventual understanding could be achieved, it was, realistically, a forlorn hope. The pessimism was justified. Babayan's invitations had always sounded hollow and designed for propaganda purposes. The request for an on-site inspection was presumably considered by Ivanov and his superiors but found to be indigestible. No reply came from the Embassy and the sole link with Soviet political officialdom evaporated as rapidly as it had appeared. That anything substantial would emerge from the contacts had been dubious from the outset, but the opportunity to apply pressure directly on an official representative of the USSR had been useful, particularly the College's unyielding reiteration that the responsibility for preventing expulsion lay exclusively with the Russians—it was incumbent on them to introduce the required reforms and their failure to do so would automatically mean the College's active pursuit of its resolution.

During these communications with Ivanov, a reply was received from Andrei Snezhnevsky to Rawnsley's dispatch of the resolution of expulsion.[21] Its thrust was one of admonition: by adopting the resolution, the College was "betraying its professional duty" and demonstrating its failure "or perhaps unwillingness", to appreciate the political nature of the fabricated charges. The Soviet Society had no intention of immersing itself in the politicization of international psychiatry, and would accordingly not recognize the legal competence of the Review Committee. Then followed two barbs. The fate of the "so-called dissidents" treated in the Soviet Union who had emigrated to the West would be of interest—the implication being that they were still ill and in need of medical help. Secondly, Western colleagues who had acquainted themselves with Soviet psychiatry had been impressed by its "humane principles and achievements". No bridge-building here, and no effort to dissuade the College from pursuing its resolution. More a rebuke from a peeved and offended old man, in response to his having been brought to task by the college two years earlier for unprofessional conduct not befitting Honorary Membership (see chapter five). This impression was reinforced by the fact that the letter was in his own name; not that of the Soviet Society.

Interestingly, Snezhnevsky adopted a quite different tack when faced by the Danish decision of February 1982 to support the College's resolution. Two months after his sullen rebuke to the College, he wrote a sharply contrasting letter to the Danish Psychiatric Association—conciliatory and courteous.[22] The motive was a decidedly different one: the hope that the Danes might be persuaded to reconsider their position. For the prospect was looming, awful in the Russian eyes, of a bandwagon effect—first the British, then the Danes, then perhaps other national bodies which were still sitting on the fence (as we shall see later in this chapter, the concern of Snezhnevsky and his associates was well founded, inasmuch as seven other associations opted to support Soviet ejection during the rest of 1982). Given the indomitable stand taken by the British since Honolulu *vis-à-vis* Soviet abuses, the likelihood of any softening of their position was negligible. The Danes, on the other hand, might be more pliable. They had opposed the Honolulu motion criticizing the Soviet Society (such was suggested by an unofficial tally of votes cast) and in the preceding four years had displayed a moderate, even-handed attitude.

For these reasons Snezhnevsky appealed to them "to consider the situation being created in relations between our associations" in the wake of the Danish resolution. At Honolulu the Danes had acted in an objective, professional manner and since the Russians shared those qualities, would it not be useful to enter into joint discussions about the issue that was dividing them? Snezhnevsky would be pleased to set up a meeting where the associations could confer. What the Soviet agenda would consist of was clear from other points made by him, points with which we are by now well acquainted: the illegality of the Review Committee, the inattention to the summarized case histories of dissenters circulated at the General Assembly in Honolulu, and the political motives of those "who make an artificial fuss about the problem of the so-called dissidents".

Little did Snezhnevsky know with whom he was dealing. True, Danish psychiatrists had during the 1970s hovered on the periphery of the tussle between the Soviet Society and its critics. But with the emergence of overwhelming evidence of the perversion of Soviet psychiatry accumulated by the Moscow Working Commission since 1977, the Danes had been galvanized into action. Particularly under the presidencies of Tove Aarkrog (1980–81) and Neils Reisby (since 1982) the Danes had committed themselves to the fray. One of us (SB) had the opportunity to meet the two leaders in November 1982 and was impressed by their sensitivity to the overall subject of human rights in psychiatry. Their sense of commitment was abundantly clear. It would have been astonishing, at least to SB, if Snezhnevsky's assessment of them as malleable had been confirmed by any subsequent backtracking from their resolve to press for Soviet expulsion. In the event, the Danes stuck to their guns and declined Snezhnevsky's proposal. Moreover, as we discussed earlier in this chapter, they also refused an invitation, along with Sweden, extended later in 1982 to all Scandinavian psychiatric societies to visit the USSR.

Apart from Snezhnevsky's responses to the two Western moves for expulsion, the Soviet Society was tight-lipped about its reactions and intentions. That it considered expulsion a real possibility, however, became indirectly apparent in March 1982. Now, for the first time, co-operation began with the WPA, in the form of a reply about the cases of Iosyp

Terelya and Anatoly Ponomaryov. As we noted in our account of the Review Committee in chapter four, this co-operation proved half-hearted and dilatory, more a form of filibustering than a genuine effort to assist with the investigation of cases alleged to be examples of abuse. It probably represented a tactic devised to destabilize the expulsion bandwagon. If the Russians could be *seen* to liaise with the WPA, other societies might be deterred from imitating the British and the Danes.

However, this was not to be the case. Two interrelated factors contributed to the tactic's failure. Firstly, the Russians' resistance to participation in the Review Committee's investigations had by 1982 become so entrenched that it seemed impossible to take the apparent change of heart as genuine. Second, the bandwagon effect so feared by the Russians had begun to roll, and short of something more radical could no longer be stopped.

The decision taken by the American Psychiatric Association in June 1982 was the clearest confirmation that an expulsion movement had gathered momentum during the first half of the year. But the American initiative also brought into view a new dimension. Instead of calling for expulsion, the Americans carefully specified the concept of suspension. Their resolution read: "If the All-Union Society of Psychiatrists and Neuropathologists of the USSR does not adequately respond to all enquiries from the World Psychiatric Association regarding the issue of psychiatric abuse in that country by April 1, 1983, that the All-Union Society should be suspended from membership in the World Psychiatric Association until such time that these abuses cease to exist."[23]

Although the wording of the College's resolution, as we previously noted, also amounted to a call for suspension, the American version was obviously intended to sound less harsh, as it explicitly offered the Russians a further opportunity to co-operate. The time limit of April 1983 suggested that in the event of non-co-operation by that date, the resolution for suspension would automatically come into play three months later in Vienna. Perhaps the question of what constituted an "adequate response" had been left ambiguous intentionally, in order to allow the Americans room for manoeuvre. Although the Americans and British saw eye-to-eye on most issues pertaining to the Soviet issue, the former did later convey their uneasiness about the College's emphasis on expulsion. The word "expel" was emotive and not specified in the WPA's statutes. A suggestion was therefore made that it be changed to "withdrawal of membership", a phrase used in the statutes. The College regarded this as reasonable, but in the wake of the subsequent resignation of the Soviet Society (see chapter seven) did not pursue the matter.[24]

So by mid-1982 three national bodies—in Britain, Denmark and the United States—had committed themselves. What about the other 70-odd societies in the WPA? With the British resolution distributed to 25 of them in November 1981 and the American alternative circulated to all societies in August 1982, the issue was becoming well publicized among world psychiatrists. Would any of them pursue a similar course of action? Conversely, would any oppose the movement to expel or suspend with a contradictory motion?

The Swiss became the fourth association to vote for ejection of the Soviet Union. On 23 September 1982 their annual assembly passed by a large majority a resolution calling for suspension.[25] Introducing the debate, Charles Durand, a central figure in the fight against abuse for several years, emphasized that suspension had the advantage of not making ordinary psychiatrists who could not criticize abuses because of the risks involved, feel rejected. On the contrary, they would feel supported by the fact that the WPA was condemning their leaders, that is, those who had compelled them to connive in the perversion of their profession. The Swiss action was to be expected in the light of their longstanding opposition to the abuses, which had included a range of protests and appeals on behalf of dissenter-patients and Soviet critics of political psychiatry.[26]

Within weeks the number of associations favouring expulsion more than doubled, to nine. Resolutions were adopted by two of the four French societies holding membership in the WPA (a unified psychiatric association does not exist in France)—the French Association of Psychiatrists in Private Practice and the French Association of Psychiatrists in Public Service; by the Royal Australian and New Zealand College of Psychiatrists; by the Norwegian Psychiatric Association; and by the Netherlands Psychiatric Association.[27] The last held a referendum on the issue, in which, of the votes cast, 409 were for expulsion, 204 for suspension and only 53 against either step. Active debate that was taking place in other national associations, in France and Japan, had not as yet yielded any decisions.[28] However, the resignation of the Soviet Society at the beginning of 1983 brought the bandwagon to a stop—the need for action had been pre-empted.

But the matter was not as one-sided as our account so far suggests. Opposition to expulsion became evident in spring 1982. The Canadian Psychiatric Association, which had been in the vanguard of recognizing the abuses and the first to condemn them in January 1971, and which also supported the condemnatory resolution at Honolulu, was, paradoxically, also the first to voice opposition to expulsion. Its Board of Directors decided to adopt a neutral position at its meeting in May 1982, when a motion calling for Soviet suspension was defeated.[29] Notwithstanding, a motion was tabled at the annual business meeting four months later. An independent pressure group, Psychiatrists Against Psychiatric Abuse, founded in 1976, attempted on this occasion to persuade their colleagues to reverse the Board's position. As only 48 members were present, two short of a quorum, only an informal vote could be taken. The result was a three to one majority in favour. This, however, was not binding, and was merely brought to the board's attention.[30]

The Association's president, Dr Q. Rae-Grant later explained his reluctance to vote for Soviet expulsion.[31] Foremost was the conviction that dialogue was preferable to "excommunication" (a view diametrically opposed to that of the British who had argued that more than a decade of dialogue had proved fruitless). A year later he would take the same line in Vienna during the WPA World Congress. Vladimir Bukovsky, when approached by a Canadian journalist to opine on the merit of dialogue, responded succinctly: "Excommunication *is* communication. It sends the strongest possible message that these activities are unacceptable and must stop."[31] The second reason given for caution—that Yuri Andropov, who had recently taken over the reins of Soviet leadership, was entitled to a fair chance—was also sharply rejected by Bukovsky: Andropov had presided over the widespread deployment of psychiatric repression on becoming head of the KGB in 1967; his disrespect for human rights had been truly proven. The third reason was based on the "glass house" argument—other countries also misused psychiatry to political ends: why pick out the USSR alone? On this point, Rae-Grant was ill-informed, citing South Africa as another offender. He clearly had not studied the report of a special committee of the American Psychiatric Association.[32] This group had visited South Africa and concluded that political abuse had not in fact occurred.* Indeed, in no other country (except possibly Romania) had it become a State-inspired and State-directed policy as in the Soviet Union, although reports of individual cases of political psychiatry did periodically emerge from some Eastern European countries.

The Canadians' rationale was somewhat baffling in the light of their previous stand. We can only assume that the leadership was sincere in its first conviction, namely, that diplomacy was preferable to the absence of dialogue, and, if patiently persevered with, could prove effective. But the hypothesis is somewhat shaken by another Canadian decision, taken in 1981, not to accord honorary membership to Anatoly Koryagin.[33] Were the Canadians *that* anxious about offending the Soviet psychiatric establishment? Notwithstanding the board's refusal to budge from its position not to support Soviet ejection from the WPA, or perhaps because of it, sections of Canadian psychiatry took the initiative into their own hands with the aim of prodding the board into action. For example, in January 1983, the Ontario Psychiatric Association passed a resolution which called on Canadian psychiatry as a whole to vote for Soviet suspension.[28]

The position of the Egyptian Psychiatric Association made more explicit what was evidently an underlying concern of the Canadian board—that Soviet ejection could lead to a possible "breakdown of mutual relations between member societies and division of the WPA into camps each with its opponents".[34] Professor M. Gawad, the Association's president, believed that the chief purposes of the international body were to encourage amiable and scientific ties between its

---

* One of us (SB) had similarly visited South Africa on a fact-finding mission in 1978 and reached the same conclusion—see *Bulletin of the Royal College of Psychiatrists*, June 1983, p. 115, for the College's position statement on South African psychiatry.

members and to stimulate research in psychiatry. Political differences were always controversial and therefore best avoided. Interestingly, the Egyptians agreed with the American Psychiatric Association on one point (their remarks were in response to the circulation of the American resolution for suspension), namely that the United Nations Commission on Human Rights (see chapter seven) was a suitable forum for dealing with the Soviet problem, but differed by advocating this as the "proper place". The Americans had by contrast deemed the United Nations as an *additional* venue for action. Finally the Egyptians, like the Canadians, posed the rhetorical question of why only the USSR had been picked out, but did no more than hint that psychiatric abuse was practised elsewhere.

The debate at Honolulu had revealed a tendency for psychiatrists from third world countries to adopt a neutral position *vis-à-vis* the Soviet practices although the delegate from Cuba had not surprisingly defended the Russians (see chapter two). The pattern of support was akin to the contemporary non-aligned movement which, while subscribing to an ethos inherent in its name, has tended in recent years to assume an anti-Western stance (especially towards the United States) if not an explicit pro-Soviet one. The Egyptian attitude was therefore more or less predictable. What could be foretold with greater confidence was the reaction of the Eastern bloc to the expulsion moves. Only one member of that bloc, however, made its position public, the Hungarians. This was undoubtedly the result of a visit made by the Soviet psychiatric leadership to Hungary in early January when the Hungarians were presumably "leaned upon" to take a public initiative. It is most doubtful that they would have proceeded otherwise. Whether the pressure was simply confined to psychiatrists or originated at a political level is open to speculation. In any event, the Hungarians made their contribution in the form of a reply to the memorandum sent out by the American Psychiatric Association calling for support to combat Soviet political psychiatry.[35] Interestingly, Professor P. Juhász, the president of the Hungarian Psychiatric Association, penned his letter some five months after the American initiative, but on the very day of his meeting with Professor Morozov. Juhász made three points, in courteous fashion. The first dealt with philosophical and diagnostic differences between various psychiatric schools. This widely-recognized phenomenon in psychiatry, he claimed, was the root cause of the misunderstanding; the Soviet theoretical approach to mental illness simply differed from that of other schools. In the absence of universal consensus, and where judgements were discordant, the opinion of the psychiatrist assuming care of the patient should prevail. In other words, the Russians should be permitted to get on with their clinical work in accordance with their own best judgements.

Whilst we would agree that psychiatric diagnosis still awaits considerable refinement, the discrepant judgements made on dissenters between Soviet and Western psychiatrists go well beyond inter-school differences. More relevant in this context is the point we have made previously in rebutting the argument of those who hold that different diagnostic theories account for the Soviet problem, namely, that even if some dissenters have suffered from mild forms of mental illness, it certainly has not been severe enough to necessitate their forcible hospitalization, and particularly not in a prison psychiatric hospital. Moreover, the conditions of the dissenters' treatment have been blatantly designed to be punitive rather than therapeutic: the internment in prison-like conditions, the inappropriate prescribing of medication, the threat of indefinite internment, the pressure for recantation, and the unsympathetic harsh attitudes displayed towards the dissenter's family and friends.

Professor Juhász's second concern was to praise Soviet psychiatry for its achievements in the sphere of community psychiatry, pinpointing its "organization and sense of responsibility towards society [which] sets a valuable example for various countries". But whatever the merit of this appraisal, the corollary that follows it is thoroughly illogical. Juhász insists that there is no justification—because of Soviet psychiatry's achievements—to condemn any of its practices. Obviously, abuse of the discipline remains an abuse, whether it occurs within the framework of an outstanding service or a thoroughly defective one. Soviet psychiatric organization may indeed be a model for emulation, at least in theory; Soviet psychiatric misuse is, contrariwise, clearly unworthy of imitation. We may want to praise the first but still condemn the second.

The final Hungarian argument refers to the "necessity for international collaboration" to advance the profession. "Mutual visits, meetings at international forums are occasions to know one another better and to render mutal assistance." How true, but, also, how tragic the paucity of such collaboration with the broad mass of Soviet psychiatrists (and indeed with psychiatrists generally from the Eastern bloc), an issue we highlighted in the context of the Kazanetz affair in chapter five. We shall return to Professor Juhász in chapter eight.

Other associations that debated the issue of expulsion and decided against it were the West Germans and the Swedes. In mid-1982 the Germans issued a statement about political psychiatry in which, *inter alia*, they deplored the fact that a case they had submitted to the WPA in 1980, Anatoly Ponomaryov, "has not been able to be verified because the Soviet Union has refused its co-operation".[25] Their decision on expulsion would depend on how this case and others submitted to the WPA were clarified. In October 1982 Dr Friedrich Weinberger, the chairman of an independent pressure group, the German Association Against Political Misuse of Psychiatry, which had done an impressive job in raising the consciousness of his German colleagues on ethical issues since Honolulu, addressed a special session on political psychiatry at the annual congress of the German Society. He argued for expulsion as the most effective means to combat the abuses. Later that day, at the general assembly, Professor Walter von Baeyer, a distinguished senior German psychiatrist, made a similar appeal for expulsion, unless all dissenter-patients were released by summer 1983. The two appeals were however opposed and a compromise resolution adopted—the Germans would "consider" expulsion if before the Vienna congress the Russians had not manifested any "tendency" to assist in the investigations of the WPA. The wording was ambiguous, leaving it unclear just how the Germans would vote in Vienna.

The Swedes, whose position, we noted earlier, moved gradually from a neutral to a more critical one in the late 1970s, debated the question of expulsion in January 1983.[28] Curiously, their board proposed expulsion, but this was defeated at a members' meeting by a ratio of three to two. Opponents, with Professor J. Ottosson prominent among them (we previously noted his role at the General Assembly in Honolulu), argued that the removal of the Russians would hinder the exertion of pressure for change. An alternative resolution of condemnation was passed instead.

Eleventh-Hour Efforts to Prevent Soviet Expulsion

By the time the Executive of the WPA met in Marrakesh in October 1982, the movement to suspend or expel the Russians was in full swing. That it might succeed at Vienna was becoming a distinct possibility. This prospect was no doubt uppermost in the minds of Professor Morozov and his associates. As we have already noted, their co-operation with the WPA leadership over alleged cases of abuse, though still intermittent and slow, had been in evidence for some months. They had conceivably calculated that their efforts were, for the time being, adequate to forestall any increase in the ranks of WPA members calling for their removal. But the approach adopted by Marat Vartanian, the Soviet representative at Marrakesh, was intriguingly baffling—a mixture of derision of the WPA Secretariat's efforts to grapple with the threat of disintegration overhanging the organization, and reasonable co-operativeness.[36] On the one hand, Vartanian attacked the draft paper on "The Issue of Abuse, 1977–1983" prepared by the Secretariat (see chapter four) as being "subjective", and criticized the previous Executive for not having circulated in 1977 the document in which the Soviet account of a group of mentally-ill dissenters had been presented. He also claimed, spuriously, that there had been no response to the Soviet invitation of 1977 to Western psychiatrists to visit hospitals in the USSR. Then followed an unsavoury *ad hominem* attack on Dr Alexander Voloshanovich, the independent Moscow psychiatrist whom we discussed in chapters three and five. Vartanian asserted meretriciously that Voloshanovich had denounced his own reports, and then proceeded to defame him, without foundation, as an unscrupulous alcoholic.* Finally, Vartanian indicated his society might resign from the

---

* Such defamation was not a new type of behaviour for Vartanian. In 1976 he had cast aspersions on the reputation of General Grigorenko, and in 1973–74 he had published a falsehood about the WPA Executive, even after it had been rebutted to him in private; see details in *Russia's Political Hospitals* pp. 315, 317, 335–336.

WPA in January 1983, that is, a matter of two or three months later. Was this mere bluff, a strategy deployed to gain the support of the Executive and then mount a counter-offensive to the movement of expulsion? Conversely, was it an implicit message that the Russians had indeed arrived at a decision to quit, but were biding their time until a propitious moment?

The issue became even more blurred when Dr Gérard Bles, another observer at Marrakesh, representing the Association of French Psychiatrists in Private Practice, responded at once to Vartanian's claim about visits by Western psychiatrists by stating that his society wished to take up the Soviet offer there and then, and to organize an international delegation of eminent psychiatrists. This initiative provoked positive comment, even from Vartanian. The latter, would, however, have to consult his colleagues and they would reply within a few weeks of receiving a definite proposal. He added, joking, "Don't be afraid we will substitute phony patients for the real ones!" Bles found it impossible to ascertain from Vartanian's overall response whether the Russians would treat the matter of a visit seriously.[37] Nonetheless, he proceeded to communicate with other societies about the proposed visit, on the grounds that there was a faint possibility of Soviet permission being granted. If, on the other hand, the Russians declined, their bluff would have been called. "Yes, you did extend an invitation to foreign psychiatrists to visit Soviet mental institutions. We took up your invitation but then you promptly withdrew it."

The Bles initiative was quite enough to complicate an already intricate situation but the matter became even more involved when another observer at the Marrakesh meeting, Professor Vianna, a Brazilian with close ties to the WPA and a member of its Ethics Committee, also set about organizing a delegation to visit the USSR, scheduled for spring 1983.[38] He had evidently discussed his plan with Vartanian and the WPA leadership as early as April 1982, and received their backing, although Vartanian had indicated that the chairman of the Review Committee, Professor Gosselin, would not be acceptable; two other members of that committee, whom he named (they were from Norway and Czechoslovakia), would however be welcomed in their personal capacity. Vianna conveyed these developments to the Royal College in late November

1982. He added that the WPA Secretariat was concerned about the possible fragmentation of the organization as a result of the expulsion resolutions. As he was pressing ahead with the Secretariat's approval and support, the visit would enjoy official or semi-official backing. Vianna hoped that the delegation would include, in addition to British psychiatrists, members from the United States, South America and Europe.

The College was explicit in its response. It would be prepared to participate in the venture but subject to certain conditions. The visit should be under WPA auspices, the WPA and participating societies should be free to select the visitors, they should have access to named Soviet institutions and be permitted to interview named patients, possibly with relatives in attendance; and the delegation should be accompanied by interpreters of its own choice. These conditions had been carefully considered in the light of the risks attendant on foreign psychiatrists visiting the USSR in the past. The Soviet record of misusing previous visits through misquotation and even outright specious reporting was too well-known by then. The inspection had to be as foolproof as possible to prevent any subsequent misunderstandings.

However, Vianna's initiative soon faded from the picture when the Soviet Society opted to take it over and negotiate directly with the WPA Secretariat. On 8 January 1983 Morozov and an associate arrived in Vienna and had several meetings with Berner and Pichot. They said that the desire of WPA members for an on-site examination of patients would be considered in Moscow on their return. The meetings took place in a friendly atmosphere. By this stage the Russians had paid membership dues for 1982 but not for 1983 (the latter were needed by 31 January to give the Russians voting rights at the General Assembly in Vienna).

By the time of this apparent Soviet willingness to co-operate, the number of societies voting for expulsion or suspension had increased to nine. The picture then looked like this: if, hypothetically, all the member-societies were to pay their dues and thus gain full voting rights, the maximum number of votes available to be cast in the General Assembly would be about 315. Out of this total, the nine societies would wield about 160 votes, that is, one half. By contrast the societies of the USSR and other Communist countries would wield about

60. Although the remaining 95 were still floating votes it was clearly inconceivable that the USSR could win over all of them. In other words, to repeat the Soviet tactics used for the previous General Assembly in 1977 would prove ineffective. A policy of "toughing it out" at home—that is, refusing to make substantive reforms—and intensive lobbying of allies and wavering societies, a policy which had just failed at Honolulu when the stakes were much lower, had no chance of success in 1983. This had become obvious as the nine societies had shown determination not only in proposing their resolutions in the first place, but also by the readiness of some of them to take part in a delegation to visit the USSR and by their insistence on proper conditions for such a visit. It would clearly be impossible to confuse, side-track or deceive such a delegation.

In these circumstances there were, in theory at least, two other options. First, political psychiatry could be quickly abolished—its leading practitioners demoted and replaced by psychiatrists respected abroad; its victims released; Dr Koryagin and his colleagues freed. This option presented serious difficulties. To convince the many sceptics, the reforms would have to be conducted quickly and thoroughly. But this is not how the Soviet bureaucracy normally operates—especially when, as in this case, it is essential to lose as little additional international "face" as possible, and therefore no public admission can be made that anything done in the past was actually improper. Moreover, although the advent of the new Andropov leadership potentially facilitated the option of abolition, this leadership had not yet sufficiently consolidated its power for decisive, clear-cut reforms to be feasible.

So the second option—prompt resignation from WPA—was now the only realistic one. This course, although profoundly humiliating, would avoid the even greater humiliation of Soviet expulsion in Vienna, amidst a blaze of publicity. It would remove one particular pressure—the necessity of responding to the WPA investigators. And it would provide a breathing-space—time in which to observe how the WPA and the world medical and political communities would react, time in which to review policy, and time in which—if abolition of political psychiatry then seemed the best course—to conduct the abolition quietly, gradually and unobtrusively, prior to re-joining the WPA at some point in the future.

The final decision to quit the WPA was clearly taken in the light of Morozov's report on his trip to Vienna, i.e. in the second half of January 1983. The frantic Soviet manoeuvres of the preceding months had produced no acceptable way out: expulsion was seen to be virtually inevitable. However, even though suspension or expulsion had now been pre-empted, the drama was not yet at an end. The General Assembly was bound by the statutes of the WPA to accept formally the resignation of a member society and thus to ratify the action taken by the Secretariat. Just conceivably, some societies might propose, for the congress in Vienna, that the Assembly should refuse to accept the Russians' resignation and, moreover, should press them to reconsider their action. In that case, however, the nine societies supporting moves to suspend or expel might proceed with their resolutions to ensure the Russians' definitive ejection. In fact, the Royal College voted in February 1983 to retain its original expulsion resolution on the agenda of the Assembly[24] while the American Psychiatric Association submitted its previously adopted suspension resolution in slightly amended form the following month.[39] Alongside this prospect, other resolutions concerning political psychiatry were scheduled for debate by the General Assembly—that Dr Koryagin should be made an Honorary Member of the WPA (a position of distinction held by only two dozen of the world's psychiatrists); that the Honolulu resolution should be widened to include the investigation of both victims *and resisters* of psychiatric abuse; that the Review Committee should be strengthened financially; and constitutionally; and finally two general resolutions: one deplored the continuing Soviet abuse but hoped for its abolition and Soviet readmission to the WPA; the other called on the WPA to continue its efforts to combat political psychiatry in the USSR and elsewhere, and to support those who resist it. So, although the Soviet Society might not be present physically at Vienna, it would be bound to occupy centre-stage. The events of the Seventh World Congress constitute chapter eight but before we can deal with them, we must first consider more closely the resignation of the Russians and its ramifications.

CHAPTER SEVEN

THE RESIGNATION: THE RUSSIANS RETREAT

IN THE LIGHT of the incipient if sluggish Soviet co-operation with the WPA Executive, the resignation of the Russians from the world body on 31 January 1983 came as a thunderbolt.[1] Perhaps because the battle lines had been drawn up over the previous year, and the site and timing of the decisive episode were still regarded, at least in Western eyes, as Vienna and the imminent World Congress, the sudden, unilateral withdrawal of one side, while explicitly foreshadowed, as we have seen, was startling news. Professors Pichot and Berner learnt of it on February 8 in London, by phone. Ironically, they were on a visit to the Royal College of Psychiatrists to try to persuade it to take part in the inspection tour of the USSR which they had discussed the previous month with Morozov (chapter six). The hope was that the College would then soften its stand and thus avert precisely what now, suddenly, had occurred.[2]

The letter of resignation, signed by Morozov and eighteen leading colleagues (see appendix V), was unrestrained and bristled with anger and hostility. Many of the points were old and familiar, others had a new twist. The most notable grievance was essentially a variation of an old theme: the politicization of international psychiatry. According to the Russians, the leadership of the WPA and several member societies, especially the Americans and the British, had been pressurized by "certain circles" to participate in a "slanderous campaign alleging that psychiatry is being abused in the USSR for political purposes". This was "in the spirit of the 'cold war' against the Soviet Union". The letter specified one of these "circles"—the US Department of State—and pinpointed a letter from the American Psychiatric Association to WPA societies of six months earlier as evidence of political entanglement. As we mentioned in the previous chapter, such a letter had indeed been circulated in which the recipients were recommended to imitate the Americans by contacting their foreign ministries with a view to using the United Nations Commission on Human Rights in the campaign to combat the Soviet abuse.

Because of the emphasis given to this American initiative by the Russians, we may briefly digress to consider how it arose and the potential implications of such a move. The Commission on Human Rights was set up in 1946 with the aim of promoting human rights worldwide. Its elected 43 member States hold a six-week session each year at the United Nations in Geneva during which various issues in the field of human rights are considered and acted upon. The Commission operates under the aegis of the Economic and Social Council, which in turn reports to the UN General Assembly. The human rights aspect of the misuse of psychiatry to suppress dissent was first brought to the attention of the Commission by Britain in 1977. Subsequently the Commission's Sub-Commission on Prevention of Discrimination and Protection of Minorities was authorized to prepare a report on the rights of people detained compulsorily in psychiatric hospitals. The document was duly completed in September 1982.[3] Thereafter, the Commission was expected to study, *inter alia*, the misuse of psychiatric facilities in the context of human rights and to take appropriate action. The options available to it included the adoption of a resolution condemning psychiatric abuse, the preparation of a set of guidelines in the form of a treaty or declaration designed to protect the rights of persons detained in psychiatric hospitals, or the setting up of an investigatory body to survey the problem of abuse and to report its findings to the Commission. None of these courses of action could, however, be accompanied by power of enforcement—the Commission's source of influence has always been limited to publicity and associated public pressure.

The Committee on Abuse of the American Psychiatric Association had first recognized the potential of the Commission to deal with the Soviet matter in 1981, at which time it broached the possibility with one of the American representatives to Geneva.[4] At a subsequent meeting with relevant officials of the State Department, the Committee on Abuse learned about the intention of the American delegation to propose the creation, under the auspices of the Commission, of a monitoring body to investigate political psychiatry on a worldwide basis.[5] It was this proposal which gained the backing of the American Psychiatric Association. The Association thereupon decided to inform other WPA members of these developments and to suggest that they might wish to contact their own delegates to the Commission (if applicable) and their foreign ministries.[2] The Russians had highlighted this communication as evidence of the political pressure to which some national associations had been subjected.

Notwithstanding that the letter had been distributed by the Americans, the WPA leadership—much to its chagrin—was accused of "having allowed itself to become involved in outright political activity", consequently harming the interests of world psychiatry.

Other Soviet grievances cited in the letter of resignation were familiar ones. As on many previous occasions, complaints about the voting procedure at Honolulu were churned out. It was described as discriminatory, with the views of a small group of countries being imposed on the majority of members, particularly from the developing countries. Moreover, and this was a novel complaint, the undemocratic nature of the organization was seen in its co-operative links with the member society of the "racist regime" in South Africa. Such a rationale was odd, but one hypothesis occurs to us: was this focus on the third world and the invocation of South Africa—obviously a target of contempt for the former—designed to win the support of societies from developing countries, either in the form of a "resignation in sympathy" or as allies in any future showdown within the WPA? It was after all not inconceivable that the WPA leadership might still—in co-operation with part of the membership—try to persuade the Russians to withdraw their resignation and to return to the fold in order to forestall the WPA's fragmentation.

The Soviet letter also included three untrue claims. First, many "outstanding" Western psychiatrists had examined dissenter-patients during visits to the USSR and had agreed with the diagnoses applied to them. This was a device which the defenders of Soviet psychiatry had used regularly in the past but with a progressive lack of credibility. Secondly, "certain national associations [had] evaded the official invitations" issued by the Soviet Society "to visit the USSR and to participate in a discussion of the above-mentioned problems". We know of two associations which did not take up invitations—the Swedish and the Danish (for the circumstances, see chapter six). By contrast, at least two member societies—the Association of French Private Psychiatrists and the Royal College—had expressed willingness to visit the Soviet Union in the event of a firm Soviet initiative. That the Soviets resigned just at a time when two international inspection visits were being set up—by Dr Bles (to which five member societies had responded positively[6]) and Professor Vianna—illuminates the speciousness of the Russian claim regarding evasion. Thirdly, the letter referred to "a whole number of mental patients" who had received, or were currently receiving, treatment following their emigration from the Soviet Union. "Such facts are being hushed up," the signatories claimed, unquestionably in their own full knowledge that they themselves were distorting these "facts". As previously mentioned, out of about 43 such people to leave the USSR, the Soviet statement appeared to be true of only three of them. Most of the 43 led normal working lives and, to our knowledge, were not receiving psychiatric treatment.

Overall, Morozov and his colleagues had gone to extraordinary lengths, indeed to outright deception, in framing their letter of withdrawal. Why was this necessary? We can only speculate that resignation from a world body constituted a great source of embarrassment to the Soviet psychiatric establishment. Although the indignity and humiliation of expulsion from the WPA later in the year had been averted, resignation in whatever form was tantamount to an oblique admission that the Russians had dirty linen to hide. The content and tone of the letter therefore had to reflect at all costs a sense that Soviet psychiatry was the maligned and aggrieved party, and the WPA the offender.

Furthermore, the psychiatric leadership was saddled with an uncomfortable dilemma. The resignation was in a sense their personal responsibility and they obviously felt that the events required a vigorous self-justification. The World Service of Moscow Radio and foreign-language Soviet periodicals were used for this purpose. Meanwhile only one article appeared at home—in the *Medical Gazette*[7] two months after the event (discussed below)—and a blanket censorship of the resignation was imposed on all other domestic media. In general, Morozov and Vartanian, selected for the task of defending the Soviet position, stuck quite closely to the points made in the letter of resignation. Occasionally Morozov exercised "poetic licence" and went further than the letter. In a broadcast on 16 February 1983 he commented: "Our diagnoses have always been endorsed by the foreign specialists. They have regarded the tactics and methods of treatment as the only correct ones."[8] In another interview he took off into higher flights of fantasy regarding Soviet "ex-patients" now living in the West: "Putting them on television programmes and the like often resulted in a deterioration in their mental state, with the result that they found themselves in psychiatric wards in the countries to which they had gone. I have no right to violate professional secrecy and give you the names of these patients. However, they are well-known to our Western colleagues."[9] In fact, not one such case is known of. On the contrary, about a dozen ex-victims have appeared on television, but with no ill-effects.

Vartanian, by contrast, had no ethical qualms during a broadcast on March 17: "We suggested on several occasions," he said, "that our Western colleagues should examine the so-called mentally sane dissidents who had emigrated to the West, especially as many of them had already been 'regulars' in psychiatric hospitals."[10] He then gave three examples to prove his point: An émigré called Lev Konstantinov (who was not a dissenter and whom no one had ever heard of, let alone campaigned for, prior to his emigration to Austria), Natalya Gorbanevskaya and Alexander Volpin.[11]

The facts were different. In Paris, Gorbanevskaya was examined by French psychiatrists at their request. They found her to be mentally normal and concluded that she had been interned in a psychiatric hospital in 1969–1972 on political, not medical grounds. When Vartanian's statement was read to her, she retorted that she had not had any contact with Western psychiatrists except on a few occasions like that just mentioned, that is, when the initiative was that of psychiatrists who wished to judge for themselves the basis of her forcible treatment in the USSR. She also suggested, plausibly enough, that Vartanian and Morozov were becoming even more irresponsible than before in their desperate efforts at self-justification. Since her emigration in 1975 she had consistently performed a demanding job as an editor.[12] Volpin had the same pattern of non-involvement with psychiatry as Gorbanevskaya.

Elsewhere in the interview Vartanian inflated another of Morozov's deceptions by making it more specific: "On numerous occasions we have provided our Western colleagues with the opportunity to examine the so-called mentally sane dissidents, and all agreed with the diagnosis established by Soviet doctors—all, even the leading Western psychiatrists from the US, Great Britain, West Germany, and so on."[10]

As indicated earlier, at home the Soviet loss of face in being forced to resign was limited by the media simply not divulging to the general public what had happened. This apparent inability to present a convincing explanation for such a humiliating event probably incurred a certain price: the accounts broadcast in Russian from abroad by such services as the BBC and Radio Liberty received no domestic reply and were therefore more likely to be perceived as credible by Soviet listeners.

Even doctors who read the one article (by G. Morozov and a colleague) published in their profession's newspaper may have remained sceptical, as it simply ignored such key issues as the psychiatric examination of Grigorenko abroad, the consistent refusal by the Soviet authorities to allow foreign psychiatrists to examine named dissenters in the USSR, and the parallel bar on any visits to special hospitals. Readers will also have been puzzled by a strange and apparently new twist to Morozov's position. Regarding the individuals whom the West described as wrongly interned for their dissent, the authors wrote: "Some of these patients were treated by psychiatrists when children, and only a few of them manifested mental disturbances during the period of in-patient examination." This passage was puzzling, as all the official psychiatric reports on such people which have reached the West purport to demonstrate what the law requires, namely that mental illness was severe enough *at the time of the offence* for the offender to be considered not responsible for his actions.

None of the reports has argued that mental illness occurred in childhood but was not operative (merely latent, as Morozov clearly implies) when the crime was committed.

Readers may also have been unimpressed by this comment on the Soviet Society's resignation: "Such a serious decision represents the outcome of a prolonged and all-round analysis of the evolving situation." If it was so serious, why was the membership in no way consulted? And why was it not even informed, until two months after the event?

The angry tone of the letter of resignation was matched in turn by the embittered reaction of Professors Pichot and Berner. They were clearly upset about the resignation in general and specifically indignant about the Soviet innuendo that they had conspired with political forces and acted dishonourably. They were quick to reject such an allegation. In a press release they announced the Soviet resignation and immediately launched into a stern rebuttal: ". . . [we] strongly refute this accusation and declare that the Executive Officers who were elected to administer the Association . . . have merely implemented the mandates given them by the Association's General Assembly".[13] They then detailed the events preceding the resignation—the establishment of the Review Committee, the Soviet Society's refusal to liaise with the Committee, and their own role subsequently to gain its co-operation. Pichot and Berner also sent a formal letter to the Russians. They did not mince their words. The reasons advanced for resigning were "unfounded accusations levelled against the Officers of the WPA and, as such, cannot be too strongly refuted".[14] A more comprehensive rebuttal than appeared in the press release took up the body of the letter. First, the memorandum from the American Psychiatric Association to member societies suggesting the UN Commission on Human Rights as a forum for action was dealt with: this was a private initiative which the WPA had had no wind of until three months later. Therefore, the criticism that the WPA was under the influence of the American State Department was completely without foundation.

The letter then tackled another criticism made by the Russians. Comments about the Honolulu voting system were ludicrous. Moreover, it was odd that events going back to August 1977 could determine a resignation five and a half years later. Pichot and Berner must have felt especially peeved at this point, when penning their letter, for they then proceeded to chide the Soviet Society for failing to pay its dues and thus forfeiting some of its voting strength at the Honolulu ballots. They had only themselves to blame! Their anger was also apparent in the final paragraph, in which they referred to the resignation as "uncalled for and unnecessary and. . . . detrimental to the advancement of [psychiatry] and destructive to the purpose of the World Psychiatric Association". Paradoxically juxtaposed was a request for Soviet reappraisal: "On behalf of the entire psychiatric community, the World Psychiatric Association deplores this latest development and would wish for a reconsideration of this decision." "Uncalled for", "obstructive", "deplores"—this array of words appeared considerably more cogent than the brief request to think again. The inclusion of the latter was however significant. While the request clearly lacked the authority claimed for it, it presumably reflected the Executive's desire to be conciliatory enough to reduce the chances of a walk-out from the WPA by Russia's allies and supporters.

The obvious pique which permeated the entire letter stemmed from a sense of betrayal. However misdirected, an unceasing effort had been expended by the Executive in trying to solve the critical issues facing the WPA. Just at the moment when it seemed that Soviet co-operation had at long last been secured, what had come instead was a hostile repudiation of their own endeavours. The leadership had obviously been delighted to welcome Morozov and the medical data he brought with him to Vienna. The assumption that this presaged a better spirit of co-operation seemed perfectly reasonable, particularly as the meeting was described as "amiable and conciliatory". Even more significantly, Morozov had agreed to consider an on-site visit of Russian psychiatric hospitals, by then an essential pre-requisite to mollify his critics.

The real reasons for the Soviet turnabout within three weeks is an intriguing subject on which we have already speculated in the previous chapter. Did the WPA leadership, by chance and quite unwittingly, steer a wavering, reconnoitring Morozov into feeling that his chances of evading censure and humiliating expulsion in Vienna were non-existent?

Whilst not adequate in and of itself to explain the abrupt change in Soviet policy, we suspect that the January meeting may well have contributed. Consider the following scenario. Morozov arrives in Vienna and presents the long sought-after documentation to the Secretariat. He breathes a sigh of hope—surely this step will satisfy them? Hereafter, he can rest assured that Pichot and Berner—who are obviously reluctant to oversee the WPA's disintegration—will now be able to use their considerable influence and clout. Now they can praise the Soviet collaboration and help to sway uncommitted members to retreat from such a radical measure as expulsion.

But what does Morozov encounter in Vienna? Pichot and Berner are unrestrainedly blunt. Nine societies have passed resolutions calling for expulsion or suspension unless the Soviet Society proves its intent of co-operating with the WPA. This will inevitably necessitate an on-site inspection of Soviet special psychiatric hospitals (SPHs). It would be prudent, indeed essential, to permit the visit (which they would help to facilitate) to take place. This last point must, despite his stated willingness to mull it over, have led Morozov and his colleagues to conclude that the level of distrust and opposition was so high among key members that there was no realistic chance of dissipating it in the mere six months before the General Assembly. To reform the SPHs and release the dissenter-patients simply could not be done so quickly—for both practical and "face" reasons. In any event, Morozov would hardly dare propose such a policy, as its implementation could easily sweep him away too. No, the previous deflections of Western attacks, wholly successful at Mexico City and partially effective at Honolulu, were obviously doomed to failure at Vienna.

With no alternative but to resign, the next questions for Morozov and his colleagues were how to limit the damage such a development would inevitably wreak, and how to save face. We have already noted the aggressive tenor of their letter of resignation—the Executive was the guilty party and it was they who had allowed the politicization of the organization, which in turn had led to the victimization of the Soviet Society. To the astute observer, however, this claim was hollow. Something more was needed by the Soviet psychiatric leadership, namely explicit support by other member societies of the WPA. This was to be confidently expected from one quarter—some, at least, of the societies of Eastern Europe which had demonstrated their allegiance in Honolulu six years before.

Thus, it came as no surprise when the East Germans voiced strong protest in March 1983 about recent developments. Their letter to the Executive bristled with resentment.[15] Asserting that their Soviet colleagues' integrity had been impugned without justification, they lashed out at the Executive. Pichot and his committee had "failed to undertake effective steps in order to counteract the anti-Soviet activities", and in particular to condemn unequivocally "those factions which have been instrumental in introducing the methods of the cold war into an international medical scientific organization". Finally, the East Germans insisted on a "prompt solution" to the problems facing the WPA, but also issued a veiled threat that they might themselves resign. What precise steps they expected the Executive to take remained unclear, though the objective was spelled out— nothing less than the readmission of the Soviet Society.

The East Germans had in all likelihood been in close touch with Morozov from the time of the Soviet resignation. But to what extent he had exerted pressure on them to act the way they did we can only conjecture. The same applies in the case of the Czechs and the Bulgarians although by the time they took action—on the same day—two months later, added Soviet pressure had probably been applied, resulting in formal resignations rather than mere threats.[16] The reasons advanced for their decisions were by now familiar—the WPA had become a political body, the Review Committee's activities were directed against the USSR, and so on. Ironically, the Czechs referred to these developments as alien to the "humanitarian mission" of Czechoslovak psychiatry.

Why the Czechs and Bulgarians resigned after a delay of three and a half months is puzzling, but might be attributable to their initial adoption of a policy of wait-and-see. Well into the waiting period, the Czechs were still in friendly contact with Berner about the holding of a WPA regional symposium in Prague.[17] Conceivably, the absence of any decisive action by the WPA Executive following the East

German intervention, may have led the Soviet Society to turn to other "dependable allies" in order to press them for a more radical contribution.

What now about the reactions to the resignation of WPA member societies which had adopted resolutions to expel or suspend? They perhaps had reason to welcome the news in the light of their original action, but, on the contrary, they responded in subdued fashion. Their victory, if it could be so labelled, was regarded as mainly Pyrrhic in nature. Leading spokesmen for the Royal College and the American Psychiatric Association, for example, were in agreement that the resignation *per se* did not solve anything. Peter Sainsbury voiced his regret that the College had not succeeded hitherto in modifying the situation, and felt that pressure on Soviet psychiatrists would have to be maintained in order to combat the abuses. The resignation, however, was a tacit admission that political psychiatry was taking place,[18] and he hoped the Russians might "now re-examine their practices out of the glare of publicity".[19] The president of the College, Professor Rawnsley, entertained a similar hope when he commented: "I hope that what might happen when the dust settles a little is that they might decide to change their policy."[18] In his view, the use of psychiatry for political purposes was not vital to Soviet interests since the authorities had many other methods at their disposal to quell dissent.

Harold Visotsky, of the American Committee on Abuse, like his British counterpart, claimed that the Soviet withdrawal was "an admission of guilt".[20] He alluded to the origin of the decision to quit by surmising that it was politically-based and in line with the tough posture of the newly-elected Soviet leadership of Yuri Andropov (who had entered office two months earlier).

What of our own views about the reason for the Russian withdrawal? If we examine the period following the Honolulu resolutions, the pattern of Soviet reaction to mounting international pressure was a combination of evasion, delaying tactics and vacillation—in practice a series of ploys designed to wear down the opposition. The approach, as we saw in earlier chapters, was not altogether unsuccessful. After all, nearly six years passed before the Russians finally threw in the towel, and then only because they could not devise any further strategies to counteract an apparently implacable foe. In fact, the options open to the Soviet psychiatric establishment were ultimately so whittled away by the march of events that expulsion or resignation loomed as the only two possible outcomes. This extremely limited choice, akin to that between Scylla and Charybdis, no doubt served to sharpen thoroughly the minds of Morozov and his associates. Their goal was to extricate themselves from an essentially insoluble predicament with the least loss of face. The double-barrelled calculation was probably made that to pre-empt the attack at Vienna would be least harmful to Soviet interests in the long term, and that the most effective mode of such pre-emption was to mount the counter-offensive described above, with the aid of Soviet allies.

The Mechanism of the Soviet Resignation

An obvious question, which we have yet to tackle, concerns the mechanism involved in the decision to resign. Formally speaking, the latter emanated from the Board of the Soviet Society, but the reality was certainly more complex.

The Communist Party of the Soviet Union controls all aspects of the country's life through an elaborate mechanism of parallel hierarchies. In particular its own hierarchy of committees—from the centre down to the grass roots— "shadows" every institution of state and society.[21] At the centre, each of the 20 permanent departments of the Party's Central Committee monitors and directs the policy of half-a-dozen government ministries or equivalent bodies, plus a number of non-state bodies—such as the Society of Psychiatrists. For routine matters the latter is presumably supervised by the Central Committee's Department for Public Services. But for unusual issues—and certainly in the case of possible Soviet expulsion from the WPA—other departments would take over. These are probably the International Department (responsible for overseeing foreign policy) and the Administrative Organs Department (responsible for supervising police, courts, KGB, labour camps, SPHs, and so on). As the KGB has been involved on a day-to-day basis with aspects of political psychiatry, almost certainly it joined these departments in formulating policy on Soviet relations with the WPA. The four bodies may well have set up a small, *ad hoc* committee, which probably consulted the politically less important Ministries of Health and Foreign Affairs, Morozov himself, and perhaps Vartanian.

Thus we may speculate that before Morozov set off for Vienna in January 1983, he was given by the committee fairly precise instructions and guidelines for the different contingencies foreseen. As Soviet policies have tended to evolve slowly under the collective leadership of the last twenty years, and as Vartanian revealed that resignation from WPA was already an active policy option in October 1982, we imagine that the committee had by January discussed this option further, and Morozov's trip was a reconnoitring operation. It would provide the information on which the timing, details and follow-up of resignation, if decided upon, could be planned. Probably, to secure maximum information about WPA attitudes and intentions, he gave an impression, genuine or otherwise, of starting to make substantial concessions, thus drawing his hosts out on the likely responses to these.

On his return home he must have written a report for the putative *ad hoc* committee. Its view about the resignation option confirmed, this group would then have worked out the guidelines for Morozov's letter of resignation and his orchestration of the counter-offensive described earlier. The precise drafting of the letter was probably done by Morozov in conjunction with Vartanian and one or two other colleagues, then presented to the presidium of the psychiatric society for signature. It is unlikely that any member questioned the decision taken in the society's name, or even small points of drafting.

Preliminary Responses to the Resignation
With the World Congress imminent, the WPA Executive faced an almost insurmountable problem. The "prompt solution" insisted on by the East Germans seemed as elusive as ever. The resignation of the second-largest society was an irretrievable fact. With the prospect of further withdrawals on the cards, the WPA's future welfare hung in the balance.

The organization's fate was much to the fore when the Executive met in March 1983 in Buenos Aires for its last meeting before the World Congress.[22] Particularly evident was the divisiveness spawned by the resignation. One

camp—in which the chief protagonists were Professor Gosselin (in his capacity as chairman of the Review Committee)
and Dr M. Sabshin (an observer representing the American
Psychiatric Association)—agreed in essence on the continuation of WPA policy *vis-à-vis* abuse. Despite recent developments, there was no turning back. Sabshin was forthright
when noting that the Soviet Society's tactics of prevarication
with the Executive had forced the Americans to adopt a tough
stand; moreover, the Russians' strategy to shift the responsibility for their withdrawal on to the WPA was unjustified. He
repudiated the suggestion made by Professor Pichot that his
association's initiative regarding the UN Commission on
Human Rights had precipitated the Soviet action.

Gosselin was equally direct. If Pichot was correct, why had
the Soviet Society not resigned until five months after the
American initiative? Turning to the lack of Soviet co-operation with his Review Committee, he criticized the Executive's
acceptance of the Russians' refusal to recognize that Committee. If the WPA believed what it preached, the existence of a
monitoring body was fully justified and apt—all member
societies, he implied, were thus beholden to collaborate with
it. He argued further that psychiatry's reputation would be
considerably tarnished if it failed to acknowledge the possibility of unethical conduct by some of its practitioners.

This was candid talking. The other camp, in which
psychiatrists from Greece and Spain figured prominently, was
no less direct. Professor Costas Stefanis (present in his
capacity as chairman of the Ethics Committee) attributed the
Soviet resignation directly to the operations of the Review
Committee. The establishment of the Committee had led to
the current predicament, and only with its abolition and
restoration of the *status quo ante*, could the WPA be spared
further traumas. Pragmatism seemed to dominate his thinking: first, the unity of the Association was a foremost priority;
second—and here his logic was somewhat odd—since the
Review Committee could not possibly expect co-operation
from member societies accused of "misdemeanour", it should
be scrapped as unworkable. Stefanis was obviously ignoring
the victims of political psychiatry (whose existence he did not
apparently negate) in his recommendations. In a sense, he
was reverting to the WPA position at Mexico City in 1971

when the organization had wriggled out of the troublesome area by declaring that its mandate did not cover the political misuse of psychiatry.

Professor Lopez-Ibor of Spain argued in similar fashion—the WPA simply lacked the power to deal with the issue. Like Stefanis, he believed all the WPA's tribulations stemmed from the resolutions passed at Honolulu. The current situation was harming the reputation of psychiatry, with the public developing an image of the psychiatrist as jailer. How exactly Lopez-Ibor thought this impression might go away was not dealt with. Then, in a striking revelation, he contended that Soviet psychiatrists, as well as their colleagues in other countries, were obliged to comply with their Governments' directives. In other words, he seemed to be saying that psychiatrists in the Soviet Union had no choice but to collude with their political masters. Moreover, if the latter were pressed by the WPA, they would react by hindering the psychiatrists even further. Dr Mesones, an Argentinian psychiatrist present, was more explicit—incredibly so: Soviet psychiatrists should not be condemned; on the contrary, they had fulfilled a benevolent role by admitting dissenters into their hospitals, thus sparing them from the "Gulag"! This was tantamount to saying: "Yes, the psychiatrist does serve as jailor, but his regime is kind and decent."

Both Stefanis and Lopez-Ibor were burying their heads in the sand. They seemed to be saying: extricate the WPA from the whole murky business, let it resume its former, exclusively scientific stance, and all will be well. Their opponents, as we have seen, adhered to the diametrically opposite view that the clock could not be turned back, and the WPA had the moral responsibility to wrestle with the problem, however demanding and complicated. The gulf between the two camps was clearly immense; compromise would be hard to achieve. That a similar split would affect the membership in Vienna less than four months later was beyond doubt. The tenor of the debate at Buenos Aires coupled with what looked like the start of a resignation bandwagon in May augured badly for the WPA. Its survival hung in the balance. The General Assembly at Vienna was faced with the task of averting the Association's fragmentation. In the final chapter, we examine how it fared.

CHAPTER EIGHT

VIENNA AND BEYOND

PROBABLY TO HEAD off the domination of the World Congress at Vienna by the issue of political psychiatry—a striking feature of the preceding congress at Honolulu—the WPA Executive scheduled the main General Assembly meeting for the day preceding the official opening. Although the Soviet resignation had to some extent defused the crisis facing the WPA; the known divisions within the Association on what policy it should adopt *vis-à-vis* the abuse were bound to intrude at Vienna, and their repercussions were potentially harmful. At least by attempting to deal with the divisions promptly, before they had a chance to escalate during the conference, damage might, the Executive thought, be minimized. The decision that the press would not be permitted to observe the proceedings of the Assembly—unlike at Honolulu—was no doubt taken for similar reasons (in fact the coverage by the local and international media was scanty).

In great measure, the Executive succeeded in containing discussion of the issue of abuse; unlike at Honolulu, it was barely perceptible, and few of the seven thousand psychiatrists in Vienna were much aware of what was happening in the Assemby. In 1977 the congress had been electrified by the then major question of whether the WPA would censure the Soviet Society by condemning its unethical practice. In the intervening six years psychiatrists worldwide had become acquainted with the issue and, to some extent, habituated to it.

While these comments are true of the conference overall they do not apply to the Assembly, where the subject of political psychiatry completely dominated the proceedings.[1] For example, nine of the ten resolutions submitted by member societies, as well as all the resolutions tabled during the sessions, were directly or indirectly related to it; the election of the new Executive was influenced critically by the attitudes held by candidates towards psychiatric abuse; and the divisions in the Association over the policy it should adopt towards the Russians were much to the fore.

One obvious manifestation of division would be reflected in the failure of certain member-societies to send representatives to the Assembly; another would be any resignations in Vienna itself. Of great interest, therefore, was the attendance of the East Germans—who had, after all, threatened to resign in March, and of the Hungarians—who had expressed their support for the Russian position in January (see chapters 6 and 7). Czechoslovakia and Bulgaria were, of course, absent following their official resignation two months earlier. But it is interesting to note that a contingent of Czech psychiatrists had planned to participate in the conference and had made contact with the WPA Secretariat.[2] Even though their Society had withdrawn from the organization, these psychiatrists would have been free to attend, since WPA conferences had always been open to any psychiatrist. They were, however, refused visas by the Czech government, a refusal based almost certainly on political grounds. The non-attendance of Romania may not have been politically inspired, inasmuch as it had neither paid its dues nor been an active member of the WPA. But intermittent criticism of alleged political psychiatry there may also have played a role.[3]

The Polish absence, however, was noteworthy. Professor Berner announced that he had received word from the Poles that their failure to attend in no way signified a lack of support for the WPA; on the contrary, they wished to retain membership and would resist any pressure on them to withdraw. This communication was tantamount to a declaration of professional independence. Their inability to obtain visas from their government—the reason given for the absence—was left enveloped in mystery. Whether this was merely a technically-based travel restriction (a genuine obstacle facing Eastern European professionals wishing to participate in conferences in the West is the critical shortage of foreign currency) or a politically-motivated decision designed to display solidarity with the Soviet Union, could only be conjectured. The fact that the Secretariat of the WPA offered to reduce or waive the rather hefty registration fee is of little help in answering the question.[4]

Thus, further resignations by societies from the Eastern bloc, which had been a distinct possibility up to the eve of the conference, did not materialize. In Vienna itself the only society to withdraw was Cuba. Having participated actively in the first session of the Assembly, the Cuban delegate announced his society's resignation rather unexpectedly a few days later. In so doing he criticized the alleged conversion of the WPA into a political body, a transformation he claimed was supported by countries in favour of the arms race. The attack on Socialist countries by the American Psychiatric Association was regrettable. In the light of these developments, Cuba had no choice but to resign. By the end of the congress it seemed that the remaining societies intended to retain their membership and to commit themselves to the preservation of the WPA.

Let us now turn to the Assembly's deliberations regarding the Soviet issue. The first major item on the agenda was not directly pertinent. It was obviously linked to the earlier possibility—prior to the Russians' resignation—that a member society might have to be ejected. A working group had set about revising the statutes in 1981 and its proposals were now brought before the delegates for appraisal and adoption. The ensuing discussion was a relatively tame affair, since most of the changes recommended were more than reasonable. The proposals that withdrawal of membership would be exclusively in the hands of the Assembly (the Executive had previously also had this power) and would require a two-thirds majority (instead of a simple majority as in the past) were sound. Withdrawal of membership, it was unanimously agreed, was too grave a matter to be dealt with in any lesser way. Similar support was forthcoming for changing the Ethics Committee from a working group to a permanent constitutionalized body, charged with the task of identifying and studying "areas of ethical concern to psychiatrists". This was deemed necessary in the light of constantly changing circumstances in the clinical and research practice of psychiatrists. Later in the session a revised text of the WPA's code of ethics, the Declaration of Hawaii, which had been prepared by the Ethics Committee, was readily accepted (see chapter two and appendix I).

The most contentious issue dealt with by the Assembly was

unquestionably the resignation of the Soviet Society. The Czech and Bulgarian withdrawals were, by contrast, relatively ignored. In ordinary circumstances the Assembly would have simply noted the report of the secretary-general of any resignations. There was precedent for this. Societies were free to resign, and some had done so in the past, invariably for straightforward reasons such as an inability to pay the required dues. On this occasion a lengthy discussion ensued. The East German delegate, Professor H. Schulze, perhaps acting as a Soviet surrogate, immediately launched the discussion by expressing his regret at the resignations; the WPA should firmly oppose them (i.e. presumably seek to reverse them), as well as the general politicization of the organization that had taken place in recent years. The latter had brought the WPA and the profession into disrepute. The Mexican delegate echoed these sentiments, and also sought an explanation for the reasons behind the withdrawals. Implicit was a criticism of the Executive's handling of the affair; in merely accepting the resignations, it had not acted neutrally. Professor Pichot, the WPA president, disputed this portrayal of his Executive: "We behaved properly," he retorted. The evidence was in the correspondence between the WPA and the Soviet Society; all member societies had been circulated with this correspondence and could confirm that until the very point of the Russians' withdrawal there seemed a reasonable chance for a favourable outcome. The abrupt resignation had, however, radically changed the prospects.

Professor Vianña, the Brazilian delegate, supported Pichot. As a close witness of the events, he could testify to the Executive's assiduity in its efforts to prevent the resignation (as we saw in chapter six, Vianna had himself tried in the autumn of 1982 to implement an on-site inspection of Soviet psychiatric facilities by Western psychiatrists, with the aim of solving the WPA's predicament). In any event, even at this stage perhaps all was not lost; the Assembly itself could now intervene, by appealing directly to the Russians to re-appraise their action.

The theme of this discussion was beginning to crystallize, and it seemed as if an *ad hoc* resolution was in the offing; namely that the Soviet Society—presumably the Czechs and the Bugarians too—should be invited to reconsider their decision and thereby return to the fold. A dissenting voice was then heard for the first time. Professor Rawnsley, representing the Royal College of Psychiatrists, argued that while the resignations were regrettable, they must be permitted to stand. Implicitly reminding his fellow delegates of the reason for the Russians' decision and the original British resolution calling for expulsion until the abuses had been brought to an end, Rawnsley expressed his preparedness to welcome back Soviet colleagues, but only when they had demonstrated an "amelioration" of the situation. This intervention was to prove crucial later by serving as the foundation of a formal resolution that would be voted on.

For the moment, however, it was only one of a series of contributions and several more were to follow. The Israeli delegate, for instance, felt that psychiatry and politics could, and should, be distinguished. A corollary was that the WPA should have trust in the psychiatric profession, but act against governments which tried to subvert it from its true purpose. His Egyptian counterpart was clearer and more to the point: he proposed a reversal of the Executive's decision to accept the USSR's resignation, and its re-enrolment in the WPA. He also reiterated a position he had advanced some months earlier—that the abuse of psychiatry was a matter for the UN Commission on Human Rights, not for the WPA (see chapter six). Other contributions, by the Cuban and Argentinian delegates, were variations on this theme.

The pendulum continued to swing back and forth, with one delegate arguing for acceptance of the resignation, another advocating that the Russians be urged to rejoin. The Canadian representative finally confronted the Assembly with a concrete reality, that a resignation is a resignation; the delegates had no choice but to accept it. Pichot, from the chair, proclaimed similarly: "The resignation is a fact." A compromise was, however, proposed by Pichot at this point: delegates who wished to table a motion concerning the Soviet withdrawal were free to do so; this would be voted on at the appropriate time.

The culmination to all this was that when the hour was late, and time pressing, the resolution submitted by member societies months before, as stipulated by the statutes, and the *ad hoc* resolutions invited by Pichot at the meeting itself, were dealt with *en bloc* in what can best be described as confused fashion. Indeed, there was a distinct incongruity between Berner's insistence some months before the Assembly on punctual submission of resolutions, and Pichot's virtually open-ended invitation to delegates to table resolutions during the Assembly itself. Considering the significance of both sets of motions, the hasty and disorderly discussion of them was decidedly inappropriate.

Confusion was the order of the day. At one point in the proceedings the Australasian delegate was convinced that he had voted for a procedural motion to link two resolutions of similar intent, whereas a French delegate was equally convinced that he had voted for a substantive resolution (the first of the pair). The disarray reached its zenith in the final minutes of the session when a resolution was passed, by a show of hands, to the effect that the WPA should abandon political activity, return to its customary medical, scientific and social pursuits, and inform the public about all this. No delegate queried the credentials of Dr William Sargant, the author of the motion. Subsequently, it emerged that Sargant's status, as both proposer and voter, was invalid, and his motion was as a result quietly annulled.

The voting on resolutions associated with Soviet abuse was subject to similar confusion. In a flurry of baffling events, the Australasian delegate precipitously withdrew his resolution. This had called for the WPA "To continue its efforts to bring to an end the misuse of psychiatry for political purposes within the Soviet Union and elsewhere in the world" and to support psychiatrists who had drawn attention to such misuse. His action followed a procedural muddle regarding a resolution submitted by three French member societies, similar in content but tougher in form. Its thrust was that the Soviet resignation had in no way resolved the issue of abuse; the WPA should therefore re-affirm its opposition to political psychiatry and welcome back the Russians only when abuse had ended and its victims and critics had been freed. The French delegates withdrew their motion under pressure. One of them, Dr Gérard Bles, reported later how bewildered he had been during this part of the session, and expressed his sense of frustration and resentment that the debate had been so mishandled.

At this point the American delegate indicated his preference for the motion that had been drafted earlier in the session by Professor Rawnsley. With the Australasian and French resolutions now withdrawn, Rawnsley's motion was promptly put to the vote. It read: "The World Psychiatric Association would welcome the return of the All-Union Society of Neuropathologists and Psychiatrists of the USSR to membership of the Association, but would expect sincere co-operation and concrete evidence beforehand of amelioration of the political abuse of psychiatry in the Soviet Union." The outcome was striking: 174 votes for, eighteen against, and 27 abstentions (the total of 219 votes cast represented the 57 paid-up member societies entitled to participate in the ballot; the remaining sixteen societies were either not present or had not paid their dues).

Considering the conflicting viewpoints expressed on whether or not the Soviet resignation should be accepted, the substantial majority for the resolution came as a surprise to many delegates. But an analysis of the voting strength of the main protagonists reveals why it was so resoundingly won. Societies from Britain, the United States, Australia and New Zealand, Canada and France—all of whom had argued for the resignation as a *fait accompli*—accounted for 91 votes (on the voting system see chapter two). The societies from Cuba, Argentina, East Germany, Egypt, Israel, Mexico and Brazil, which may have opposed the resolution, were in some cases not entitled to a vote because subscriptions had gone unpaid, but in any event would have rated only eighteen votes between them.

Another explanation for the overwhelming support of the resolution undoubtedly lay in its moderate wording. Unlike the French resolution, which was tough in tone and called for the cessation of political psychiatry, and the Australasian resolution, which failed to mention the potential return of the Russians to the WPA in the event of a change in policy, the British motion was more conciliatory, being designed to win wide endorsement. The phrase "The World Psychiatric Association would welcome the return . . ." was unambiguous, and also had a ring of optimism about it—that such a prospect was not altogether absurd or fanciful. Then the conditions set for their return—"sincere co-operation and concrete evidence beforehand of amelioration"—were not so utopian or ideal as to be utterly unattainable. Overall, the terminology expressed a call for Soviet goodwill. As long as it was accepted that the Russians had a case to answer, the resolution could be viewed as reasonable and fair, even if its mild tone did not correspond to the suffering of the dissenters interned in mental hospitals. In the light of the above result, the resolutions calling for Soviet expulsion (submitted by the British and the Danes) or suspension (proposed by the Americans) were withdrawn. These had intentionally been left on the agenda at the request of the proposers lest an *ad hoc* motion seeking Soviet re-enrolment was introduced during the Assembly (see chapter six).

A variegated assortment of *ad hoc* resolutions proposed by, among others, the Brazilian, Israeli and Cuban delegates, and relating to the Soviet issue, were either withdrawn, or discarded after a vote because most delegates had abstained. For example, an Israeli motion, vague and incomprehensible, at least to judge by the delegates we consulted, received a mere five votes, with four against.

The inept treatment by Professor Pichot of the Assembly's debate on the Soviet matter, which had led to such utter confusion, was later matched by Professor Berner's handling of another prominent item on the agenda—the proposal to confer honorary membership of the WPA on Dr Anatoly Koryagin. As we noted in chapter five, Koryagin had already been awarded membership of both the Royal College of Psychiatrists and the American Psychiatric Association in recognition of his exceptional courage in promoting the ethical practice of psychiatry. He had also won, together with an Argentinian physicist, the Scientific Freedom and Responsibility Award of the prestigious American Association for the Advancement of Science, in March 1983. Against this background Berner's statement to the Assembly that no WPA precedent existed for conferring honorary membership on a psychiatrist who was not a scientist, sounded mean and even disingenuous. It was also factually wrong, as Koryagin held a PhD and had also written research reports.

Berner's attitude from the moment the French Association of Psychiatrists in Private Practice had first proposed in May 1981 that Koryagin be honoured was one of reluctance and ambivalence. Later that year he and his colleagues on the Executive declared their inability to take a clear position on the issue and therefore advised the French to submit an official motion for debate at Vienna.[5] At first sight, this might seem to have been a reasonable recommendation. But we should note that in terms of the statutes there was no justification for the Executive's hesitancy: "Honorary membership may be conferred upon individuals considered so worthy. Recommendations may be sent to the Executive Committee, which will submit its choice to the General Assembly for approval."

Considering that the Executive was in the process of preparing a list of fourteen other psychiatrists for approval by the Assembly (in the case of eleven it would appear simply for being the president of a society which had hosted a WPA conference), its evasive and vacillating behaviour *vis-à-vis* Koryagin was revealing.

The Executive's clumsy actions were in fact easily explicable. Since Koryagin's arrest in 1981 he had, as we saw in chapters three and six, become the main symbol of professional opposition to the Soviet abuse, the embodiment of the unswerving commitment to the ethical practice of psychiatry, whatever the personal cost might be. Berner almost certainly concluded that conferment of honorary membership would be interpreted by many societies as a political, partial act, and might undermine his own efforts to gain Soviet co-operation in an investigation of the abuse. He was sharply reminded of that prospect in November 1981 when the East Germans lodged a protest at the possibility of Koryagin being honoured, declaring that this would, because of its political nature, constitute an abuse of the distinction.

The upshot of the Koryagin episode was the inclusion on the Assembly's agenda of the original French resolution. It read:

1. The General Assembly of the WPA nominates as an honorary individual member Dr Anatoly Koryagin of Kharkov, who has demonstrated in his struggle against the perversion of psychiatry for non-medical purposes, professional conscience, courage and devotion to duty, all in exceptional measure. In doing this he has acted in

accordance with the principles of the Declaration of Hawaii, adopted unanimously by the WPA General Assembly in 1977, and with the Charter of Psychiatry published in 1980 by the French Association of Psychiatrists in Private Practice and strongly supported by Anatoly Koryagin.

2. The General Assembly of the WPA asks the USSR's All-Union Society of Neuropathologists and Psychiatrists to intervene urgently on behalf of Dr Koryagin with the competent authorities, so that Dr Koryagin, who has been imprisoned since 13 February 1981, may be released without delay and allowed, as a practitioner who does honour to the medical community of his country, to resume his practice.[6]

A much briefer resolution, from the American Psychiatric Association, to the effect that Koryagin should be made an honorary member, had also been submitted. Although it was unclear which motion was being voted on, the result was a convincing two to one majority, with 119 votes for, and 58 against.

The Assembly also addressed itself to the future of the Review Committee. The WPA's Working Group on the statutes had proposed that both this committee and the Ethics Committee should be converted from working groups of the Executive into permanent, constitutionalized bodies.[7] This alteration in status was clearly necessary in the wake of the Soviet long-standing refusal to recognize the Review Committee's legal basis (see chapter four). Once embedded in the statutes, the Committee would enjoy the authority to function autonomously and would, at least theoretically, command the respect of all member societies. The proposed new statute was brief and to the point: "The Committee to Review the Abuse of Psychiatry will be appointed by the Executive Committee and shall have the responsibility to review individual complaints. Its activities will not be limited in time."

Apart from modifying the Review Committee's legal and temporal status, the working group recommended a third fundamental change, the widening of its remit to encompass the investigation not only of cases of political psychiatry but also of other forms of abuse. The rationale offered was ostensibly pragmatic in nature, and was based on the claim that submission of complaints of abuse of a non-political type had increased to a point where they imposed a considerable burden on the secretary-general. Because of its original mandate, the Review Committee was not empowered to deal with these cases. However, since it had the expertise and experience to investigate all forms of abuse, its operational guidelines should now be extended to cover any complaints, "regardless of their specific nature".

This proposed remit was so vague as to be almost meaningless; the only possible clue to its dimensions was a reference to abuse of a "private, a professional, or a political nature". Mr Anthony McNulty, the legal expert chiefly responsible for devising the original guidelines (see chapter four), was rather mystified by the terminology, but expressed the view that new guidelines could be formulated, and that the submission of complaints via member societies only, as hitherto, would tend to filter out inappropriate cases, and thus save the Committee from being inundated.[8] Many delegates with whom we raised the issue informally in Vienna felt that a widened remit was in principle a desirable step but shared a concern about the practicability and workability of a committee with such undefined boundaries. One of their main concerns centred around adequate financial backing; for the committee to work efficiently with an increased work-load, it would have to have the wherewithal.

As for the discussion in the Assembly of the three changes proposed for the Review Committee—regarding its constitutional status, permanency and widened remit—an assortment of views was expressed. These ranged from a proposal for its total abolition to one for its constitutional and financial reinforcement. The former came predictably from the East German delegate. His cardinal point was that the political activities of the WPA, as reflected in the work of the Review Committee, had brought the Association into disrepute. Delegates had to accept the inevitable conclusion that the Committee had been a failure; moreover, it had led to the frittering away of valuable resources. It ought to be dissolved. The Egyptian delegate was equally keen on dissolution. Another proposal came from the American and Norwegian delegates, who suggested that the Review Committee and Ethics Committee could be combined, but it remained unclear whether the new body would continue to investigate individual complaints or deal only "theoretically" with the subject of unethical psychiatry. Could not the Executive take over the function of the Review Committee, asked a delegate from Spain. Could the WPA not pass the "problem" over the UN, suggested a French representative. The only delegate who argued forcibly for the retention of the Committee was another French delegate, Dr Bles. He called on the WPA to continue supporting it, and to increase its resources. The primary reason for its paralysis hitherto had been a lack of statutory status; the proposed constitutionalization would therefore enhance its role.

With this mélange of views, it was no surprise that a vote was ultimately called to decide the Committee's fate, and specifically the triple-barrelled proposals for change. Perhaps unexpected was the support they received—158 votes for, 43 against. Apparently, despite any misgivings or reservations societies might have harboured about the Committee, its work was deemed necessary. Although there was no substantial discussion regarding the widened remit, delegates no doubt assumed that appropriate guidelines would be formulated in due course to cover the extended functions.

The question of a widened remit for the Review Committee arose in another context during the Assembly. In 1979 the Royal College of Psychiatrists (joined later by the Australasians) had proposed that the Committee's mandate should be extended to include the investigation not only of alleged victims of psychiatric abuse, but also of individuals who had been punished for publicizing it. The College had in mind a psychiatrist like Semyon Gluzman who, as we saw in chapters one and five, was then serving a ten-year sentence solely because he had openly criticized the Soviet abuse. Professor Berner had sought clarification of the College's proposal, and pointed out the legal snags which would confront the Review Committee with such an extended remit.[9] Since the persecuted critics of abuse were usually punished through the courts, the Committee would necessarily have to become entangled with the legal machinery of the countries involved. The result of this interchange was a revised proposal which called on the WPA to oppose the misuse of psychiatry "as well as the persecution of individuals who bring this abuse to the attention of the world . . .".

An American-sponsored resolution, narrower than the British-Australasian one in the sense that it was confined to psychiatrists, but wider inasmuch as it referred to their vulnerability to abuse generally ("The WPA resolves to establish a mechanism for review of alleged abuses of psychiatrists.") had met with the same cautious response from Berner.[10] The Americans thereupon recommended a specific procedure which might be pursued: the proposed committee, which would be akin to the Review Committee, would tackle a case of the alleged abuse of a psychiatrist by requesting the member society of the country involved to conduct an *in situ* investigation, and to report its findings to the WPA. Such action would clearly demonstrate the Association's concern for any of its members who were subject to unjustified persecution (for whatever reason). Presumably this approach—essentially humanitarian—would circumvent any legal hurdles.

In the event, the version suggested by the British and Australasians was put to the vote and won the Assembly's support (the ballot was curiously by a show of hands with 21 societies for and five against). The American resolution was inexplicably withdrawn. It was apparently felt that a similar motion had already been passed and that Berner's caution was warranted. Thus the WPA had committed itself to oppose the punishment of critics of abuse, whether psychiatrists or lay people.

How this would be translated into action by the Executive remained to be seen. Pious, abstract statements of the "sin is bad" variety would probably be of little value. That an initiative could be taken for a specific case was, however, realistic and precedented. The British and American Special Committees on Abuse had shown this in their regular activities on behalf of members of the Moscow Working Commission; so had many other member-societies, particularly those which had campaigned on behalf of Gluzman and Koryagin (see chapter five).

With the resolutions out of the way the next major item of Assembly business was the election of a new Executive (and new Committee*). Although the Executive takes care of the Association's affairs for no less than six years, that is for the period between two World Congresses, its election in the past had never been viewed as particularly noteworthy. The procedure had been straightforward—nominations were invited from member societies and from members of the Committee, these were studied by the Executive, and a slate prepared by the latter for automatic acceptance by the Assembly.

On the occasion of the Vienna congress, two developments ensued which suggested that the election would be taken much more seriously. First, the Executive had prepared two alternative slates of candidates (instead of the customary one) and, second, the Americans had requested that voting should be for each office individually, not by slate.[11] In conjunction, these changes would facilitate a more democratic process, even though the selection of candidates to be voted on still remained in the hands of the Executive.

During the conference itself, however, more radical developments were to occur, and then quite unexpectedly. When the two lists of candidates were appraised informally by a group of delegates from Britain, the United States, Canada, Australasia, Sweden, Norway, Denmark and France, a consensus was soon reached that the range of choice was slender. Furthermore, there was a shared concern that the candidates nominated for the two key posts of president and secretary-general might not lead the Association well *vis-à-vis* the issue of abuse.

At this point it is useful to distinguish between two main bodies of opinion regarding the WPA's future path that had evolved since Honolulu and which crystallized in Vienna. We have alluded to these two contrasting positions in our account of the debates on the Soviet Society's resignation and on the constitutionalization of the Review Committee. One path might well have borne the signpost: "To the original scientific purpose of the WPA"; the other path's sign might have read: "To the WPA's commitment to the abolition of psychiatric abuse." Although these positions were not entirely contradic-

---

* The Committee consists of 24 members plus the retiring Executive, and serves as an advisory body to the new Executive, most importantly just preceding the meeting of the General Assembly.

tory, an emphasis on one would inevitably be at the expense of the other.

The first position was clearly favoured by the WPA leadership and had influenced the Association's policy in recent years. It is best embodied in a key paragraph of Berner's official report to the 1983 General Assembly:

> The officers that have administered the WPA during the last election period have been obliged, through a mandate from the last General Assembly, to countenance open confrontation between the national member societies, and have thus been unable to prevent the ultimate outcome of that confrontation, namely the withdrawal of psychiatric societies from membership with the Association. In consequence the Association's image has been seriously impaired and its international influence has decreased. A most dangerous precedent has been set, moreover, which does not augur well for the future of the organization.[12]

In other words, unity should be the foremost priority; criticism of a member society, however justified, could lead only to schism and disintegration; and the WPA should revert to its former scientific purposes.

Those holding the alternative position—essentially the nine member societies that had proposed the ejection of the Russians—argued that while the WPA should continue to pursue its customary scientific interests, it should view ethical concerns as paramount. As John Grigor, the Australasian delegate, put it, "The WPA must take a clear and continuing line; otherwise we stand for nothing".[13] Paul Chodoff, the American psychiatrist who had unequivocally criticized the Soviet practices at the Honolulu congress (see chapter two), insisted that "to hide behind the rationalization of dialogue was tantamount to moral cowardice"; the WPA would be guilty of the "sin of omission" if it failed to voice its opposition.[13]

Upholders of this view argued that the campaign to combat abuse, wherever it might occur, took precedence over the attempt to preserve the WPA at all costs. Moreover, the Association could afford to lose members such as the Russians and their supporters. Indeed, in reacting sturdily to the abuse issue it would acquire a more impressive image. Further, temporary ostracism could pave the way for a resolution to the problem by convincing Soviet political authorities that ditching the use of psychiatry as a punitive weapon was in their interests.

The picture was not as clear-cut as the above schematic account suggests. Running between the two paths lay several connecting tracks. One track is epitomized by the attitude adopted by the Canadian delegate. At a forum held during the congress and devoted to an open discussion on abuse (it was sponsored by the American, British, Canadian, Danish and Australasian societies), Dr Quentin Rae-Grant argued for an intermediate position, namely that reprimand of and dialogue with the Russians could go hand in hand (see chapter six). The abuse was undoubtedly a fact and had to be condemned, but the pivotal question was how to bring it to a halt. Dialogue was a crucial tool and on occasion one was obliged to resort to it even when the partner involved offended one's sensibilities, and the progress achieved was slow and modest. Ostracism, by contrast, was a blunt instrument with as many negative as positive effects. A practical recommendation followed: the WPA should set up a body like the Review Committee to maintain a line of communication with Russian colleagues.[14]

If we bear these different viewpoints in mind, the significance of the election of the new office-bearers becomes obvious. The Executive would hold office until 1989 and it was probable that during this extended period the Soviet affair would reach its finale, whatever form it took. Most candidates presented for election by the retiring Executive bore the stamp of the first position described above, that is the preservation of the WPA by concentrating on its scientific functions and relegating the abuse issue to a circumscribed, limited sphere. For example, Peter Berner was one of the two nominees for the presidency. Of the two candidates for the post of secretary-general, one was unknown with respect to both his opinion about the Russian problem and his experience as an administrator but was regarded as closely allied to Berner; the other had a few months before expressed opinions which clearly bore the stamp of "WPA first, abuse second".

We mentioned earlier the realization by delegates from

Britain, North America, Australasia, France and Scandinavia (excluding Finland) that the range of choice for the two pivotal posts of president and secretary-general was exceedingly narrow. At an informal meeting a mere 24 hours before the election, the idea was raised of a write-in candidate for the office of secretary-general in order to widen the selection.[15] The Scandinavians had originally nominated a distinguished Danish psychiatrist, Fini Schulsinger, for an executive post and they now recommended that his candidacy should be pressed. After his credentials had been evaluated, a rapid consensus was reached about his suitability: he was an eminent scientist, a proven administrator, and resolute in his opposition to political psychiatry. Less clear were the group's thoughts about who should be supported for president, although a feeling did emerge that Berner's continuing presence on the Executive would provide for continuity, and together with Schulsinger constitute a balanced force.

The election at the Assembly was almost as chaotic as had been the debate on the resolutions. A secret vote, for example, was required to decide which office should be voted on first. Some candidates originally selected by the retiring Executive withdrew from the race while Schulsinger's candidacy was added. The first upshot of these changes was the election of the Dane as secretary-general by a convincing majority. The election of the president came next, and with it utter confusion. Berner declared that in the absence of any knowledge about Schulsinger's likely policies for the WPA, he was withdrawing his candidacy. Since Schulsinger, an eleventh-hour write-in candidate, was not present, various moves were made to resolve the predicament, ranging from a suggestion for an adjournment to a concerted endeavour to persuade Berner to reconsider his decision. But he would not budge. Several substitute candidates were then nominated but immediately declined. Ultimately, the contest between three psychiatrists—from Iceland, Holland and Greece—was won by the last, Professor Costas Stefanis, with a handsome margin. Stefanis had played an active role in WPA affairs, especially in his role as chairman of the Ethics Committee. His attitude to the Soviet issue was not dissimilar to that of Berner; probably it was held even more tenaciously. As we noted in the previous chapter, he had advocated at the

Executive meeting in Buenos Aires in March 1983 the dissolution of the Review Committe on the grounds that it was
unworkable. He had also expressed the view that the unity of
the Association was the foremost priority. He thus clearly trod
the first of the two paths we outlined earlier in the chapter.

At a press conference the following day Stefanis was,
perhaps understandably, cautious in his replies to a flurry of
questions about his future priorities for the WPA.[16] The
Association would have to strive to regain a sense of unity; at
least nothing should be done to deepen the rifts that existed
between member societies. What strategies could be employed
to achieve "détente", he candidly did not know at this early
juncture. How he would tackle the problem of Soviet abuse
and the question of the Russians' readmission to the WPA was
left unanswered. No real clues emerged from this first public
appearance as to the type of leadership Stefanis would
provide. This was not surprising—Stefanis had been elected
less than a day before and had not conferred with his newly-
elected fellows on the Executive, especially Fini Schulsinger,
who would be a key figure in future policy-making.

Who were the other new office-bearers? Professor Pal
Juhasz, the president of the Hungarian Psychiatric Society,
was elected to the vice-presidency. His victory by a thumping
majority reflected a widespread conviction that the presence
of a psychiatrist from Eastern Europe was essential for the
future welfare of the WPA (in fact there had been such
representation since 1971). The nomination of a Hungarian,
and specifically of Juhasz, had been a sagacious move on the
part of the retiring Executive. Hungarian psychiatry was a
relatively autonomous profession, not wholly subservient to
governmental and Soviet pressure. A reflection of this could
be seen in the fact that, unlike Czechoslovakia and Bulgaria,
the Hungarian Society had neither resigned from the WPA
nor withdrawn Juhasz's candidacy. But its autonomy was far
from complete. As we saw in chapter six, Juhasz had supported the Soviet position in a letter to the American Psychiatric
Association earlier in the year. The timing of this communication was highly revealing—on the very day of a visit by
Professor Morozov to Budapest on his way home from
deliberations with the WPA Secretariat in Vienna. Morozov
had undoubtedly pressed the Hungarians to lend their sup-

port. That this may have been given reluctantly is suggested by the tone used by Juhasz in his letter. Unlike the correspondence from the Russians, Czechs and Bulgarians, the Hungarians were relatively courteous and discreet.

Juhasz's actions in supporting the Russians and accepting nomination for the Executive were like walking a tight-rope. His actual election would call for more of the same. Further pressure from the Soviet Society was more than likely but would have to be off set by the striving of Hungarian psychiatrists for a relatively independent posture and Juhasz's need to display a sense of co-operativeness with his fellow Executive members.

The other three members elected—Mel Sabshin from the United States, Neils Reisby from Denmark, and J. Costa e Silva from Brazil—were spared Juhasz's dilemma of dual loyalty. The first two had shown in recent years a consistently strong commitment to a role for the WPA as "ethical ombudsman", and could be expected to maintain their position. The Brazilian was a relatively unknown quantity.

With the Executive elected, and a few other items of business attended to, the Assembly completed its work. As the delegates emerged from the session the question uppermost in their minds was what shape the WPA would be in by the time the Assembly next convened in six years' time. Would the unity to which Professor Stefanis had referred be re-established? Would the Russians and their supporters seek re-enrolment in the Association? Could the Review Committee continue to investigate Soviet cases of abuse in the absence of the Soviet Society? Would the Committee begin to examine other forms of abuse? Would the Association take initiatives on behalf of those who had been punished for their criticism of political psychiatry? These were but some of the questions preoccupying delegates and other psychiatrists concerned with the future welfare of the WPA and indeed of world psychiatry.

Some pointers for answering such questions were, perhaps, already available. The Assembly debates had lacked discipline, but not led to the WPA's dismemberment by centrifugal forces. The active opponents of Soviet abuse had won the key votes handsomely, but at the expense of softening their central resolution. The new Executive contained—if partly by chance—a rough balance of viewpoints on the Soviet issue. In other words, enough elements of compromise had emerged for disaster to be averted and hope for the future maintained.

For unity to be fully restored, however, much would depend on the reactions of the Soviet political and psychiatric authorities to the decisions taken in Vienna, in particular to the resolution proposing the conditional return of Russian psychiatrists to the WPA. The same *ad hoc* working group of the Central Committee which we hypothesized in chapter seven had been responsible for the Russian decision to quit, would in all likelihood monitor the events of Vienna and their immediate aftermath, conduct a searching review òf policy, and then take the appropriate political decisions.

One potential policy, which we might aptly label the "optimistic scenario", is best outlined in terms of the rationale the Central Committee's working group might favour. The gist of it is as follows:

First and foremost, the political abuse of psychiatry is not an essential instrument of our rule. As the president of the Royal College of Psychiatrists has correctly said of us, "I don't really believe that this policy is vital to their interests. They could deal with dissenters in other ways if they wanted." And indeed we do—we sack them, exile them, imprison them, deport them abroad, and so on. The alarming precedent of our first *de facto* expulsion from an international organization may lead on to action against us in other international forums, as Soviet psychiatry is increasingly seen as a new version of the Lysenkoism which destroyed our reputation in biology for a generation, and the trend could spread to other professional fields like physics, mathematics, and the Churches, where our vulnerability is already clear.

So now we must do what we did to Lysenko and his empire in the 1960s and prepare for the following reforms. Morozov, Snezhnevsky and their colleagues must be quietly retired or demoted, and replaced by psychiatrists respected abroad. The theoretical and organizational stranglehold of the former on Soviet psychiatry must be gradually ended by a range of personnel changes in institutes, hospitals, medical schools, ministerial bodies, publishing-houses, societies and journals. The dissenters interned in mental hospitals must be unobtrusively and gradually released. And Dr Koryagin and his colleagues must be quietly freed from imprisonment.

All these developments will take time, as of course no clear-cut admission of past guilt can be made and everything must seem to be happening routinely and naturally, not in response to foreign pressure. But the policy must be undertaken. For if it is not, our forced resignation from the WPA is likely to be the first of a series of international reversals—in the UN Commission of Human Rights, in other UN bodies, in professional associations, and in our international diplomacy as a whole.

Obviously, to conclude, anyone concerned about the interwoven issues fates of dissenters victimized by political psychiatry, the future of the psychiatric profession in the Soviet Union, and the future welfare of the WPA, would heave a sigh of relief if this "optimistic scenario" came to fruition. Its failure to do so could only lead to further tragic consequences for a profession bedevilled by dissension and fragmentation. Will reason ultimately prevail, and bring to an end an unsavoury saga in the annals of psychiatry?

APPENDIX I

The Declaration of Hawaii, 1983

This code of ethics was adopted by the General Assembly of the World Psychiatric Association in July 1977 (see chapter two). Minor amendments were approved by the Assembly in July 1983.

Ever since the dawn of culture, ethics has been an essential part of the healing art. It is the view of the World Psychiatric Association that due to conflicting loyalties and expectations of both physicians and patients in contemporary society and the delicate nature of the therapist-patient relationship, high ethical standards are especially important for those involved in the science and practice of psychiatry as a medical specialty. These guidelines have been delineated in order to promote close adherence to those standards and to prevent misuse of psychiatric concepts, knowledge and technology.

Since the psychiatrist is a member of society as well as a practitioner of medicine, he or she must consider the ethical implications specific to psychiatry as well as the ethical demands on all physicians and the societal responsibility of every man and woman.

Even though ethical behaviour is based on the individual psychiatrist's conscience and personal judgement, written guidelines are needed to clarify the profession's ethical implications.

Therefore, the General Assembly of the World Psychiatric Association has approved these ethical guidelines for psychiatrists, having in mind the great differences in cultural backgrounds, and in legal, social and economic conditions which exist in the various countries of the world. It should be understood that the World Psychiatric Association views these guidelines to be minimal requirements for ethical standards of the psychiatric profession.

1. The aim of psychiatry is to treat mental illness and to promote mental health. To the best of his or her ability, consistent with accepted scientific knowledge and ethical principles, the psychiatrist shall serve the best interests of the patient and be also concerned for the common good and a just allocation of health resources. To fulfil these aims requires continuous research and continual education of health care personnel, patients and the public.

2. Every psychiatrist should offer to the patient the best available therapy to his knowledge and if accepted must treat him or her with the solicitude and respect due to the dignity of all human beings. When the psychiatrist is responsible for treatment given by others he owes them competent supervision and education. Whenever there is a need, or whenever a reasonable request is forthcoming from the patient, the psychiatrist should seek the help of another colleague.

3. The psychiatrist aspires for a therapeutic relationship that is founded on mutual agreement. At its optimum it requires trust, confidentiality, co-operation and mutual responsibility. Such a relationship may not be possible to establish with some patients. In that case, contact should be established with a relative or other person close to the patient. If and when a relationship is established for purposes other than therapeutic, such as in forensic psychiatry, its nature must be thoroughly explained to the person concerned.

4. The psychiatrist should inform the patient of the nature of the condition, therapeutic procedures, including possible alternatives, and of the possible outcome. This information must be offered in a considerate way and the patient must be given the opportunity to choose between appropriate and available methods.

5. No procedure shall be performed nor treatment given against or independent of a patient's own will, unless, because of mental illness, the patient cannot form a judgement as to what is in his or her best interest and without which treatment serious impairment is likely to occur to the patient or others.

6. As soon as the conditions for compulsory treatment no longer apply, the psychiatrist should release the patient from the compulsory nature of the treatment and if further therapy is necessary should obtain voluntary consent. The psychiatrist should inform the patient and/or relatives or meaningful others, of the existence of mechanisms of appeal for the detention and for any other complaints related to his or her well-being.

7. The psychiatrist must never use his professional possibilities to violate the dignity or human rights of any individual or group and should never let inappropriate personal desires, feelings, prejudices or beliefs interfere with the treatment. The psychiatrist must on no account utilize the tools of his profession, once the absence of psychiatric illness has been established. If a patient or some third party demands actions contrary to scientific knowledge or ethical principles the psychiatrist must refuse to co-operate.

8. Whatever the psychiatrist has been told by the patient, or has noted during examination or treatment, must be kept confidential unless the patient relieves the psychiatrist from this obligation, or to prevent serious harm to self or others makes disclosure necessary. In these cases, however, the patient should be informed of the breach of confidentiality.

9. To increase and propagate psychiatric knowledge and skill requires participation of the patients. Informed consent must, however, be obtained before presenting a patient to a class and, if possible, also when a case-history is released for scientific publication, whereby all reasonable measures must be taken to preserve the dignity and anonymity of the patient and to safeguard the personal reputation of the subject. The patient's participation must be voluntary, after full information has been given of the aim, procedures, risks and inconveniences of a research project and there must always be a reasonable relationship between calculated risks or inconveniences and the benefit of the study. In clinical research every subject must retain and exert all his rights as a patient. For children and other patients who cannot themselves give informed consent, this should be obtained from the legal

next-of-kin. Every patient or research subject is free to withdraw for any reason at any time from any voluntary treatment and from any teaching or research program in which he or she participates. This withdrawal, as well as any refusal to enter a program, must never influence the psychiatrist's efforts to help the patient or subject.

10. The psychiatrist should stop all therapeutic, teaching or research programs that may evolve contrary to the principles of this Declaration.

APPENDIX II

How Can Foreigners Help the Victims of Soviet Psychiatric Abuse?
by Vyacheslav Bakhmin

In 1978–1979 a lively debate took place in Psychiatric News, *the fortnightly paper of the American Psychiatric Association, about the most effective ways of combating Soviet psychiatric abuse and helping its victims. Much of the debate was read in Moscow by the Working Commission to Investigate the Use of Psychiatry for Political Purposes (see chapter three), a leading member of which, Vyacheslav Bakhmin, contributed the following letter, published in* Psychiatric News *on 15 June 1979.*

I have had the opportunity (rare in our circumstances) to read a series of letters in *Psychiatric News** which debate the most effective methods of combating abuses of psychiatry in the Soviet Union. As a member of the Working Commission to Investigate the Use of Psychiatry for Political Purposes I would like, if with some delay, to express some views on this debate, views which are broadly shared by my colleagues in the Commission.

In a letter with which I agree on many points, M. H. Nelson, MD, noted quite correctly that any attempt to act is better than complete inaction (*PN*, 20 October 1978).

---

* The whole debate involved contributions by J. Masserman (2 June 1978), Masserman and P. Chodoff (15 September 1978), M. Nelson (20 October 1978), J. Davidson and J. Hochman (3 November 1978), Masserman, H. Breen, H. Rome, J. Skirgaudas and A. Stone (1 December 1978), Nelson and H. Merskey (19 January 1979), J. Wortis, H. Fireside and Masserman (16 February 1979), A. Halpern (6 April 1979), Chodoff (19 October 1979, A. Voloshanovich (7 December 1979), S. Bloch (15 February 1980), J. Wortis and T. Brocher (2 May 1980), and S. Bloch and P. Reddaway (17 October 1980).

On the other hand, to those who favour "quiet diplomacy" and private professional contacts I must say that in my view this approach calls for many caveats. First, it is not effective unless there is already a broad and vigorous *public* campaign. The authorities—who are accustomed to lying and hypocrisy, and try to spread their influence all over the world—are very sensitive to world opinion (even when it does not appear so on the surface). Only under pressure from broad campaigns of protest, or out of the desire to prevent their development, do the authorities make concessions to "quiet diplomacy" (not surprisingly this method usually works to rescue only well-known people).

The method of private contacts should not be overestimated. Sometimes it does indeed give positive results—but only in specific cases. The abuse as a whole remains unaffected. Moreover, an illusion is created that the situation has improved, while hundreds of completely unknown people continue to suffer in psychiatric prisons, and millions of ordinary people remain in ignorance of the shameful practice of psychiatric terror.

It seems to me that quiet diplomacy is also in some ways ethically unacceptable. It should be left to politicians. It belongs to the sphere of trade-offs and secret negotiations. Such an approach is often dominated by professional and group interests, not by humanitarianism and the desire to resist evil. For some reason it is always forgotten that private negotiations and contacts of this sort are usually unequal, resembling a game in which one of the players is a cheat. On the one side there are psychiatrists concerned about the prestige of their profession, speaking frankly about their problems and doubts. On the other are psychiatric politicians who do, and always will do, what they are ordered to, and who will happily distort facts and deceive, while simultaneously considering themselves patriots.

Not surprisingly, some Western psychiatrists are later upset, and assert that they were misunderstood and their statements were distorted. As M. H. Nelson correctly writes, "Private efforts are very often used as publicity to legitimize unethical practice." I would say that the authorities *never* let such chances pass.

The experience of our Commission shows that "punitive

psychiatry" in the Soviet Union fears, above all, publicity. And especially publicity reaching psychiatric colleagues, who cannot so easily be diverted by references to their lack of medical qualifications. Precisely for this reason the leaders of Soviet psychiatry reacted with such morbid defensiveness to the decisions of the WPA congress in Honolulu. For the same reason steps were taken so remarkably quickly to try to discredit the psychiatric reports of our consultant psychiatrist, Dr A. Voloshanovich.

Fearing exposure of their activities, these psychiatric politicians speak in the name of all Soviet psychiatrists, and try to appeal to the feelings of professional solidarity of psychiatrists in other countries, and in this way to turn them into their collaborators.

What methods, then, are most acceptable for honest psychiatrists in the West who appreciate the danger for mankind of psychiatric abuse and want to help the victims of "punitive medicine"? The methods can be varied—one should only not keep quiet and pretend the problem doesn't exist.

In our opinion one of the most effective methods is for pyschiatrists to send various sorts of official and private enquiries, letters and petitions, professionally composed and relating to each specific known case. These letters and petitions are best sent to those particular organizations and individuals who are directly responsible for the abuses. At the same time it is essential to inform psychiatrists and the public about both the letters and replies to them. In this way the publicity generated excludes the possibility of outright mendacity by officials (of the sort used in the Klebanov case).

The absence of replies to professionally composed enquiries of this sort is, also, in itself indicative.

30 March 1979

APPENDIX III

Open Letter to World Psychiatrists from Dr Anatoly Koryagin

This letter was written in summer 1981 and smuggled out of a Perm region labour camp in the Urals. Dr Koryagin was psychiatric consultant to the Working Commision—see chapter three.

Dear Colleagues,

I am writing to you from Soviet political labour camp No. 37 in which the authorities have incarcerated me on the basis of a perfectly absurd, stereotyped charge of anti-Soviet agitation and propaganda.

As I did not at all have the intentions which the court arbitrarily attributed to me, I can only regard the judgement as an act of revenge against a specialist who has fulfilled his doctor's duty by obeying the voice of conscience and not subordinating it to the purposes of the KGB. It is only because I examined some dissidents who had been persecuted through psychiatric means, and because I communicated the results of my investigations to the world community, that I was sentenced to seven years of imprisonment followed by five years of exile in a remote area.

Earlier, all the members of the Working Commission to Investigate the Use of Psychiatry for Political Purposes had also been sentenced.

Dear friends, let there be no doubt about the fact that the Soviet authorities have turned our most humane branch of medicine into an instrument for achieving a main aim of their internal policy—the suppression of dissent in our country. Psychiatry in the totalitarian Soviet state brings not only succour to the ill but also harm to the healthy.

The facts about the use of psychiatry to suppress dissidents in the USSR have now angered the world community for some years. At the world psychiatric congress in Honolulu in 1977

Soviet psychiatry was condemned as punitive. Since then, however, the dirty stain on its white coat has spread still further. Thousands of dissenters have spent time in psychiatric hospitals since that time, and many with names that mean little to anyone are still there now.

Continuous criticism has forced the Soviet authorities to change their tactics somewhat. The main weight of psychiatric persecution, the scale of which has grown still more, has now been redirected to the provinces. Here the "success" of punitive psychiatrists is, as before, assured by the KGB and the Procuracy, while in the central institutions (e.g. the Serbsky Institute) the number being ruled mentally ill has been considerably reduced. In this way the authorities are trying to achieve their dual purpose; to suppress all dissent in the outlying areas of the country, and also to rehabilitate Soviet psychiatry in the eyes of the world community: the opinions of foreign colleagues are formed in the course of contacts with, after all, representatives of the central institutions.

Questions about the direct involvement of particular Soviet psychiatrists in the anti-humane role which the Soviet authorities have assigned to their profession can be answered clearly. First among the guilty, without doubt, are those doctors who diagnose non-existent illnesses in healthy people. But no less guilty are those leading psychiatrists of our country who—at the top administrative level—organize and facilitate the execution of this ugly policy.

Not surprisingly, the leaders of Soviet psychiatry do everything possible, and more, to conceal the shameful facts and to whitewash, at one go, both themselves and the KGB. A. Snezhnevsky, G. Morozov, E. Babayan and others have "covered their names with glory" by making absurdly stupid statements at international forums and in the press, where they hold forth about "the sallies of bourgeois propaganda" and the "humanism" of Soviet psychiatry, while carefully not replying to questions about particular individuals whose cases have been documented by the Working Commission. They talk a lot about "medical confidentiality" while in fact shamelessly exploiting that principle in order to conceal a system based on the "creative" procedures of oppressors from psychiatry and the KGB.

Remember, colleagues, that all contacts with foreign psychiatrists are used by the leaders of Soviet psychiatry as a means to rehabilitate themselves. They widely and untiringly advertise such contacts, trying to convince everyone that they are accepted internationally not as violators of medical ethics and norms, but as colleagues and equal partners.

The importance of the USSR in the world is well-known. Nonetheless, the interests of High Policy and the natural desire for professional contacts should not weaken in any of us a feeling of common guilt and responsibility for the lives of those people who are suffering at the hands of psychiatrists. Their crippled careers (and sometimes health too) call out for effective sorts of resistance to the evildoing, for constant, widespread and public exposure of those responsible, for their boycotting.

Is it tolerable that the World Psychiatric Association (WPA) should have member societies from countries where psychiatry is assigned punitive functions? Is it ethical to have any professional contacts with the official psychiatric representatives of those countries? Has the time not come to form an international commission of psychiatrists on medical diagnosis, the effectiveness of whose action would be ensured by the states represented by the WPA? These and other questions could become subjects for debate in psychiatric forums if psychiatrists developed a widespread interest in resolving the problem of psychiatric oppression of dissenters in various countries.

Soviet politicians have always, and specially recently, trumpeted across the world their appeals to live in peace, friendship and co-operation with others. It is, however, impossible to believe that politicians who keep their own people deprived of all rights and incarcerate critics in concentration camps and psychiatric prisons, really care about the happiness of all peoples. Only since the Madrid conference [on European security and co-operation] began [1980], hundreds of Soviet dissenters have been imprisoned or interned in mental hospitals. The authorities have shown special hatred towards those who have exposed their repressive policy and tried to counter its implementation.

In my case the court ruled my activity to be "incompatible with the calling of a Soviet scientist" and demanded that I be deprived of my Doctor of Science degree. KGB officials tried to force me to renounce my views, subjecting me to exhausting interrogations of many hours and locking me up in a punishment cell. They also threatened me, saying that I would never be freed from captivity, that I would be reduced there "to a vegetable", that I would never again be able to work as a doctor, and so on.

Now, in the camp, they deny me not only the chance to extend my professional range [through work in a new situation], but even to read specialist literature on psychiatry. Every line I write is inspected, letters are confiscated or delayed, and a meeting with my wife is barred.

Our professional duty demands of us that we care for others. I appeal to you, my colleagues, not for a moment to forget those who have stood up for the rights and freedoms which people need, and now are condemned to spend years in the nightmarish (for a healthy person) world of psychiatric wards, exhausting themselves in a debilitating struggle to preserve their psyches, a struggle against torturers armed with drugs. To remember them and to do everything possible for their release is our obligation. Their fate is a reproach to our conscience, a challenge to our honour, a test of our commitment to compassion. We must brand, brand with shame, those who out of self-interest or anti-humanitarian motives trample on the ideals of justice and on the doctor's sacred oath.

Your colleague, psychiatrist A. Koryagin

APPENDIX IV

The Psychiatric Internments of Alexander Shatravka

In 1974 a 24-year-old sailor, Alexander Shatravka, crossed the Soviet border into Finland with three comrades. Soon he was handed back by the Finns under a Soviet-Finnish treaty which covers such cases. Believing that a mental hospital would be preferable to a labour camp, he simulated mental illness and was duly interned by court order in a succession of psychiatric institutions, including the special hospitals of Dnepropetrovsk and Chernyakhovsk, and the Serbsky Institute. Eventually he was released in 1979. He then wrote a remarkable 400-page book about his experiences, which reached the West in 1981. He also made contact with the Moscow-based commission on psychiatric abuse (see chapter three), and assisted it in various ways. As a result he underwent renewed hospitalizations which he describes in the following slightly abridged document of 1981. His account starts in May 1980, two months before the Moscow Olympic Games.

In 1982 Shatravka was arrested and given three years in a labour camp for assisting the unofficial Soviet peace movement. Western publicity about his book probably helped to avert further persecution through psychiatry.

Sensing that nasty things were in the offing for me, I set off for the remote wilds of the Tyumen taiga [in West Siberia], where I lived quietly in a woodman's hut, alongside the bears and the elks. Soon some strangers appeared in the forest. But they weren't hunters, and weren't looking for elks or hares. Their job was to catch me, and to deliver me, for the duration of the Olympic Games, to the mental hospital in Urai.

For two days they pursued me, pushing me from the forests of Tyumen into the forests of Karelia. . . . I was [later] detained. . . . The Kandalaksha KGB officers . . . quickly deposited me in the Apatity mental hospital.

There the head doctor of my section greeted me with this

happy news: "Sasha [familiar form of Alexander], your case notes show that I have to give you a course of Haloperidol by injection." So while I was being pumped with Haloperidol, the KGB boys were combing the woods in search of my comrade [whom they eventually put into the Petrozavodsk mental hospital].

In October both he and I were sent under guard to Geikovka mental hospital [in the south Ukraine]. The papers on both of us contained the same barefaced words: "Detained in Karelia when planning to cross the [Finnish] border." We were much too far, not just from the border, but even from the frontier zone, for this to be true.

In mid-October the unseen hand [of the KGB] gave the word for me to be discharged.

A postscript to this episode was that my comrade earned himself the status of a socially dangerous person, and a corresponding red stripe on his record card in the psychiatric clinic. As for me, I have long been labelled a socially dangerous person because of my unsuccessful escape to the West and my continuing attempts now to emigrate from the USSR.

The November holidays [around 7 November—Revolution day] were approaching. I was not fearful of a new hospitalization, as I had promised the KGB officials that I'd stay at home [in Krivoi Rog] the whole time, and phone them each day. My parents, too, hoping that nothing would happen to me in the next few months, went on holiday to visit relatives in the north, leaving my sick brother and me at home. As my brother constantly needs medicine, I decided to go to the psychiatric clinic to get a new batch for him.

I had hardly entered the office of psychiatrist Stanislav Borisovich Mrachko when he rushed out and quickly shut all the clinic doors. Before I could open my mouth they had put me in the top-security block. This block is a sort of transit point, to which ambulances bring sick people from all over the city, and where doctors place patients before their dispatch to mental hospitals. New arrivals are rarely washed. For this reason the block swarms with lice and other parasites. The bedding is changed only on fixed days, irrespective of how many people use it, and the blackened mattresses, rotting from all the urine, are better not discussed. It is also quite usual for an orderly to take over from a nurse and clumsily give patients injections.

Horror seized me, not so much for myself as for my sick brother. With great difficulty I managed to persuade a nurse to let me use the phone. I straight away called the KGB. Fortunately my case-officer was at his desk. I explained the whole situation to him. Two hours later Dr Mrachko ran into the section and said he would release me—on condition that I came back on Monday [27 October 1980]. I came as promised, and was again put in the security block. It was crammed full. Some people were bawling songs, other just screaming. Some woman had stripped herself naked in the corridor, but the orderlies paid no attention: they were hauling away an incontinent old man who had just emptied his bowels.

But this time I did not have to stay in the section for long. An ambulance came for me from Geikovka mental hospital, and collected just me. This time I arrived at the hospital without any accompanying papers.

"I'll discharge you after the holidays," promised section-head Popov on his rounds.

"But don't prescribe me any drugs, please," I said, reconciling myself to my position.

"What d'you mean, no drugs? Once you're in the hospital, we're obliged to treat you."

"Treat me for what?"

"How do you mean, for what? At least as a prophylactic measure," the doctor replied calmly.

5 February 1981. The bus set off from Kharkov to Krivoi Rog through a sleeping city. Stretching out in my seat, I looked back over the wonderful days I had just spent with the family of the Kharkov psychiatrist Anatoly Koryagin. [During a formal examination of Shatravka, Koryagin had found no trace of mental illness in him].

The bus pulled in to the Krivoi Rog bus station and stopped. [Shatravka then describes how the police arrested him there.] A few minutes later men in white coats appeared, who seized me and shoved me into an ambulance.

The first section of the clinic's security block was quiet. The patients were sleeping in threes—each threesome lying on two beds pushed together—or on stinking mattresses on the floor. In the two male wards there was no spare place. "Sleep in the female ward. There's a spare bed there," said the nice orderly Liza, in a friendly way.

In the morning, after breakfast, I drank the prescribed neuroleptic drugs, watched by an orderly. Apart from these tablets, another of the doctor's "surprises" awaited me—injections of Chlorpromazine. Three ampoules, twice a day.

In the office, apart from section head Nina Dmitrievna Pavlova, sat the clinic head doctor himself, Georgy Dmitrievich Dynovsky.

"Why did you visit Sokolov [an interned dissenter] in Rostov region, and why, in general, do you interest yourself in other people's affairs?" the head doctor asked in the cold tone of an investigator, considering it his medical duty to ask this question, which had been supplied to him by the KGB. . . .

"The man is an acquaintance of ours, and my mother sent me to the Novoshakhtinsk mental hospital so that I could receive him on his discharge."

"So this means you've converted your mother to your views, eh? Has she started supporting you? And what conference of dissidents did you just go to Kharkov for?"

"That's all nonsense. I went to Kharkov so that the psychiatrist Koryagin could examine me," I answered wearily, overcoming the weakness induced by the Chlorpromazine.

"No! You don't want to tell us the truth. Answer! Why did you go to Kharkov, and what did you all do at that conference?"

Now Pavlova intervened: "Shatravka! What *is* all this? We're constantly being bothered about you. Why don't you just stay at home, and stop your constant travelling? Why don't you want to work in the clinic's workshops?"

[Shatravka explains that as he is officially a disabled person, he is not obliged to work. He also describes the work available to patients—for an average wage of up to 50 roubles a month (30 roubles below the minimum wage of 80)—and says that doctors often blackmail patients into this work by threatening them with transfer to Geikovka.]

The following days were an indescribable nightmare. I languished in the female ward in a semi-conscious state, not noticing anyone around me and losing almost all idea of time. Sometimes my mother came. . . . Gathering all my strength, I spoke with her through a fine-meshed grill in a small window.

Only then, after those few short visits, was it wholly clear to me that my hospitalization had occurred because of the approach of the 26th Party Congress. I couldn't forgive myself for failing to anticipate this and to find a safe refuge for myself during the congress. Yes, I was like that eccentric of [the fable-writer] Krylov's who visited a zoo but didn't notice the elephant.

To my great relief the clinic administration decided to get rid of me. "All roads lead to Rome," but all my roads, as ever, end up in the Geikovka mental hospital. . . .

Looking at me through his glasses, the head of section 1, Nikolai Petrovich Popov, said in a friendly tone: "This time you've come to us for a long stay. I see you became very active while you were free. Now the prosecutor's office has just asked me to phone regular reports to them. So your discharge in no way depends on me. . . ."

I always land in this first section in some sort of strange circumstances. None of the doctors can ever tell me the reason for my hospitalization, nor exactly who gave the order for it. . . .

The congress ended, and everything duly reversed itself. The unseen hand made itself felt at once.

"Sasha, we'll discharge you on 16 March, that's a Monday. Try not to land here again," the head doctor of the hospital said kindly.

All I could answer was: "I'll try. But soon the May holidays [around Labour Day] will be looming up. What can I do about it?"

Geikovka, 6 March 1981

APPENDIX V

Letter of Resignation from the USSR's All-Union Society of Neuropathologists and Psychiatrists

This letter was signed by President G. Morozov and eighteen other members of the presidium of the board of the Soviet Society and sent to the World Psychiatric Association on 31 January 1983 (see chapter seven).

Dear Prof. P. Pichot, Prof. P. Berner and Members of the Executive Committee:

The All-Union Society of Neuropathologists and Psychiatrists has been a member of the World Psychiatric Association since 1967. Having expressed their desire to participate in the work of the WPA, Soviet psychiatrists were guided by the premise that this non-governmental professional organization, in accordance with its Charter and the interests of National Associations, should direct its efforts towards pressing scientific problems, promote progress in studying the nature of mental diseases, as well as to improve the organization of psychiatric aid to the population.

Regretfully, we must declare that in recent years, due to the fault of certain circles exerting unprecedented pressure on a number of national societies and the leadership of the WPA, this Association found itself a participant in a campaign having absolutely nothing to do with its fundamental professional activity. The case in question concerns the utilization of the WPA in a slanderous campaign alleging that psychiatry is being abused in the USSR for political purposes.

An active role in this campaign is being played by the leadership of the American Psychiatric Association and the Royal College of Psychiatrists (United Kingdom). Things went so far that the WPA leadership did not respond to the slanderous letter of the American Psychiatric Association dated August 12, 1982, which was sent to all psychiatric societies. This letter with reference to the State Department of the USA, which is an indication of its active participation in this propaganda campaign, contains slanderous accusations directed against Soviet psychiatrists concerning alleged abuse of psychiatry.

Therefore, a US government body is actively interfering in the work of national non-governmental organizations, and indirectly, in the work of the WPA. Once again, this fact confirms the political anti-Soviet nature of the given campaign.

This whole slanderous campaign, blatantly political in nature, is directed against Soviet psychiatry in the spirit of the "cold war" against the Soviet Union.

We would like to emphasize once again that there have been no grounds and there are no grounds for such slanderous attacks.

Soviet psychiatrists, just like their colleagues in many countries, are seriously concerned over the unfavourable situation which has developed in the WPA, and also over the fact that the WPA leadership has not undertaken and is not undertaking the necessary measures for its normalization.

In the course of decades, the efforts of Soviet scholars and physicians, of specialists from other countries promoted the advance of psychiatric science, improved the system of organizing aid for the population, and tremendous efforts were directed towards overcoming a prejudiced attitude in respect to the mentally ill and to psychiatry.

Slanderous fabrications about the abuse of psychiatry create a barrier between patients and doctors, and depict psychiatry, in the understanding of patients and society, as a body of suppression. This disrupts the mutual relationships between the patient and the doctor, and results in an improper formation of public opinion concerning the tasks and functions of psychiatry.

Soviet psychiatrists, displaying a spirit of co-operation at the request of the WPA leadership, submitted detailed medical documents concerning the mentally ill, who in the West were pronounced mentally healthy "victims" of Soviet psychiatry.

Many outstanding psychiatrists from Western countries,

including WPA members, during their visit to the USSR, at their request, had the opportunity to examine the corresponding patients in whom they were interested, and no one expressed any doubts as to the correctness of the diagnosis of the mental diseases in these individuals.

Unfortunately, at the same time, certain National Associations evaded the official invitations from the All-Union Society of Neuropathologists and Psychiatrists to visit the USSR and to participate in a discussion of the above-mentioned problems.

It is noteworthy that a whole number of mental patients who left the USSR, and who prior to that, in the West had been pronounced mentally healthy people, had received treatment and even at the present time, periodically receive treatment in psychiatric hospitals. Such facts are being hushed up, which is an obvious indication of the ill-intentioned nature of this whole campaign.

The system of voting in the WPA is discriminatory and undemocratic, since the number of votes allotted to member-countries depends on the number of psychiatrists, and first of all, on the amount of dues. This has enabled a small group of countries to implant their decisions on the rest of the WPA members, first and foremost, on the developing countries.

We would like to recall to your attention that this discriminatory mechanism was employed in Honolulu against Soviet psychiatry when a slanderous resolution was pushed through with 33 countries voting against it, and only nineteen for it.

It is also necessary to emphasize that the co-operation of the WPA with the Psychiatric Association of the racist regime in South Africa is confirmation of its undemocratic principles.

It would seem that the WPA leadership, following the Charter, should concentrate its efforts and guide the activity of all psychiatrists towards resolving the professional tasks standing before it, however, the real activities of the WPA have been geared to another direction. The leadership of the WPA, instead of taking the road to uniting psychiatrists, has embarked upon the path of splitting them, and has turned into an obedient tool in the hands of the forces which are using psychiatry for their own political goals, aimed at fanning up contradictions and enmity among psychiatrists of different countries.

Consequently, it is quite apparent that the WPA leadership has allowed itself to become involved in outright political activity and has supported the slander against the Soviet Union. We have no doubts whatsoever that the WPA leadership, by its activity, is doing irreparable harm to the common interests of world psychiatry and to the unity of psychiatrists from different countries of the world.

In connection with this, the All-Union Society of Neuropathologists and Psychiatrists no longer considers it possible to remain a member of the WPA, and hereby officially notifies the leadership of its departure from the WPA.

At the same time, the All-Union Society of Neuropathologists and Psychiatrists has notified all the National Psychiatric Societies of the reasons for its departure from the WPA.

APPENDIX VI

List of Victims of Psychiatric Abuse, 1977–1983

This list of 346 victims excludes individuals whose psychiatric intern-ment amounted to no more than an in-patient examination resulting in a decision that they were responsible and could stand trial. It includes 84 individuals also listed in our Russia's Political Hospitals *(appendix I), as further information has become available on them since 1976. The identity of these people is indicated. The list includes a dozen individuals whose internment was connected with the exercise of some sort of violence by them, but where there is nonetheless reason to believe that psychiatry was abused for political reasons. These people have been allocated below to the category of motivation underlying their violent acts.*

Abbreviations

E,N,R and S indicate the real, underlying reason for an internment.
  E = in connection with emigration—desired, or attempted or performed illegally (30% of cases)
  N = nationalist activity (7% of cases)
  R = religious activity (13% of cases)
  S = socio-political activity (50% of cases)
I   = *Information Bulletin* of the Moscow Working Commission — for details see reference 8 to chapter 3.
B   = *Information Bulletin* of the International Association on the Political Use of Psychiatry (IAPUP)—for details see the introductory note to the References section below.
SPP = *Soviet Political Psychiatry*, IAPUP, 1983—see note under B above.
W   = *News Bulletin on Psychiatric Abuse in the Soviet Union*, Working Group on the Internment of Dissenters in Mental Hospi-tals—see note under B above.
U   = *USSR News Brief: Human Rights* (Russian edition), fort-nightly, 48 rue du Lac, 1050 Brussels.
CCE = *A Chronicle of Current Events*, Moscow, a journal published

regularly (63 issues to date) by Amnesty International
Publications, London.

P   = A. Podrabinek, *Punitive Medicine*, Karoma, Ann Arbor,
       USA, 1979.

V   = Psychiatric report by Dr A. Voloshanovich.

List = The annual *List of Political Prisoners in the USSR* (same
       address as under U above).

K   = Psychiatric report by Dr A. Koryagin.

*   = Also listed as one of the 210 tabulated cases in appendix 1
       of our *Russia's Political Hospitals*.

†   = Also listed as one of the 60 untabulated cases in *ibid*.

‡   = Has emigrated to the West.

Agapova, Antonina
  Romanovna—E; I-20
Akinkin, Ivan—R; B2
*Alekseyenko, Sergei
  Sergeyevich—S; I-5, 11, 14,
  15; P
†Anisimov, Anatoly
  Alekseyevich—S; I-2, 16;
  CCE 39
Antipov, Igor—E; I-8; B2
Artsimovich, Viktor
  Vasilevich—S; B5, 6; U7
  (1983)
Arutyunyan, Eduard
  Bagratovich—S; I-19, 23
*Asselbaums, Teodor—E; I-24
*Avramenko, Vladimir Ilich—
  S; I-2, 7, 15; W3
*Baranov, Nikolai Ivanovich—
  S; I-4, 12, 15, 17, 20, 21; W3;
  B1–3, 5, 6; CCE 63; SPP
Barats, Vasily
  Martynovich—E-R; B1, 4, 5;
  CCE 61
Batovrin, Sergei Yurevich—S-
  E; B5, ‡
Baturov, Yury—E; I-23
Bebko, Vladislav
  Vladimirovich—S; I-16, 17,
  22

Belikova, Liliana Ivanovna—E;
  B2; V
*Beloborodov, Leonid—E-I; I-
  2, 5; B2
Belov, Sergei Pavlovich—S-E;
  I-24; B1, 2, 4, 6; K
*Belov, Yury Sergeyevich—S;
  I-1, 2, 4, 5, 7, 10–12, 14–18;
  W2; CCE 45–47; V; ‡
Berozashvili, Mikhail
  Ivanovich—E; I-24; B1
Besov, Andrei—S; I-14, 15, 17;
  W3
Bezzubov—S; P
Biletsky, Vladimir—E; I-12; B2
Bondarenko, Aleksei
  Tikhonovich—S; I-16
†Bondarev, Yury (or P.Yu.)—S;
  I-10, 15; CCE 39; P
*Borisov, Vladimir
  Evgenevich—S; I-1, 2, 11, 15,
  22; W3; ‡
*Borisov, Vladimir
  Sergeyevich—S; I-18; P
Borodin, Nikolai Ivanovich—S;
  B4
†Borovik, Pavel Ivanovich—S;
  W3
Borovsky, Aleksei N.—E; I-14,
  17

Borovsky, Viktor—S; I-1; CCE 46;‡
*Boss, David Yakovlevich—S; P
Bragunets, Evgeny—E; I-13, 19
*Breslavsky, Nikolai Ivanovich—E-R; I-18; W3; U (Supp. 7, 1983)
*Bublik, Vitaly Kuzmich—S; I-10, 11
Bulakh, Eduard Petrovich—E-R; B2; CCE 62–63
Bushin, Viktor Petrovich—S; I-13
Buterus, Gergard Teodorovich—E; I-21; W3
Butko, Anatoly Aleksandrovich—E; I-13, 22, 24; CCE 51; V; K
Bykov, Alexander Nikolayevich—S; I-10, 16; W2
Bykov, Sergei—S; P
Bykovsky, Ivan Andrianovich—S; I-24; B1
Čekanavičius, Arvydas—S; I-5, 7, 9, 12, 14–21; W3
Cherkasov, Anatoly Aleksandrovich—E; B1; List 1982
*Chernyshov, Vasily Ivanovich—S; I-10, 15, 20
Cherpakov, Gennady Grigorevich—E; I-16
Chertkova, Anna Vasilevna—R; I-5, 7; W3; B2, 5, 6; CCE 48, 61
Chudakov, V. S.—R; I-11; CCE 39
*Cidzikas, Petras—S; I-10, 15; W3; B2
Danchev, Vladimir—S; U-10-12 (1983)
*Davletov, Kim Saifullovich—S; I-4, 5, 7; W3; B2, 3

Davydov (Ryzhov), Viktor Viktorovich—S; I-16, 19, 22, 23; B1–3, 5, 6; CCE 58; SPP; V; U16 (1983)
†Demyanov, Nikolai Ivanovich—S; I-5, 12, 15, 17–19; W3; CCE 52–54
†Denisov, Alexander Ivanovich—S; B4
Dmitrienko, Vladimir—S; I-15
Dobromyslov, Vyacheslav—S; I-5, 7, 8
Domnitsa, Anatoly—R; CCE 56
Dubrovin, Valery—S; I-18; List 1981
Duvanov, Anatoly—S; I-17
Dvoretsky, Fëdor Pavlovich—S; I-18; W2
*Dzibalov, Vyacheslav Anisimovich—S; I-5, 9, 12–16; W3; CCE 49
†Efimov, Aleksei (not Leonid)—S; I-16, 19; CCE 39
Ekimov, Andrei Alekseyevich—S; I-8
Erygina, Evgenia Nikolayevna—R; I-15
*Evdokimov, Boris Dmitrievich—S; I-4, 5, 9–19, 24; W3; CCE 47, 48, 51, 53
Fadeyev, Nikolai—E; B6
Fedorenko, Ivan Grigorevich—N; I-15, 21; W3; B1, 2; CCE 60
Fëdorov, Vladimir—S; B1
*Fedotov, Georgy Alekseyevich—R; I-2, 21; W3
Fedyanin, Viktor—S; I-12, 16; W3
Finkel, Fëdor—S; B6
Galko, Kazimir Andreyevich—E; I-13, 21; B4
Gallyamov, Salavat—R; I-17, 19, 21; W3; CCE 53–54

Zaitsev, Vyacheslav
Kondratievich—R; I-17–20,
23; W3
Zakirov, Shavkat—S-E; I-15, 17
Zaks, Valery—E; B6
Zavalnyuk, Vladislav
Matveyevich—R; B2, 3; CCE
47, 48, 53, 55
†Zharov, Yury Sergeyevich—S;
U20 (1980); I-2; B1
Zhikharev, Mikhail
Nikolayevich—S; I-3, 4, 8, 10,

14, 16, 19, 22, 23; W3; B1, 5,
6; CCE 47, 49
Zotov, Mikhail Vasilevich—S;
I-24; B2–6; U (Supplement 4,
1983)
Zotova, Valentina Vasilevna—
R; B2
Zuyev, B.—S(?); P
*Zverev, Mikhail Stefanovich
—S; I-5, 13, 17; W3
*Žypre (not Žipre), Algirdas
Pranas—N; I-15; W3; B1, 2

Note: List of Ex-Victims who have Emigrated

The following is as full a list as we can compile of ex-victims who have emigrated since their internments. They figure in the above list and/or in the list of 210 in our first book.

Britain: Zh. Medvedev. *USA*: P. Grigorenko, A. Esenin-Volpin, I. Belau, M. Bernshtam, V. Kharitonov, A. Tummerman, G. Kukarskikh, V. Sevruk, V. Bukovsky, T. Shatalova and V. Ivanov (later returned to USSR) V. Borovsky; *Canada*: R. Fin, B Naudžiunas. *Israel*: I. Rips, G. Feigin, E. Pargamanik. *France*: N. Gorbanevskaya, L. Plyushch, V. Fainberg, V. Borisov, Y. Titov, E. Stroyeva, O. Iofe, P. Egides (Abovin), L. Konin, N. Bokov, V. Smirnov. *Germany*: V. Grigas (H. Mickoleit), J. Vishnevskaya, E. Nikolayev, Y. Belov. *Austria*: A. Dubrov, O. Vorobyov. *Switzerland*: V. Tarsis. *Italy*: Y. Maltsev. *Unknown countries*: S. Batovrin, V. Golikov, A. Plenainen.

NOTES AND REFERENCES

Note: Some frequently quoted sources below are not available through most commercial and library channels. These are publications of the International Association on the Political Use of Psychiatry (IAPUP) and the Working Group on the Internment of Dissenters in Mental Hospitals. These publications can be obtained from Peter Reddaway, London School of Economics, Houghton St, London WC2A 2AE, England.

Chapter 1: Political Abuse: What is it? (notes pp. 13–44)
1. McGarry, L. and Chodoff, P., "The Ethics of Involuntary Hospitalization", in Bloch, S. and Chodoff, P. (eds.) *Psychiatric Ethics*, Oxford, Oxford University Press, 1981, pp. 203–219.
2. Szasz, T., *The Myth of Mental Illness*, New York, Delta, 1961.
3. See Reich, W., "Psychiatric Diagnosis as an Ethical Problem", in Bloch, S. and Chodoff, P. (eds.) *Psychiatric Ethics*, Oxford, Oxford University Press, 1981, pp. 61–88, for an excellent account of this aspect.
4. Halleck, S., *The Politics of Therapy*, New York, Science House, 1971.
5. Bloch, S. and Reddaway, P., *Russia's Political Hospitals*, London, Gollancz, 1977 (*Psychiatric Terror*, New York, Basic Books, 1977 in the US).
6. *Ibid.*, p. 44.
7. *Ibid.*, p. 50.
8. Letters in *American Journal of Psychiatry*, 1970, Vol. 126, pp. 1327–1328; 1970, Vol. 127, pp. 842–843; 1971, Vol. 127, pp. 1575–1576; and 1974, Vol. 131, p. 474.
9. Bloch and Reddaway, *op. cit.*, p. 61.
10. Tarsis, V. Y., *Ward 7*, London, Collins/Harvill, 1965.
11. Bloch and Reddaway, *op. cit.*, p. 73.
12. *Ibid.*, p. 75.
13. *Ibid.*, p. 152.

14. *Ibid.*, p. 157.
15. *Ibid.*, p. 219.
16. *Ibid.*, p. 208.
17. *Survey*, 1970, No. 77.
18. Bloch and Reddaway, *op. cit.*, appendix VI, pp. 419–440.
19. *Ibid.*, p. 212.
20. *Soviet Political Psychiatry: The Story of the Opposition*, London, International Association on the Political Use of Psychiatry, 1983, pp. 80–83.
21. *Information Bulletin* of the International Association on the Political Use of Psychiatry (henceforth referred to as *Bulletin*), London, No. 1 (May 1981) and No. 3 (March 1982).
22. *Bulletin*, Nos. 2 and 6 (October 1981 and March 1983).
23. *Bulletin*, Nos. 4 and 5 (June and October 1982).
24. *Bulletin*, No. 4 (June 1982).
25. *Bulletin*, Nos. 1, 3, 5 and 6 (May 1981, March 1982, October 1982 and March 1983).
26. Bloch and Reddaway, *op. cit.*, p. 272.
27. *Survey*, No. 81, p. 114.
28. Bloch and Reddaway, *op. cit.*, p. 243.

Chapter 2: The Honolulu Congress: The First Great Clash (notes pp. 45–71)
1. Most of the material in this chapter is derived from the personal participation in, and observation of, events at the congress by one of the authors (SB).
2. *The Times*, 13 August 1977.
3. *The Times*, 12 March 1971.
4. Agenda, General Assembly of the WPA, 29 and 31 August 1977.
5. *Ibid.*
6. Bloch and Reddaway, *op. cit.*, p. 92.
7. *American Journal of Psychiatry*, 1979, Vol. 136, pp. 1498–1506.
8. *Moscow News*, 24 September 1977.
9. Bloch and Reddaway, *op. cit.*, pp. 311–319.
10. Minutes, General Assembly of the WPA, 31 August 1977.
11. *The Guardian* and *The Times*, 1 September 1977.
12. In letter dated 20 January 1978.
13. Memorandum of Soviet delegation to Sixth WPA World Congress, 1 September 1977.
14. See *Soviet Weekly*, 10 December 1977, and *Soviet News*, 27 September 1977, for the sort of attacks Dr Babayan was making at the time.
15. There is only one case about which we have doubts and whose inclusion may not have been warranted, namely Oleg Smirnov.

It is notable that he is the sole dissenter out of the 210 we listed who has been presented to Western psychiatrists since the list was published.

16. *Washington Post*, 29 October 1977.
17. *International Herald Tribune*, 31 October 1977.
18. Resolution of the All-Union Society of Neuropathologists and Psychiatrists, 14 December 1977. Published in *Korsakov Journal of Neuropathology and Psychiatry*, 1978, No. 4, pp. 624–625.
19. Press conference of 4 October 1977, reported in the Austrian press on 5 October, also in a Reuter dispatch of 4 October; personal communication from Dr I. Hutter. See also the transcript of a radio interview given by Dr Sluga on Austrian Radio's "Mittagsjournal", 4 October.
20. See, e.g., *Kurier*, Vienna, 17 December 1978; *Le Monde*, Paris, 19 December 1978.
21. *Die Volksstimme*, Vienna, 7, 9–11, 13–16, 18 and 20 September 1977. See also other reports in the same paper of 30 August, 1 and 4 September, and 6 October 1977. For a typical Austrian press attack on Wolker's version see *Die Presse*, 31 August. For a point-by point rebuttal of many of Wolker's distortions see the ten-page document widely distributed and quoted in Austrian papers, "Corrections of Untrue Assertions" by Dr I. Hutter of the International Executive Committee of Amnesty International, 29 September 1977. For a typical Soviet exploitation of Wolker's reports see *Literaturnaya gazeta*, 7 September 1977, which favoured the "big lie" approach: "Soviet doctors . . . organized meetings and conversations for them [the Austrian psychiatrists] with the individuals listed by Amnesty International" (i.e. the six we have referred to).
22. News release, American Psychiatric Association, 15 August 1977.
23. *Psychiatric News*, 7 October 1977.
24. *Honolulu Advertiser*, 2 September 1977.
25. *Psychiatric News*, 7 October 1977.

Chapter 3: Resistance at Home: Growth and Suppression (notes pp. 72–110)
1. Since 1976 solid information has in fact reached the West on 347 individuals, not just the 275 mentioned. The additional 71 featured in our earlier list of 210 for 1962–76: the recent information updates their stories by, typically, documenting either their transfer to a different institution, or their release, or their reinternment—i.e. a new episode of psychiatric abuse. For this reason the alphabetical list of victims in appendix VI gives

347 names. The 80-odd individuals not included because the evidence is too fragmentary are made up of (a) 42 of those listed on pp. 347–48 of our first book, on whom, still, insufficient data are available (the other 23 are now well documented enough to feature in appendix VI); (b) the following 29 reported on by the Working Commission: Aksentovich (*Information Bulletin* 20), B. B. Bodanin (11), Bogdanas (18), Ivan Bogdanov (14), Ivan Bogu (13), Bozhbatov (19), Yury I. Bushkov (14), Alexander Y. Chernogorov (5, 8), Viktor N. Degtyarev (13), Mikhail Gershov (8), Alexander N. Grigorev (13), Anatoly Ivanov (5), Egidijus Jonaitis (18), Kalyush (5), Kapitsky (5), Kapranov (8), Komissarov (15), Kremets (19), Genrikh Lapochkin (20), Latyshev (16), Mikhail Leukhin (14), Ivan F. Lom-Lopata (18), Pëtr V. Losik (15), Mark M. Mezhibovsky (17), Shatalov (5, 19), Fëdor F. Shneibel (10), Valery Sorin (8), Verba (5), and Vitaly Zhuk (5); and (c) half a dozen cases reported since 1980. Nearly 80 per cent of all the information that reached the West in the years 1977 to mid-1983 came from the Commission during its four years of existence.

2. The figures are: 1962–15, 1963–3, 1964–7, 1965–9, 1966–11, 1967–6, 1968–29, 1969–23, 1970–28, 1971–54, 1972–46, 1973–32, 1974–37, 1975–24, 1976–21, 1977–27, 1978–31, 1979–24, 1980–42, 1981–14, 1982–20, 1983 (first half)–5. Total–508.

3. The main reasons for this change were the need to purge dissent before the Moscow Olympic Games, followed by the convenience of doing so in the wake of the Soviet invasion of Afghanistan in December 1979. At this time the USSR was the subject of so much world criticism that the political price to be paid internationally for continuing the pre-Olympic purge indefinitely went sharply down.

4. See our *Russia's Political Hospitals*. esp. pp. 223, 227, 443–447.

5. The study is called "The Consent of Mentally Ill Persons to Hospitalization, and Associated Problems Regarding the Organization of Psychiatric Care". It has not been published, but a four-page summary of it was printed in a volume of abstracts of papers presented at the Seventh Congress of Soviet Psychiatrists in May 1981. Although the volume was not put on sale, a photo-copy of the four pages (pp. 488–491) was given to Western journalists by a reliable source whose identity we know. Further proof of authenticity is the fact that although the most interesting findings of the paper were given widespread coverage in the Western press, no comment has since issued from Moscow— except for an eloquent silence. The other

authors are B. P. Shchukin, N. N. Maslov, Yu. O. Musayev, V. V. Ostrishko, and A. N. Skrobansky. It is interesting to note the authors' statements: (a) that 61.8 per cent of the 817 patients were schizophrenics, and (b) that of the 817, "20.8 per cent were admitted voluntarily, 31.1 per cent passively, and 48.1 per cent resisted in one way or another . . . 5.3 per cent were hospitalized in connection with suicidal tendencies or attempts". A full translation is available from us on request. An oblique reference to the paper did appear in the *Korsakov Journal of Neuropathology and Psychiatry* (in Russian), 1981, No. 10, p. 1589. The Western press reports appeared mostly on 1 June 1981, e.g. in *The Daily Telegraph*, London. They seem to have been the main if indirect reason why Dr E. Babayan gave a widely publicized interview to *New Times*, Moscow, 1981, No. 29, pp. 18–20, denouncing Western critics of abuse.

6. Published in English by Karoma Publishers (3400 Daleview Drive, Ann Arbor, Michigan 48103, USA), 1979, and in Russian by Khronika Press, New York, 1979.

7. *Information Bulletin* (hereafter *IB*) No. 9, June 1978 (see ref. 8 below).

8. All issues (1–24) are reflected and/or summarized in *A Chronicle of Current Events*, Amnesty International Publications, London, Nos. 46–58. Issue No. 6 was published in full in English by Amnesty's International Secretariat, London, and No. 11 by its British Section. Nos. 1–5 and 7–9 appeared in Russian in *Volnoe slovo*, Possev, Frankfurt, 1978, Nos. 31–32. Each issue was published in Russian, with annotations, in the *Materialy samizdata* series of Radio Liberty's Samizdat Archive (Munich).

9. *IB* No. 14, January 1979.

10. See ref. 8 above.

11. *IB* No. 12, October 1978.

12. *IB* No. 23, May 1980.

13. *IB* Nos. 2, September 1977, and 7, February 1978.

14. *IB* Nos. 14, January 1979, and 15, March 1979.

15. *IB* No. 21, February 1980. The speech was delivered in Geneva by Menno Kamminga on 4 September 1979.

16. *IB* No. 17, June 1979.

17. *IB* No. 20, December 1979.

18. Private communication, June 1979.

19. *IB* No. 11, September 1978.

20. *IB* No. 21, February 1980.

21. *IB* No. 20, December 1979. Solovyov's memoir appeared in *Kontinent*, No. 18, and in English in Harvey Fireside, *Soviet Psycho-prisons*, Norton, New York, 1979.

22. *IB* No. 14, January 1979. Matveyev later, in 1981, tried to make his statement sound less ambiguous. See document AS 4505 (ref. 35 below).
23. *IB* No. 1, July 1977.
24. *IB* No. 5, December 1977, describes these episodes in more detail.
25. *IB* Nos. 4, 5, 9–19, 24. See Also *Chronicle of Current Events* Nos. 47, 48, 51, 53. Under the pen-name Sergei Razumny, Evdokimov was one of the earliest people to expose the political abuse of psychiatry. See his essay of 1970 in *Kaznimye Sumasshestviem*, Possev Verlag, Frankfurt, 1971, pp. 472–490.
26. E.g., A. Podrabinek's and A. Shatravka's visits to the hospitals where, respectively, V. Rozhdestvov and V. Sokolov were held. See *IB* No. 3, October 1977, and Appendix IV.
27. *IB* No. 5, December 1977.
28. *IB* No. 16, April 1979.
29. *IB* No. 17, June 1979.
30. *IB* No. 14, January 1979.
31. *IB* No. 24, September 1980, which also prints Koryagin's article "Unwilling Patients".
32. *IB* Nos. 23, May 1980, and 24, September 1980.
33. *IB* No. 15, March 1979.
34. *IB* No. 5, December 1977. His apparent subsequent denial of these circumstances (see ref. 35 below) does not strike us as wholly convincing.
35. *IB* No. 11, September 1978. By 1981 he was working in Belorussia, outside the SPH system. He was a witness in I. Grivnina's case, but failed to appear in court. See document AS 4505 in the Samizdat Materials series of Radio Liberty, Munich.
36. On Barabanov see *IB* No. 5, December 1977. In 1978 he was reportedly working in Vladivostok, outside the SPH system. See *IB* No. 11. On Totenko see *IB* No. 23, May 1980.
37. *IB* No. 5, December 1977, which also publishes a long letter by E. Nikolayev about his first-hand experiences of the system.
38. *IB* No. 16, April 1979.
39. *IB* Nos. 2, September 1977, and 15, March 1979.
40. *Information Bulletin* No. 6, International Association on the Political Use of Psychiatry (IAPUP), March 1983. See also the account in the "Materialy Samizdata" series of Radio Liberty, Munich, by I. Terelya (document AS 4984).
41. *IB* No. 2, September 1977.
42. *Ibid.*
43. *IB* No. 4, November 1977.

44. *IB* No. 3, October 1977.
45. *IB* No. 8, April 1978.
46. *Ibid.*
47. Written 15 April, 1979, published in *Psychiatric News* on 7 December 1979 (see full reference for the debate in appendix II). Translation by the authors from the original text.
48. Letter dated 15 January, 1981. Published in *Information Bulletin*, IAPUP, No. 1, May 1981.
49. The cases of V. Albrekht (*IB* 1), V. Igrunov (*IB* 4), V. Borisov (*IB* 5), V. Gornostayev and V. Nechayev (*IB* 7), V. Kuvakin and T. Los (*IB* 9), M. Niklus and G. Rytikova (*IB* 10), Y. Belov (*IB* 18), R. Popova and O. Solovyov (*IB* 20), M. Landa (*IB* 21), V. Senderov (*IB* 23) and M. Zotov (*IB* 24).
50. Those of V. Konovalikhin (*IB* 9, 24), S. Ermolayev (*IB* 17–19), V. Bebko (*IB* 16–17), I. Polyakov (*IB* 17, 19), I. Koreisha (*IB* 18, 20, 23), V. Sichko (*IB* 18, 19), V. Sysoyev (*IB* 19), V. Goncharov (*IB* 22), and V. Kishkun (*IB* 24).
51. Those, for example, of P. Sebelev (*IB* 21) and E. Nikolayev (see below in chapter).
52. E.g., that of S. Purtov (*IB* 12).
53. *IB* No. 9, June 1978.
54. *IB* Nos. 14 and 15, January and March 1979.
55. *IB* No. 18, August 1979.
56. Published by Farrar, Straus and Giroux, New York, and Gollancz, London, 1980; summarized in our *Russia's Political Hospitals*, pp. 147-151.
57. *IB* Nos. 9, June 1978, and 24, September 1980.
58. On Nikolayev's internment see *IB* Nos. 7–10, February 1978–August 1978, and 12, October 1978.
59. E. Nikolajew, *Gehirnwaesche*, Munich, 1983.
60. *IB* No. 16, April 1979.
61. *IB* No. 5, December 1977.
62. *IB* Nos. 3–5, 6 (special issue exclusively about him), 8, 9, 18, 21; *Information Bulletin*, IAPUP, No. 6, March 1983.
63. *IB* No. 6, February 1978. Author—S. Kallistratova, a lawyer and member of the Moscow Helsinki Group. She wrote a similarly lengthy analysis of Alexander Podrabinek's trial in 1978. See *IB* No. 11, September 1978.
64. *IB* No. 9, June 1978.
65. *IB* Nos. 12, October 1978, and 14, January 1979.
66. *IB* No. 15, March 1979.
67. *IB* No. 23, May 1980.
68. *A Chronicle of Current Events* (hereafter *Chronicle*), 1977, No. 45.

69. *IB* Nos. 2 and 3, September and October 1977; *Chronicle* No. 47, 1977.
70. In the year after the congress the following were among those freed: V. Merkushev, S. Potylitsyn, M. Shatravka, Z. Krasivsky, Y. Belov, M. Vorozhbit, A. Butko, G. Klimašauskas and M. Lutsik (on the Serbsky's remarkable decision to annul his previous diagnosis as resulting from his simulation, see *IB* No. 13, November 1978).
71. For searches in October 1977 see *IB* No. 3, October 1977.
72. *IB* Nos. 5, December 1977, and 9, June 1978; *Chronicles* 48–50, 1978.
73. On these points see *IB* Nos. 9 and 10, June and August 1978; on the hearings see also *Soviet Opponents of Political Psychiatry in the USSR*, Working Group on the Internment of Dissenters in Mental Hospitals, London, 1980, p. 9.
74. *Der Stern*, Hamburg, 23 March to 27 April 1978.
75. *IB* No. 11, September 1978, is wholly devoted to the case. Further materials appear in subsequent issues, notably No. 14, January 1979. See also *Chronicle* 58, 1978.
76. *IB* No. 11, September 1978.
77. *Ibid.* The authorities had been trying to find out about these examinations for at least the previous two months. See an account of an interrogation of Bakhmin in *IB* No. 9, June 1978.
78. *IB* No. 13, November 1978.
79. An exception was the warning given to Dr Ternovsky in an inter- view with the head of his institute. See *IB* No. 16, April, 1979.
80. *IB* Nos. 19, October 1979, and 20, December 1979.
81. Extracts published in *IB* No. 20, December 1979. The full text is document AS 3827 in the Materialy Samizdata series of Radio Liberty, Munich. The Fainberg episode appears in our *Russia's Political Hospitals*, p. 334.
82. See *IB* No. 21, February 1980, for Bakhmin's arrest and an official warning to Ternovsky; No. 23, May 1980, for the hearings and material on the two men's cases; and *Soviet Opponents* . . . (reference 73 above), pp. 9–13, for the hearings.
83. *Chronicle* No. 58, November 1980.
84. *Ibid.*
85. *Chronicle* No. 60, December 1980.
86. *Chronicle* No. 63, December 1981.
87. *Ibid.*
88. *Chronicle* No. 62, July 1981.
89. *Ibid.*
90. See references listed for him in appendix VI.

Chapter 4: The Review Committee: An Attempt to Investigate (notes pp. 111–133)

1. Minutes, WPA Executive Committee, Cairo, 5 December 1978.
2. Letter, 10 October 1978.
3. Letter, 9 November 1978.
4. Letter, 6 December 1978.
5. Letter, 5 December 1978.
6. Letter, 12 February 1979.
7. Letter, 13 April 1979.
8. Minutes, WPA Executive Committee, Moscow, 23 May 1979.
9. Minutes, WPA Executive Committee, London, 11 November 1979.
10. Bloch and Chodoff, *op. cit.*, pp. 346–349, and Recommendation 818, Parliamentary Session of the Council of Europe, adopted 8 October 1977, respectively.
11. See news release, American Psychiatric Association, 15 August 1977.
12. Letter, 11 January 1979.
13. Letter, 11 May 1979.
14. Letter, 15 August 1979.
15. Bloch and Reddaway, *op. cit.*, p. 391 and *Bulletin*, Nos. 1, 3 and 6 (May 1981, March 1982 and March 1983).
16. Terelya, I. M., *Notes from a Madhouse*, Baltimore, Smoloskyp, 1977.
17. These two documents appear in *Information Bulletin* Nos. 1 and 5, Working Commission to Investigate the Use of Psychiatry for Political Purposes, Moscow, July and December 1977.
18. Letter, 31 August 1979.
19. Minutes, WPA Executive Committee, Madrid, 9 October 1980.
20. Minutes, WPA Executive Committee, New York, 30 October 1981.
21. Minutes, WPA Executive Committee, Kyoto, 8 April 1982.
22. *The Issue of Abuse* 1970–1983, WPA, January 1983.
23. These were: Nikolai Demyanov, Valeria Makeyeva, Viktor Rafalsky, Vladimir Rozhdestvov, Vasily Spinenko, Mikhail Zhikharev, Evgeny Nikolayev, Iosyp Terelya, Anatoly Ponomaryov, Vladimir Klebanov, Aleksei Nikitin, Mykola Plakhotnyuk, Arvydas Čekanavičius, Anna Chertkova, Nikolai Baranov, Vera Lipinskaya, Sergei Purtov, Algirdas Statkevičius, Vladimir Kislik, Gennady Kuznetsov, Anna Mikhailenko, Anatoly Lupinos, Teofils Kuma, Alexander Kuzkin, Alexander Lyapin, Fyodor Parasenko, Boris Evdoki-

mov. See *Bulletin*, Nos. 1–6 (May 1981–March 1983). We may note here that one additional case was submitted in 1983 by the Austrian Psychiatric Society regarding the treatment in Austria of Lev Konstantinov.

Chapter 5: Honolulu to Vienna: The Opposition Intensifies (notes pp. 134–164)

1. Minutes, Executive and Finance Committee, Royal College of Psychiatrists, 9 June 1978.
2. Cited in memorandum by Dr P. Sainsbury, 20 April 1982.
3. Minutes, Committee on International Abuse of Psychiatry and Psychiatrists, American Psychiatric Association, 26 September 1980.
4. Report to the Royal College of Psychiatrists, 12 May 1978.
5. See Bloch and Reddaway, *op. cit.*, p. 385.
6. See Bloch and Reddaway, *op. cit.*, p. 376.
7. See, for example, *The Observer*, 28 May 1978; *Financial Times*, 21 April 1978; *The Guardian*, 21 April 1978 and 29 May 1978.
8. See Bloch and Reddaway, *op. cit.*, chapter five, and Grigorenko, P., *Memoirs*, London, Collins/Harvill, 1983.
9. Reich W., "The Case of General Grigorenko: A Psychiatric Re-examination of a Soviet Dissident", *Psychiatry*, 1980, Vol. 43, pp. 303–322. See shorter version in *New York Times*, 13 May 1979.
10. Letter from Soviet Society to WPA, 31 January 1983.
11. *New York Times*, 30 January 1983.
12. See also the Moscow Working Commission's reports on these developments in chapter three.
13. At various points in this chapter, and elsewhere in the book, we refer to the efforts of *independent pressure groups* in the fight against political psychiatry. The first of these, the Working Group on the Internment of Dissenters in Mental Hospitals, was founded in February 1971 in London. A small, *ad hoc* research group, composed mainly of psychiatrists, human rights experts and political scientists, the Working Group came to play a crucial role in obtaining accurate data about the Soviet abuses and passing on relevant information to the psychiatric profession in Britain, and elsewhere, through the publication of a regular bulletin. (It also investigated political psychiatry in other countries, especially in Romania, but because of the magnitude of the problem in the USSR, tended to focus its efforts there.)

   As knowledge of the abuses became better known, so other groups similar in composition and aims sprang up in France, Switzerland, West Germany, Holland and Canada. The Moscow

Working Commission (see chapter three) was akin to these groups but obviously, at the same time, radically different inasmuch as it was based on Soviet soil and therefore enjoyed the advantage of on-the-spot research but also the severe disadvantage of being at the mercy of the Soviet authorities.

Although these groups, including the Working Commission, established close liaison throughout the 1970s it became obvious by the end of the decade that affiliation to a centralized body would enhance their effectiveness. 20 December 1980 saw the formation in Paris of such a co-ordinating body, the International Association on the Political Use of Psychiatry (IAPUP), with Dr Gérard Bles of France as its first secretary.

IAPUP immediately embarked on a number of initiatives, concentrating on the Moscow Working Commission whose members were then under great pressure—subjected to arrest, trial or punishment. This endeavour was in keeping with the second of the association's principal purposes—to campaign on behalf of "all direct and indirect victims" of political psychiatry. The first aim was to act as a body to co-ordinate various groups which opposed psychiatric abuse, wherever it occurred. IAPUP's crucial attribute was its total independence of any political or religious organization. This enabled its constituent groups to act solely with the object of combating political psychiatry. Continuing the tradition of the pioneering British Working Group, IAPUP soon began regular publication of an authoritative bulletin in which accurate information about psychiatric abuse was publicized. It came to be published in four languages. Although each issue included an editorial article, the bulletin was primarily devoted to the circulation of objective knowledge concerning political psychiatry and guided by a concern for the professional ethics of psychiatrists worldwide. At this writing six issues of the bulletin had been published and regular conference of IAPUP's liaison committee had been held. Its member groups had continued to play an important role in their respective countries—in the spheres of research, dissemination of new information, and support of the victims, both direct and indirect, of psychiatric abuse. For details of the activities of all the above groups in recent years, see *Bulletin*, Nos. 1–6 (May 1981–March 1983).

14. Letter, 4 October 1979.
15. Letter, Dr R. M. Babaev and Director Zelekh, 3 February 1983.
16. Letter, 25 May 1979.
17. Letter, 13 April 1981.
18. Letter, 4 March 1982.

19. Letter, 15 July 1979.
20. *Bulletin*, No. 1 (May 1981).
21. Letter, 28 February 1983.
22. Letter, 13 April 1981.
23. Minutes, Special Committee on Political Abuse, 3 March 1982.
24. Agenda, Annual General Meeting, Royal College of Psychiatrists, July 1979.
25. Letter from Royal Australian and New Zealand College of Psychiatrists to Royal College of Psychiatrists, 30 October 1981.
26. Letter, 27 October 1978.
27. Letter, 31 October 1978.
28. Cable, 9 May 1979.
29. Letter, 12 May 1979.
30. *Journal of the Japanese Medical Association*, 24 May 1980.
31. *Psychiatric News*, 1 February 1980.
32. *Bulletin*, Royal College of Psychiatrists, February 1981.
33. Bloch and Reddaway, *op. cit.*, pp. 419–440.
34. *Bulletin*, No. 3 (March 1982).
35. *Bulletin*, No. 4 (June 1982).
36. At quarterly meeting, 17 November 1978.
37. *Psychiatric News*, 7 December 1979.
38. Press statement, 11 March 1980.
39. Cable from American Psychiatric Association, 21 March 1981; Cable from Swiss Psychiatric Association, 9 June 1981; *Le Monde*, 23 May 1981.
40. *The Lancet*, 11 April 1981, pp. 821–824.
41. *The Lancet*, 27 November 1982, p. 1232.
42. *Psychiatric News*, 7 August 1981.
43. Press release, Royal College of Psychiatrists, 24 March 1983.
44. *Bulletin*, No. 3 (March 1982).
45. Press release, American Association for the Advancement of Science, 2 May 1983.
46. Proposal for election to membership of the Royal College of Psychiatrists, 1 February 1983.
47. *Bulletin*, No. 1 (May 1981).
48. The appeal appeared in full in *The Times*, 13 November 1981.
49. *Bulletin*, No. 2 (October 1981).
50. *Ibid.*
51. See reference 13.
52. Letter, 6 December 1978.
53. Reddaway, P., "The Attack on Anatoly Koryagin", *New York Review of Books*, 3 March 1983.
54. *Psychiatric News*, 1 January 1982.
55. *Bulletin*, No. 6 (March 1983).

56. Letter, 16 October 1978.
57. Letter, 15 November 1978.
58. See Medvedev, R. and Medvedev, Z., *A Question of Madness*, London, Macmillan, 1971.
59. Bloch and Reddaway, *op. cit.*, p. 223.
60. Report on Professor Andrei Snezhnevsky, Special Committee on Political Abuse, Royal College of Psychiatrists, 14 November 1979.
61. Letter, 20 December 1979.
62. Minutes, Committee on International Abuse of Psychiatry and Psychiatrists, 23 June 1982.
63. Kazanetz, E., "Differentiating Exogenous Psychiatric Illness from Schizophrenia", *Archives of General Psychiatry*, 1979, Vol. 36, pp. 740–745.
64. Letter, 20 March 1981.
65. Minutes, Special Committee on Political Abuse, 7 May 1981.
66. *Ibid.*, 15 July 1981.
67. *Bulletin*, Róyal College of Psychiatrists, October 1981.
68. Letter, 31 July 1981.
69. Letter, 14 August 1981.

Chapter 6: Dialogue or Confrontation?—The Movement to Expel (notes pp. 165–196)

1. Personal communication from Dr H. Blomberg, 28 May 1978.
2. Personal communications from Dr H. Blomberg, 10 February 1981 and 25 June 1983.
3. *Bulletin*, No. 3 (March 1982).
4. Reported in letter from Professor G. Eberhard to Royal College of Psychiatrists, 3 May 1982.
5. Reported in letter from Professor G. Eberhard to Royal College of Psychiatrists, 22 September 1981.
6. Letter, 2 May 1982.
7. Report to the Norwegian Psychiatric Association on a trip to the USSR, 15–21 November 1982.
8. Reported in letter from Dr S. Lystrup to the Royal College of Psychiatrists, 4 August 1980.
9. See our account of this episode in Bloch and Reddaway, *op. cit.*, pp. 120–124.
10. See reference 9, chapter five.
11. See Bloch and Reddaway, *op. cit.*, chapter eight.
12. Minutes, Special Committee on Political Abuse, 18 February 1981.
13. *The Times*, 13 November 1981; *The Lancet*, 13 November 1981.

14. Medvedev, Z., *The Rise and Fall of T. D. Lysenko*, New York, Anchor, 1971.
15. Letter, 23 January 1982.
16. Report to the Special Committee on Political Abuse, 3 March 1982.
17. Minutes, Special Committee on Political Abuse, 3 March 1982.
18. Letter, 30 March 1982.
19. Minutes, Special Committee on Political Abuse, 19 May 1982.
20. Letter, 4 June 1982.
21. Letter, 16 March 1982.
22. Letter, 25 May 1982.
23. Memorandum from the American Psychiatric Association to WPA member societies, 12 August 1982.
24. Special Committee on Political Abuse, 24 February 1982.
25. *Bulletin*, No. 5 (October 1982).
26. See *Bulletin*, Nos. 1–5 (May 1981–October 1982).
27. See *Bulletin*, Nos. 4–6 (June 1982–March 1983).
28. *Bulletin*, No. 6 (March 1983).
29. Personal communication from Professor H. Merskey, 21 May 1982.
30. Personal communication from Professor K. Rawnsley, 18 October 1982.
31. *Financial Post*, 1 January 1983.
32. *American Journal of Psychiatry*, 1979, Vol. 136, pp. 1498–1506.
33. *Bulletin*, No. 2 (October 1981).
34. Letter to American Psychiatric Association, 17 February 1983.
35. Letter, 11 January 1983.
36. Personal communication from Ellen Mercer, 15 November 1982.
37. Personal communication from Gérard Bles, 10 November 1982.
38. Memorandum from Professor K. Rawnsley to Special Committee on Political Abuse, 25 November 1982.
39. Letter, 28 March 1983.

Chapter 7: The Resignation: The Russians Retreat (notes pp. 197–211)
1. Letter to WPA Secretariat, 31 January 1983.
2. Personal communication from Professor K. Rawnsley, 12 July 1983.
3. Report of the Sessional Working Group on the Question of Persons Detained on the Grounds of Mental Ill-health, Commission on Human Rights, United Nations Economic and Social Council, Geneva, 5 September 1982.
4. Minutes, Committee on International Abuse of Psychiatry and Psychiatrists, 2 December 1981.

5. *Ibid.*, 23 June 1983.
6. Personal communication from Dr G. Bles, 23 April 1983.
7. Morozov, G., "We Condemn This Unseemly Activity", *Medical Gazette*, 25 March 1983. Translation in *The Current Digest of the Soviet Press*, Columbus, Ohio, 27 April 1983.
8. Moscow Radio broadcast, 16 February 1983.
9. *Soviet Weekly*, 29 January 1983.
10. Moscow Radio broadcast, 17 March 1983.
11. On Gorbanevskaya and Volpin, see Bloch and Reddaway, *op. cit.*, pp. 70–73 and 127–146 respectively.
12. *Bulletin*, No. 6 (March 1983) and personal communication from Natalya Gorbanevskaya, 20 March 1983.
13. Press release, 15 February 1983.
14. Letter, 15 February 1983.
15. Letter, 15 March 1983.
16. Their letters to WPA, 20 May 1983.
17. Letter to WPA, 2 May 1983.
18. *The Times*, 10 February 1983; *Daily Telegraph*, 11 February 1983.
19. *Daily Telegraph*, 11 February 1983.
20. *New York Times*, 15 February 1983.
21. See L. Schapiro, *The Government and Politics of the Soviet Union*, Hutchinson, London, 1977.
22. Minutes, WPA Executive Committee, Buenos Aires, 20–21 March 1983.

Chapter 8: Vienna and Beyond (notes pp. 212–232)
1. One of the authors (SB) attended the World Congress and was a close observer of the events covered in this chapter. He is indebted to Professor Ken Rawnsley, Professor Hugo Solms, Dr Gérard Bles and Dr John Grigor (delegates to the General Assembly representing the Royal College of Psychiatrists, the Swiss Society of Psychiatrists, the French Association of Psychiatrists in Private Practice, and the Royal Australian and New Zealand College of Psychiatrists respectively) for their generous help in providing accounts of various aspects of the congress.
2. Information from WPA Secretariat, 15 July 1983.
3. *Bulletin*, No. 6 (March 1983).
4. See reference 2.
5. *General Assembly, 1983*, WPA, Vienna, 10 July 1983.
6. *Ibid.*
7. *Statutes and Bye-Laws*, WPA, Vienna, 10 July 1983.
8. Personal communication from A. McNulty, 14 July 1983.

9. See reference 5.
10. *Ibid.*
11. *Ibid.*
12. *Report of the Secretary-General, 1983*, WPA, Vienna, July 1983.
13. Quoted from speech given at Forum on Abuse, Vienna, 13 July 1983.
14. *Ibid.*
15. Attended by one of the authors (SB).
16. Attended by one of the authors (SB); 15 July 1983.

INDEX

This is an index of proper names, organizations, key texts, and medical and other institutions referred to in the book.

An asterisk indicates that a photograph (or photographs) of the individual or building appears among the illustrations.

Abbreviations used: SPH = Special Psychiatric Hospital; OPH = Ordinary Psychiatric Hospital.